سيدنا محمد رسول الله ﷺ

OUR MASTER MUHAMMAD
THE MESSENGER OF ALLAH ﷺ

HIS SUBLIME CHARACTER & EXALTED ATTRIBUTES

VOLUME I

IMAM ʿABDALLAH SIRAJUDDIN AL-HUSAYNI

Foreword by
Shaykh Muhammad b. Yahya al-Ninowy

Translated by Khalid Williams

SUNNI PUBLICATIONS

Sunni Publications © 2008
Third Edition, December 2013
Eight Print, September 2024

ISBN 978-90-79294-23-7

Our Master Muhammad, The Messenger of Allah
His Sublime Character & Exalted Attributes
Volume I

Imam ʿAbdallah Sirajuddin al-Husayni

Foreword by:
Shaykh Muhammad b. Yahya al-Ninowy

Translated by:
Khalid Williams

Cover Design by:
Abu Nibras

Printed by:
IngramSpark

Published by:
Sunni Publications
Rotterdam, the Netherlands
www.sunnipubs.com
info@sunnipubs.com

Published in Arabic by:
Dar al-Falah
Aleppo, Syria
www.srajalden.com

بسم الله الرحمن الرحيم

Dear reader,

When you read any of my books, please recite Sūrat al-Fātiḥa, and donate the reward of your recitation to the renowned scholar and great Gnostic, carrier of the banner of the authority of the Qurʾān and Sunnah, the Qurʾānic exegete and scholar of Ḥadīth—with sound chains of transmission from many great scholars of Ḥadīth in Aleppo, Damascus, Morocco and elsewhere in the Islamic world, complete with written authorisations which I have kept with me—my Shaykh and noble father, Shaykh Muḥammad Najīb Sirājuddīn al-Ḥusaynī, may Allah ﷻ have mercy on him, and reward him well on behalf of the Muslims; Indeed, He is All-Hearing, All-Knowing.

Āmīn

—ʿAbdallāh b. Muḥammad Najīb Sirājuddīn al-Ḥusaynī

Publisher's Note

Praise be to Allah, Lord of the Worlds, and peace and blessings be upon our Master Muḥammad the Messenger of Allah, and upon his Family, his Companions and those who follow in their footsteps.

It was in the month of Rabīʿ al-Awwal 1428 H—the month in which the Best of Creation ﷺ was born—that we set into motion our plan of publishing in English the illustrious work, *Our Master Muḥammad The Messenger of Allah ﷺ His Sublime Character & Exalted Attributes*, written by the pole of Prophetic love of our times, Imam ʿAbdallāh Sirājuddīn al-Ḥusaynī ﷺ. By the grace of Allah, today we have the fruit of our efforts before us. It is a great honour to present as our second publication, the first volume of *Our Master Muḥammad, The Messenger of Allah ﷺ*, an intense expression of Prophetic love that is rare yet greatly needed in our times.

We thank Allah for aiding us in the publishing of this book, and request those who benefit from it to pray for all those who supported us. We would especially like to thank Dr. Muḥiyuddīn Sirājuddīn al-Ḥusaynī, Shaykh Muḥammad b. Yaḥyā al-Ḥusaynī al-Nīnowy, and Shaykh Galāl ʿAlī al-Jihānī—may Allah bless them and preserve them. We pray Allah showers His blessings upon the soul of our Imam, the Light of Aleppo, Shaykh ʿAbdallāh Sirājuddīn al-Ḥusaynī ﷺ, and upon his father, Imam Muḥammad Najīb Sirājuddīn al-Ḥusaynī ﷺ and we ask Him to preserve their children and grandchildren. We ask the reader to recite Sūrat al-Fātiḥa and donate its reward to these carriers of the banner of the Qurʾān and Sunnah, may Allah reward them abundantly.

Sunni Publications
4/1429 – 4/2008

PART V
OUR MASTER MUHAMMAD 🌼 THE MESSENGER OF MERCY

TRANSLITERATION TABLE

ا/آ/ى	ā	ظ	ẓ
ب	b	ع	ʿ
ت	t	غ	gh
ث	th	ف	f
ج	j	ق	q
ح	ḥ	ك	k
خ	kh	ل	l
د	d	م	m
ذ	dh	ن	n
ر	r	ه	h
ز	z	و	w/ū
س	s	ي	y/ī
ش	sh	ة	/h/t
ص	ṣ	ء	ʾ
ض	ḍ	أ	a/u
ط	ṭ	إ	i

LIST OF SYMBOLS

ﷻ	Mighty and Glorious is He
ﷻ	Exalted and Sublime is He
ﷺ	Allah's blessings and peace be upon him
ﷵ	Peace be upon him
﵁	May Allah be pleased with him
﵂	May Allah be pleased with her
﵃	Allah be pleased with them

ABOUT THE AUTHOR

THE Syrian city of Aleppo—also known as 'the city of scholars'—is considered by many to be the cradle of Islamic scholarship. One of the greatest scholars it has ever produced was the Friend of Allah ﷻ, Imam ʿAbdallāh b. Muḥammad Najīb Sirājuddīn al-Ḥusaynī al-Ḥalabī ﷺ, an extraordinary saint who dedicated his entire life to the service of Islam. His qualities were many and his skills outstanding. Imam ʿAbdallāh was a renowned spiritual master, an expert in jurisprudence, a Ḥāfiẓ and scholar of Ḥadīth as well as a brilliant exegete of the Qurʾān. He was most famous, however, for his immense and intense love for our Master Muḥammad ﷺ, the Messenger of Allah.

A descendant of the Prophet's ﷺ grandson, our Master Ḥusayn b. ʿAlī b. Abī Ṭālib ﷺ on his father's side, Imam ʿAbdallāh was born into an honourable and pious family on the verge of the collapse of the Ottoman Sultanate in 1923 CE. During his childhood, Imam ʿAbdallāh was surrounded by the love and care of his father, the esteemed Shaykh Muḥammad Najīb Sirājuddīn al-Ḥusaynī ﷺ who was himself a spiritual master and a leading jurist, exegete of the Qurʾān and scholar of Ḥadīth. Imam ʿAbdallāh began his pursuit of knowledge at an early age and memorized the Qurʾān when only thirteen years old under the guidance of his father. At that time, he was studying Ḥadīth at the Islamic school of al-Khasrawiyya. There he studied under leading scholars of the time such as the great jurist Imam Muḥammad Ibrāhīm al-Salqīnī ﷺ, the Saintly Sufi Shaykh ʿĪsā al-Bayanūnī ﷺ, Shaykh ʿUmar Masʿūd al-Ḥarīrī ﷺ, Shaykh Fayḍallāh al-Ayyūbī al-Kurdī ﷺ, Shaykh Aḥmad al-Shammāʿ ﷺ and several other prominent scholars. Imam ʿAbdallāh also frequented other scholars who did not teach at his school, such as the jurist Shaykh Aḥmad al-Kurdī ﷺ and Shaykh Muḥammad

Sa'īd al-Idlībī ﷺ. As he remained in their proximity, the great scholar of Ḥadīth and leading historian of Aleppo Shaykh Muḥammad Rāghib al-Tabbākh noticed his intelligence and intense devotion to the pursuit of knowledge and he decided to become his mentor.

He continued his studies under the supervision of his father, Shaykh Muḥammad Najīb Sirājuddīn who always attracted large crowds to his lessons. In this environment Imam 'Abdallāh was given the opportunity to further develop his skills and increase his knowledge and his fame as a scholar soon spread throughout Aleppo. He began teaching Islam in various mosques, such as the Ḥamawī Mosque where he tutored one hour in the morning, four times a week. Soon he was asked to teach at various colleges including the Sha'bāniyya School. He also taught many courses and lessons in various mosques including his own where he continued to impart knowledge upon the masses even when the funds that provided his payment were stopped. Then came one year in which his father's age prevented him from continuing his classes. Imam 'Abdallāh, still only twenty-two years old, carried the heavy load of succeeding his father as a scholar. The demands of the public and the high level of his father's classes made this a great test for him, but by the Grace of Allah ﷺ he succeeded in it, and honouring this responsibility caused the admiration of the public for him. Following the vacuum caused by the closing of the Sha'bāniyya Islamic school, Imam 'Abdallāh felt the need to found a large Islamic school in Aleppo that would take charge of training future scholars and preachers.

He decided to revive religious teaching by founding the School of Islamic Teachings in 1958 CE. Its program combined legal courses, Islamic spirituality, the life and qualities of the Messenger of Allah ﷺ as well as the sciences of Ḥadīth. In addition, he founded a Qur'ānic school whose mission it was to teach its students the Majestic Qur'ān. Generous scholarships were granted to the pupils in order to encourage the preservation of this knowledge.

Imam 'Abdallāh was known to be generous and helpful towards the poor, lenient towards the pupils of his school, and famed for his humility and devotion. As Imam 'Abdallāh became the leading scholar of Aleppo, he conveyed in his classes the quintessence of Islamic legislation and spirituality. In a moving voice, he often spoke of love towards the Messenger of Allah ﷺ and the duty to follow his excellent manners. He promoted love for the Sunnah and revived it in his behaviour and exhortations. Shaykh Nūr al-Dīn 'Itr mentions that he was *'extremely scrupulous and avoided any doubtful thing.'*

Imam 'Abdallāh was truly in love with the Messenger of Allah ﷺ. He did not cease pointing out his qualities, his ethics and the nobility of his status in nearness of Allah ﷺ, and did not accept anyone to be given the importance of our Master Muḥammad ﷺ. In light of this incredible love Shaykh 'Abd al-Raḥmān al-Shāghūrī ﷺ called him *'the Pole of Prophetic love of our times.'*

Imam 'Abdallāh wrote nearly thirty books dealing with Islamic spirituality, creed, ethics, and the noble manners of the Messenger of Allah ﷺ, the sciences of Ḥadīth and *Tafsīr* of the Qur'ān. Perhaps his most famous work, however, was the book of which we have the translation before us today, *Our Master Muḥammad the Messenger of Allah ﷺ.*

Imam 'Abdallāh's students were numerous, many of them becoming prominent scholars themselves, such as his son Shaykh Aḥmad Sirājuddīn, his nephew and son-in-law Shaykh Nūr al-Dīn 'Itr, Shaykh Sāmir al-Nass, Shaykh Muḥammad 'Awwāma and Shaykh Muḥammad al-Nīnowy, may Allah preserve them.

Following a surgical operation carried out toward the end of his life, the health of Imam 'Abdallāh deteriorated. On the 4th of March 2002 CE [1422 H] he returned to his Lord. The news of his passing was announced throughout the Muslim world and covered it with a veil of sorrow. Imam 'Abdallāh b. Muḥammad Najīb Sirājuddīn al-Ḥusayni al-Ḥalabī ﷺ was buried in the Sha'bāniyya complex, next to the graves of its Ottoman founders.

May Allah sanctify the noble Imam's secret.

PRAISE be to Allah, who sent our Master Muḥammad with guidance and blessings, and gave him the finest attributes, and chose him from the purest of peoples and the noblest of tribes; and may benedictions and salutations be upon he whom Allah elected to the station of Prophethood whilst Adam was still between clay and water, and made him the Master of the Messengers and the Leader of the Prophets; he who will intercede and be interceded for at the Resurrection; the model for all humanity; the bearer of the standard; the refuge of all who seek intercession on the Day of Judgement; the keeper of the secret of the Inscribed Book; he by whom Allah took humanity from darkness into light; the liege lord of all creation; the light of the heavens and the earth; he to whom all glad tidings first manifested; he who saw his Lord's mightiest signs; he about whom was revealed: ❨Glory be to He who raised His servant by night...❩ (Qur'ān 17:1), whereupon He revealed to him what He revealed, and revealed, and ❨the heart was not false in what it saw❩ (Qur'ān 53:11); he whose light shone out in all resplendence, and all who prostrated before Allah felt his presence; he who, upon his birth, the skies and palaces of the Levant were filled with light, and the angels rushed in droves to greet him, and the horizon was filled with signs of joy at his coming; he whose beauty inspired inanimate objects to speak, and for love of whom the palm-trunk wept at his absence; he by whose signal the moon cleaved in two; he whom the stone greeted and testified to his truth; he from between whose fingers water poured forth; he whose lofty reality cannot be expressed by words—may Allah bless him and his family with blessings equal to all knowledge, light, and wisdom, and may He be pleased with his noble and pious companions as long as angels circle the Holy House.

Thus says the humble servant, dire in need of his Lord's, Muḥammad b. al-Sayyid Yaḥyā al-Nīnowy, may Allah forgive him, and his forefathers, and all Muslims: When Allah chooses to ennoble His Friends by opening for them the doors of the unseen, and lifting from their eyes the veils of the unknown, and enlightening their inner sight so that there comes to light that which had been hidden, He raises their status after having cleaned their imperfections, and chooses them as His friends after having taken care of them, and then endows them with the blessings of truthfulness, and utter absorption in their Beloved, and moves their attention from the blessing to the One Who Blesses, and from creation to the Creator.

Then He endows them with Sainthood and Nearness to Him; and the generous do not seek to reclaim their gifts. Then He gives them to drink of the glory of ❨He loves them; they love Him❩ (Qur'ān 5:54), so they are bathed by the light of His proximity, and the secrets of His protection enshroud them, and the signs of His Love are manifested in them, and so their inner and outer states are devoted to His worship, and they are consumed by His constant remembrance: ❨Indeed, by remembrance of Allah hearts find rest.❩ (Qur'ān 13:28)

One such as this was my master, the Knower of Allah, the pious, pure, Prophetic scion, a branch upon the Hashemite tree, the noble, erudite scholar and Ḥadīth narrator, the virtuous author, the inheritor of Prophetic perfection and scholarship, the source of good character and self-purification, the authority of the seekers of knowledge and purity, whose presence among us was a divine mercy, and whose blessing remains still amongst us, Sayyid Shaykh Imam 'Abdallāh b. al-Sayyid al-'Allāmah Muḥammad Najīb Sirājuddīn al-Ḥusaynī al-Ḥalabī, may the abundant mercy and forgiveness of Allah be upon him.

My eyes were opened when I first encountered his teachings more than thirty-five years ago at the Grand Mosque in Aleppo (may Allah protect it from the schemes of the wretched), in gatherings that thronged with righteous people and scholars who drank from the well of the Shaykh's knowledge, and were enlightened by his great wisdom and sagacious intellect. I am still deeply moved by what my noble father ﷺ said as he took my hand and led me to one such gathering and whispered in my ear, 'This is one of Allah's righteous Friends.' This statement took hold of me and inspired me, and ignited in my heart a love for the gatherings of the righteous—and telling is not like seeing. Scholars and seekers of knowledge would spread the word if he was scheduled to visit their mosques, and men of high status would flood to his circles of knowledge from far and wide. His ﷺ words and prayers, distinguished as they were by the spirit of sincerity and love, continue to echo in my ears until this very day.

He took knowledge from many erudite scholars, the foremost of whom was his father, the great scholar Sayyid Imam Muḥammad Najīb Sirājuddīn ﷺ, until he surpassed the other scholars of his time, and became the leader of all his contemporaries.

He was not deceived by the delights of this world, or distracted by its temptations; he followed the way of the great-faithed ones, and followed the footsteps of the Friends of Allah.

The Shaykh ﷺ always magnified the Sunnah, and acted according to his knowledge, and was humble and devote. He was a Qur'ānic exegete, and a Ḥadīth scholar, and a scholar of the fundamentals of jurisprudence, and a linguist. He was a man of great forbearance and amiability, who pursued knowledge of all the Islamic sciences and disciplines. His serenity was unshakeable, his mind always illuminated, his memory unfathomable; it is almost impossible to enumerate his vast knowledge and fields of expertise. All in all, the Shaykh ﷺ was the beauty and pride of his age, and a well of knowledge, and a storehouse of purity, and when the scholars of the Levant are counted, he will appear as one of their leaders, may Allah be well pleased with him and benefit us with his knowledge and wisdom.

One of the finest of this great author's many noble and valuable works was **Our Master Muḥammad ﷺ: His Sublime Character & Exalted Attributes**. It is an immensely important work, which the Shaykh based upon Qur'ānic verses and rigorously authenticated Prophetic Ḥadīth, also drawing from the words of the noble scholars of the Sunni community. He followed a precise scholarly methodology in authoring the work, devoting a chapter to each separate subject, and then adducing evidence for each from the Noble Qur'ān and the Prophetic Ḥadīth, and the statements of the Prophetic Household, the Ṣaḥāba, and the Tābi'īn ﷺ, ascribing every Ḥadīth to its narrator, and every statement to the one who made it, as is the custom of all notable and elect scholars.

The merits of this work are without limit. The Shaykh reached the utmost limit of excellence in its authorship, and as a result its fame spread throughout the East and the West, and became a means of drawing both its author and its reader closer to Allah. It is sufficient honour for this book that to be occupied with it is a means of reaching Paradise, and of coming to a realisation of the greatness of the Prophet ﷺ, and of realising the Prophetic Sunnah, and of filling the heart with love for him—and this is merit enough. It will escape no one who reads the Shaykh's beautiful description of the Best of Creation ﷺ that it sprung from divine grace and heavenly bestowal. How should this not be so, given, that it alerts you to the subtleties of the perfections of our Master Muḥammad ﷺ, and the dazzling brightness of his signs, and the secrets of his lofty status, and his sublime attributes, and the immense reality of his worship, whose sweet scent is known only to the hearts of those who enter his inner circle, and whose brilliance illuminates the souls of those who love him, and all his ﷺ other miraculous signs, and gifts, and indications and proofs of his Prophethood? Allah elected the Shaykh for intimate knowledge of these great signs and secrets— and this is the bounty of Allah, which He gives to whom He wills; and Allah possesses immense bounty.

The Shaykh's collection of the attributes and secrets of the Prophet ﷺ should by all rights be written down in golden ink of pages of pure light. His words are pure pearls, and his work exceeds all expectations. Whoever reflects on the meanings of his work will see that they came from the inspiration of sainthood and nearness to Allah, and that their author was following the way of felicity. It is as though the Shaykh ﷺ was looking directly at the Messenger of Allah ﷺ before him as he wrote, deriving his beautiful expressions from the light of his ﷺ countenance, so that by divine providence his insight was opened, and he grazed in the pastures of subtle secrets, uncovering the beauty and perfection of the Messenger's ﷺ character, imbibing the fragrance of the Prophetic Sunnah, bathing in the light of the Muḥammadan reality and its meanings, and tasting of its fruits, and then gathering all of these illuminations in a work so noble and rarefied that it would not be surprising if it were to be read to a sick person and so cure him.

And so I leave you in the hands of the Imam and exemplar, the Knower of Allah, famous of his love for Him, Sayyid 'Abdallāh Sirājuddīn ☙, first asking Allah ☙ that these words might be a means for our attachment to the Beloved, our Master Muḥammad ☙ and that we might be counted amongst his servants, and members of his group, and that we might be firm upon the way of those who love him, and that we might follow in their footsteps until we reach a sea that disappoints none who seek it, and leaves thirsty none who drink from it.

I have nothing left to do except obey the request of our Shaykh that we remember him and his own Shaykh and father, Shaykh Muḥammad Najīb Sirājuddīn in our prayers: may Allah have mercy on them, and be pleased with them, and reward them on behalf of Islam and the Muslims with the best of rewards; for He is All-Hearing, All-Seeing.

MUḤAMMAD B. YAḤYĀ B. MUḤAMMAD AL-NĪNOWY
12 RABĪ' AL-AWWAL 1429

Translator's Preface

PRAISE be to Allah, He who sent His Messenger ﷺ as a mercy to the worlds, and by his means did unite peoples who were divided, and soften hearts that were hardened. May the benedictions and salutations of Allah be upon His Messenger, our Master Muḥammad, and upon his noble family and descendants, and his devoted companions, and upon all those who love him until the rising of the Hour.

Much controversy has arisen because of several instances in recent years when Muslims throughout the world have protested against what they perceive to be acts of a disrespectful nature aimed against the Messenger of Allah ﷺ from certain quarters of the Western world. Muslims have expressed frustration and anger at what they see as blasphemous and insulting attacks against their Prophet ﷺ; some fury has also been saved for what many Muslims see as media bias in the reporting of these events and the subsequent reactions to them.

What has been somewhat lost in all the debate about these issues is any kind of retrospection on the part of the Muslims as to the cause of this apparent negativity and bias. Just as we Muslims encouraged the Western powers, after the events of September 2001, to reflect upon their own conduct in their attitudes towards and dealings with the Islamic world—not because we felt they were somehow to blame for what had happened, but simply because there was an opportunity for some good to come out of the terrible events—should not we ourselves think deeply about the image of Islam that we portray to the non-Muslim world?

The biggest tragedy of all these events is that they spring from a single source: a lack of acquaintance with the Messenger of Allah ﷺ. If the non-Muslims do not know much about the true character and nature of the Seal of the Prophets ﷺ, this is indeed a shame; but if the Muslims themselves are ignorant of the one person with whom by all rights they should be most familiar, this is nothing short of a disaster. To love the Messenger of Allah ﷺ is an essential foundation of this religion. How can you love a man if you do not know him?

Imam 'Abdallāh Sirājuddīn al-Ḥusaynī ﷺ loved the Messenger of Allah ﷺ. Every page of the masterpiece of Prophetic portrait he bequeathed to the world is perfumed with the scent of this love, impossible to escape the attention of anyone who reads it. During the translation of this work by one of such lesser status than him, much of this fragrance must surely have been lost. I praise Allah for any that still remains; all success is due to Him.

KHALID WILLIAMS
SALÉ, MOROCCO
17 DHU AL-QA'DA 1428
(28 NOVEMBER, 2007)

INTRODUCTION

ALL praise is due to Allah, the Lord of the worlds. May the finest of benedictions and the best of salutations be upon our Master Muḥammad, the leader of the Prophets and Messengers, and upon his household, and all his companions and their followers.

I have collected in this book some concise examples which illustrate the Muḥammadan ﷺ character, and demonstrate some aspects of his outstanding moral disposition, and his sublime conduct, that perhaps they might remind the intellectual, and alert the heedless, and inform the ignorant.

It is incumbent upon every intelligent, responsible person to become acquainted with the attributes of this great and noble Prophet ﷺ, in order that they may follow the light of his example, and take the perfection of his characteristics as a model for themselves.

If it is the nature of intellectuals to seek knowledge of the world's great and worthies, then it is more fitting that they should aspire to become acquainted with the Master of Masters ﷺ, the pride of all creation, he whom Allah ﷻ raised to the highest status, and promoted above all other ranks.

No person, no matter how high his status may be, nor how vast his knowledge, nor how complete his intellect, is able to encompass the merits of this noble Prophet, or penetrate deeply the facets of his perfection and the shades of his beauty; all of us are incapable of expressing these qualities and attributes:

A robe weaved from the twenty-nine letters
Would fall short of expressing his noble character.

****

THE OBLIGATION OF BECOMING ACQUAINTED WITH
THE PROPHET ﷺ AND STUDYING HIS HONOURABLE
CHARACTER AND SUBLIME DISPOSITION

Allah ﷻ says in the Qur'ān: ﴾And know that amongst you is the Messenger of Allah﴿[1] He ﷻ also says: ﴾Do they not know their own Messenger, and so deny him?﴿[2] It is the duty of all intelligent, responsible people to become acquainted with this noble Messenger, and with his praiseworthy character and illustrious attributes, for several reasons:

Firstly: Allah ﷻ has commanded His servants to believe in this noble Messenger ﷺ, saying: ﴾Believe in Allah, and His Messenger, and the Light We have sent down; Allah is Aware of that which you do.﴿[3]

Belief in him ﷺ demands from the servants of Allah that they come to know the merit of this noble Messenger, and the loftiness of his rank above the rank of all others, and the perfections of personality that Allah has bestowed upon him, and the refined and noble manners that He has taught him, and the exalted character and beautiful physical attributes that He has given him, and the merits that He has created in him, and the perfections that He has gathered in him; for He has exalted the eminent nature of the Prophet ﷺ high above all other individuals and races, and he cannot therefore be compared to any other person.

How could he be compared to any other, when Allah ﷻ has singled him out for perfection, and endowed him with the noblest of attributes, and raised him up to the heights of exalted character, and adorned him with the fairest of appearances and the handsomest of forms, and distinguished him with enumerate distinctions? He has raised him with care, and watched over him

---

[1] Qur'ān 49:7
[2] Qur'ān 23:69
[3] Qur'ān 64:8

with regard, and has said: ❨Did He not find you an orphan, and give you refuge? Did He not find you lost, and guide you? Did He not find you destitute, and enrich you?❩[4]

Allah ﷻ Himself undertook the Prophet's ﷺ education and teaching, as he had grown up unlettered, and said to him: ❨Read, by the Name of your Lord.❩[5] That is, read not by your learning or education, but rather by the Name of your Lord.

And He ﷻ said: ❨We will cause you to read, so that you do not forget.❩[6]

And He ﷻ said: ❨And He taught you that which you knew not; and Allah's Grace unto you is ever Great.❩[7]

The status of ❨it is revealed to me❩ in the Word of Allah: ❨Say: 'I am but a mortal like you; it is revealed to me...❩[8] inspires deep reflection concerning the nature of this Chosen Messenger ﷺ, and indicates the unique characteristics of this eminent Prophet ﷺ, whom Allah has endowed and prepared for in soul, body, mind, intellect, hearing, sight, and all other senses and faculties, and to whom He has given the unique ability to receive Divine Revelation in all its forms from the Lord of the Worlds.

For that reason, as is reported in Bukhārī and Muslim, when the Prophet ﷺ maintained a continuous fast, and some of the Ṣaḥāba (Companions) ﷺ fasted with him, he prohibited them from doing so. They said, 'But we see you fasting continuously, O Messenger of Allah.' He replied, 'I am not like you'—and in one narration 'my condition is not like yours'—'throughout the night, my Lord feeds me and gives me to drink.'

For he ﷺ is a human being, but not like human beings, as a ruby is a stone, but not like other stones.

---

[4] Qur'ān 93:6-8
[5] Qur'ān 96:1
[6] Qur'ān 87:6
[7] Qur'ān 4:113
[8] Qur'ān 18:110

Secondly: Allah ﷻ has commanded His servants to follow the Prophet ﷺ, saying: ❨Say: 'If you love Allah, then follow me, and Allah will love you, and forgive your sins. Allah is forgiving, compassionate.❩[9] By this, Allah ﷻ has made the true proof of the servant's love for Him ﷻ that they follow the Prophet ﷺ. And He ﷻ said: ❨And follow him, that you may be guided.❩[10] That is, that you may be guided to that wherein lies your happiness in this world and in the hereafter.

This necessitates the study of his ﷺ actions, words and states, and acquaintance with his noble disposition and exalted character, that he ﷺ may be comprehensively followed in them, except in regard to those rulings and states that Allah ﷻ has ordained for him ﷺ alone.

Because of this, the Companions of the Prophet ﷺ strove with all determination to examine his actions, speech, states and manners, in order that they might imitate them. Indeed, they even extended the same effort in studying his regular habits and activities, because the habits of the best people are the best of habits, and so what of the habits of the greatest of them all ﷺ?!

The great scholar [Imam] al-Sanūsī ﷺ said in his commentary on his own *Muqaddima*:

> It is evident that the Ṣaḥāba ﷺ considered it religiously necessary to follow the Prophet ﷺ unhesitant in all of his words and deeds, except for those things which were legislated solely with regard to him ﷺ. They removed their shoes when he ﷺ removed his, and cast aside their gold rings when he ﷺ cast aside his. Abū Bakr and 'Umar ﷺ went out of their way to sit on a well the Prophet ﷺ had sat on. When the Ṣaḥāba ﷺ saw the Prophet ﷺ shaving his head to finish his 'Umra at Ḥudaybiya, they almost endangered each other's lives in the rush to shave their own heads. They would make a great effort to know his ﷺ exact way of sitting, sleeping, eating, drinking, and so on, in order to follow him.

---

[9] Qur'ān 3:31
[10] Qur'ān 7:158

They even liked and disliked the same foods as him ﷺ.[11] And so, we have mentioned in this book some of the characteristics, manners, deeds, words, and acts of remembrance and worship of the Prophet ﷺ, so that he can be followed in them.

Thirdly: Allah has made it obligatory for the believers that they love the Prophet ﷺ more than their fathers, children, spouses, families, businesses and wealth, and has warned those who fail to realise this with chastisement. For He ﷻ has said: ﴾Say: 'If your fathers, your sons, your brothers, your spouses, your families, the wealth you have gathered, the trade whose decline you fear, and the homes you enjoy are more beloved to you than Allah and His Messenger and striving in His cause, then wait until Allah brings His command to pass; Allah guides not the wicked.'﴿[12]

There is no doubt that the causes of love spring from beauty, perfection and benefit, as Imam al-Ghazālī ﷺ and others have put it.

A man is loved for his generosity, or his bravery, or his forbearance, or his knowledge, or his humility, or his piety, or his asceticism and caution, or the perfection of his intellect, or the quickness of his understanding, or the beauty of his character and manners, or his eloquence, or his good company, or his righteousness, or his care and compassion, or for other attributes of the like. What if these consummate attributes and others were gathered together in one man, and realised to their fullest and most complete extent? This is our Master Muḥammad ﷺ, in whom all attributes of beauty and perfection are gathered.

---

[11] For example, Tirmidhī related on the authority of Anas ﷺ that a tailor once invited the Messenger of Allah ﷺ to a meal he had made for him. Anas said: 'I went with the Messenger of Allah ﷺ to the meal. The host placed in front of the Messenger of Allah ﷺ barley bread and a pumpkin sauce. I saw the Prophet ﷺ eating the pumpkin, and from that day on I never lost my liking for it.'

And Muslim narrates on the authority of Abū Ayyūb ﷺ that he once presented food to the Prophet ﷺ which had garlic in it. It was said to Abū Ayyūb, 'the Prophet will not eat it.' He replied, 'is it forbidden?' The Prophet ﷺ said 'No, but I do not like it.' Abū Ayyūb said 'In that case, I do not like that which you do not like.'

[12] Qur'ān 9:24

Allah 🕊 has created his exalted image, his noble form, and has adorned him 🕊 with all forms of beauty and splendour, so that any who described him 🕊 would say: 'I never saw before him or after him anyone like him.'

It is, therefore, essential for the legally responsible person to seek acquaintance with the beauty of this noble Messenger 🕊: with his beautiful character, with his perfections of soul, heart, mind, and intellect. Only then can one attain true love for him 🕊, for knowledge is the source of love: as knowledge of the beautiful qualities of one's beloved increases, so does one's love for them.

Our Master Ḥasan b. ʿAlī 🕊 said: 'I asked my uncle Hind b. Abī Hāla—who was gifted at describing—about the beauty of the Prophet 🕊, hoping that he would describe to me something I could hold on to and cherish, and he replied: "The Messenger of Allah 🕊 had great and stately attributes, and was honoured as such by others. His face shone like the light of the full moon..."' as in the Ḥadīth which will be mentioned later.

Fourthly: A study of the Prophet's 🕊 great qualities and noble characteristics leaves a firm and clear image imprinted in the heart and the imagination, as though one has truly seen one's beloved 🕊.

The Prophet 🕊 himself would describe to his companions the Messengers who came before him, and would mention those who resembled them to further clarify these descriptions, until they arrived to a state when it was as though they had seen them. This was the most appropriate way for them to become acquainted with them and to love them.

Bukhārī, Muslim and others relate that Abū Hurayra 🕊 said: 'The Prophet 🕊 said: "On the night of my ascension, I met Mūsā," and went on to describe him thus: "He had wavy hair, and resembled the tribesmen of Shanūʾa." He then said: "and I met ʿĪsā," and he described him thus: "He was medium built, and red-skinned, and looked as fresh as if he had just come out of a bath. And I saw Ibrāhīm, and I am the closest of his sons in resemblance to him."'

Fifthly: When his ﷺ character is mentioned, and his ﷺ attributes are described, it is a source of life for the hearts of those who love him, and a means to stir their souls and intellects, and increase their love, and arouse their yearning.

The great Gnostic Shaykh Abū Madyan ؓ said:

> *We live by thinking of you when we do not see you*
> *Truly the remembrance of loved ones refreshes us;*
> *Were it not that our hearts see your graces;*
> *When we are awake, and lost in our slumber,*
> *We would die of our longing, and sorrow for your distance,*
> *But as it is, your graces are with us.*
> *To remember words from you moves us and stirs us:*
> *Were it not for your love in our hearts,*
> *We would not be moved.*

And may Allah show compassion to he who said:

> *Friends! If the beloved and his people are far-off,*
> *And meeting him is out of reach, and his home is distant,*
> *And you have lost the chance to see him with your eyes:*
> *You have not lost the chance to hear his description.*

May Allah bless him, and give him peace.

سيدنا محمد رسول الله ﷺ

OUR MASTER MUHAMMAD
THE MESSENGER OF ALLAH ﷺ

PART I

THE PHYSICAL BEAUTY OF OUR MASTER MUḤAMMAD ﷺ

THE BEAUTY OF HIS PHYSICAL APPEARANCE ﷺ

KNOW, may Allah ﷻ enrich our knowledge, that Allah ﷻ created our Master Muḥammad ﷺ with the finest and most beautiful of human appearances. He ﷺ is the epitome of created beauty, and physical and behavioural excellence. All those who saw him and described him agreed that no one like him had ever been seen.

Barā' b. ʿĀzib ؓ said: 'The Prophet ﷺ had the handsomest face and the most excellent character of all people. He was neither excessively tall nor short.'[13] He also said ؓ: 'The Prophet ﷺ was of medium height, and broad-shouldered. His hair fell to his earlobes. I saw him wearing a red shawl—I have never seen anything more beautiful than him ﷺ.'[14]

The Commander of the Believers ʿAlī b. Abī Ṭālib ؓ said: 'The Messenger of Allah ﷺ was neither short nor tall. His head was large. His hands and feet were fleshy. The complexion of his face was red. He had a thin line of hair from his chest to his navel. When he walked, it was as though he was descending from a height. I saw neither before nor after him anyone like him.'[15]

It is related from ʿAlī ؓ that when he described the Messenger of Allah ﷺ he would say: 'The Messenger of Allah ﷺ was neither excessively tall nor short, but rather was of a medium stature. His

---

[13] Agreed upon by Bukhārī and Muslim.
[14] Narrated by Muslim.
[15] Narrated by Imam Aḥmad.

hair was neither curly nor straight, but rather was wavy and flowing. He was not corpulent. His face was not completely circular, but was slightly rounded. His complexion was white with some redness.[16] His eyes were very black. His eyelashes were long. His joints were large, and his shoulders broad. He was smooth-skinned; a thin line of hair ran from his chest to his navel. His hands and feet were fleshy. He walked with vigour, as though descending from a height. When he turned to look at something, he would turn with his whole person. Between his shoulders was the Seal of Prophethood, and he was the Seal of the Prophets. His heart was the soundest of hearts. His speech was the most truthful of speech. He was the gentlest of people, and the kindest of them in companionship. Whoever saw him unexpectedly would be awe-stricken. Whoever came to know him would love him. Whoever described him would say: "I saw neither before him nor after him anyone like him.'"

Bayhaqī and others[17] related that when the Messenger of Allah 鸞 emigrated from Mecca to Medina with Abū Bakr, 'Āmir b. Fuhayra (Abū Bakr's freed servant) and their guide 'Abdullāh b. Urayqiẓ al-Laythī, they passed by the tent of Umm Ma'bad 'Ātika bint Khālid al-Khuzā'iyya, an elderly woman who used to sit in the camp ground and feed and water (those who passed). They asked her if she had any meat or milk they might buy, but they found she had none. She said to them: 'By Allah, if we had anything, we wouldn't leave you wanting, but our people have experienced a barren year.'

The Messenger of Allah 鸞 looked at a ewe which had appeared at the side of her tent, and said: 'What is this ewe, Umm Ma'bad?'

---

[16] As for that which is related in some Ḥadīth stating that his 鸞 complexion was dark, Ḥāfiẓ al-'Irāqī considered it unsound by virtue of its being related in isolation. He said: 'This word (dark complexioned) is related only by Ḥamīd from Anas; the other narrators from Anas give the word 'brightly-complexioned.' Fifteen of the Ṣaḥāba described his 鸞 complexion as white, as those who have investigated the matter have noted.'

[17] It was also related by Ḥākim, who declared it to be rigorously authentic, and also by the author of *al-Ghīlāniyāt*, Ibn 'Abd al-Barr, Ibn Shāhīn, Ibn al-Sakan, Ṭabarī, and others.
(*Sharḥ al-Zurqānī 'alā al-Mawāhib*)

'It is a ewe which fatigue has forced to fall behind the other sheep,' she said. 'Is there any milk in it?' the Prophet ﷺ asked. She replied: 'It is too weak for that.' He ﷺ said: 'Would you permit me to milk it?' She replied, 'If it can be milked, then milk it.' (And in another narration, 'Yes, my father and mother be sacrificed for you, if you feel it can be milked, then milk it.')

The Messenger of Allah ﷺ called for the ewe, and wiped his hands on its udder (in another narration: 'its back') and mentioned the Name of Allah, and called for a pail that would suffice the whole company until they slept. The ewe moved its legs apart and expressed milk in abundance until the pail was full.

The Prophet ﷺ gave Umm Maʻbad and her companions to drink, and they drank until they were satisfied, and then the Prophet ﷺ finally drank, saying: 'He who gives people to drink should drink last.' Then he ﷺ filled the pail again with milk and left it with her, and in one narration said: 'Give this to Abū Maʻbad (her husband) when he comes to you.' Then they left.

Soon afterwards, her husband Abū Maʻbad came, driving thin, emaciated sheep. When he saw the milk, he was astonished, and said: 'Where did this milk come from, Umm Maʻbad, when there is no animal that gives milk in the house, and the ewes are far from the pasture?' 'No, by Allah,' she said, 'but a blessed man passed by us,' and she told the story. 'Describe him for me, Umm Maʻbad,' he said.

She replied: 'I saw a man of visible radiance, his appearance beautiful, his face bright, with neither protruding ribs nor a small head, handsome and fair. His eyes were deep black, and his eyelashes were lush. His voice was mellow and soft. The whiteness of his eyes was bright, and his pupils were very black. His eyebrows were fine at the corners, and connected.[18] His neck was long, his beard full. When he was silent, he appeared dignified. When he spoke, he was eminent, and crowned with

---

[18] This is contrary to the upcoming Ḥadīth of Hind b. Abī Hāla, which states that the Prophet's ﷺ eyebrows were long, but did not connect—and this is the more dominant narration. This apparent contradiction can be explained by supposing that between his noble eyebrows was fine hair which became apparent when the dust of travel fell upon it, as the Ḥadīth of Umm Maʻbad took place at a time of travel. (Ibid.)

magnificence. His speech was sweet, his words precise, neither too little nor too much, like a string of pearls flowing down. He was the most striking and beautiful of people when seen from afar, and the fairest of them when seen up close. He was medium height, neither unagreeably tall nor scornfully short; a branch between two branches. Among the three he was the most radiant in appearance, the finest of them in stature. He was surrounded by companions. When he spoke, they listened attentively. When he gave orders, they hastened to fulfil them. Honoured, and surrounded by followers. He neither frowned, nor criticised.'

Abū Ma'bad said: 'This, by Allah, is the man of Quraysh we are searching for, and if I encounter him, I will seek to accompany him.' In another narration, he said: 'If I see him, I will follow him, and I will strive to find a way to do so.' Then they migrated to the Prophet 𐌰 and accepted Islam.[19]

Muslim and Tirmidhī narrated on the authority of Jurayrī that he said to Abū al-Ṭufayl: 'Did you see the Messenger of Allah 𐌰?' He replied 'Yes.' Abū al-Ṭufayl said: 'How did he appear to you?' (And in Tirmidhī's narration: 'Describe him for me.') He said: 'The Messenger of Allah 𐌰 was white,[20] with a handsome face.' In another narration, he said: 'White, handsome, and medial.'[21]

THE RADIANCE OF HIS FACE 𐌰
AND LUMINESCENCE OF HIS COUNTENANCE

Of all people, the Prophet 𐌰 had the most beautiful face, and the brightest countenance. All of the Ṣaḥāba who described the Messenger of Allah 𐌰 agreed that his face was bright and radiant, and shone with resplendent light, and clear brilliance. Some of them compared the brilliance of his 𐌰 light to the sun, others to the moon. Some of them likened the shining light of his face to

---

[19] See *Sharḥ al-Mawāhib* and *Tārīkh Ibn Kathīr*.

[20] With some redness as well, as the rest of the narrations mention.

[21] Meaning that he 𐌰 was in a middle position in his attributes; and the middle is the sum of the best elements of opposite features.

the beams of the moon. All of this confirms for us the clear radiance of his face, and his dazzling luminescence 鑿.

Let us consider the clear evidence for this from the Ḥadīth: Tirmidhī narrated that Abū Hurayra 鑿 said: 'I never saw anything more beautiful than the Messenger of Allah 鑿: it was as though the sun was shining from his face.'[22]

Imam al-Ghazālī 鑿 said: 'And they used to say: "He is as his companion Abū Bakr 鑿 has described him:

Honest, the chosen one who calls to goodness,
Like the light of the moon when it cleaves the darkness."'

And on the authority of Abī ʿUbayda b. Muḥammad b. ʿAmmār b. Yāsir, who said: 'I said to Rubayyaʿ bint Muʿawwidh: "Describe to me the Messenger of Allah 鑿." She said: "O my son, if you had seen him, you would have seen the sun rising."'[23]

Tirmidhī narrated the Ḥadīth of Hind b. Abī Hāla, on the authority of Ḥasan b. ʿAlī 鑿, who said: 'I asked my uncle Hind b. Abī Hāla—who was gifted at describing—about the beauty of the Prophet 鑿, hoping that he would describe to me something I could hold on to and cherish, and he replied: "The Messenger of Allah 鑿 had great and stately attributes, and was honoured as such by others. His face shined like the light of the full moon..."'
...as in the Ḥadīth which will be mentioned later in full.

---

[22] Also narrated by Imam Aḥmad, Bayhaqī, Ibn Ḥibbān, and Ibn Saʿd. When the Messenger of Allah 鑿 was in Medina with his companions in the mosque, ʿAmr b. Sālim al-Khuzāʿī recited a poem of support for him 鑿 when Quraysh broke the treaty:

O my Lord! I implore Muḥammad,
The oath of our father and his father of old,
You were a son, and I was a father,
Then I submitted, and never removed my hand,
So be victorious, may Allah guide you!
And call the servants of Allah to come in droves,
The Messenger of Allah is among them, unique:
White as the full moon rising above.

[23] Narrated by Tirmidhī, Bayhaqī, and others.

Jābir b. Samura ﷺ said: 'I saw the Messenger of Allah ﷺ on a moonlit night, and he was wearing a red shawl. I began to look from him to the moon, and to me he was more beautiful than the moon.[24] Abū Isḥāq al-Sabīʿī said: 'A man asked Barāʾ b. ʿĀzib: "Was the face of the Messenger of Allah like a sword?"[25] He replied: "No; it was like the moon."'[26] Muslim related on the authority of Jābir b. Samura ﷺ that a man said: 'Was the face of the Messenger of Allah ﷺ like a sword?' Jābir said: 'No; it was like the sun, and the moon, and it was round.'[27]

And we find in Bukhārī's *Ṣaḥīḥ* the narration of Kaʿb b. Mālik, who said: 'When the Messenger of Allah ﷺ was pleased, his face would light up like a section of the moon.'

Bayhaqī narrated, on the authority of Abū Isḥāq al-Hamdānī ﷺ,[28] that a woman from Hamdān (whom Abū Isḥāq named) said: 'I performed Ḥajj with the Messenger of Allah ﷺ several times. Once I saw him on a camel of his circumambulating the Kaʿba, a staff in his hand, wearing two red robes, his hair reaching almost to his shoulders. When he passed the Black Stone, he saluted it with his staff, then raised it to his lips and kissed it.' Abū Isḥāq said: 'Compare him ﷺ with something.' She said: 'Like the moon when it is full. I saw neither before nor after him anyone like him.'

When he ﷺ arrived in Medina, the people of the city began to sing:

The full moon has risen over us
Over the hill of Wadāʾ.
Gratitude is incumbent upon us,
As long as Allah is called to.
O you who has been sent among us,
You have come with a command that will be obeyed.

---

[24] Narrated by Tirmidhī.

[25] I.e. in the way it shone and lit up.

[26] Narrated by Bukhārī and Tirmidhī.

[27] Meaning that his ﷺ face was bright like the sun, and resplendent like the moon, and that it had some curvature. (*Sharḥ al-Mawāhib*)

[28] He is Sabīʿī from the above Ḥadīth. He was a famous Tābiʿī (follower of the Ṣaḥāba), from whom the six Imams related Ḥadīth.

His 🕮 face, radiant with light, overflowing with meanings and secrets, is a clear evidence that he is truly the Messenger of Allah 🕮. 'Abdullāh b. Salām 🕮 said: 'When the Messenger of Allah 🕮 first entered Medina, the people rushed to him, and I was among them. When I saw his face, and examined it, I knew that it was not the face of a liar—it was the face of the Leader of the Messengers. The first thing I heard him say was "People! Spread peace and salutations, and feed one another, and maintain your family ties, and pray at night when others sleep—and you will enter Paradise in peace."'[29]

Because of this, 'Abdullāh b. Rawāḥa 🕮 said:

> *If he had embodied no other clear signs*
> *His very appearance would be enough to give you the message.*

'Ā'isha 🕮 said: 'Of all people, the Messenger of Allah 🕮 had the handsomest face and the lightest colour. Nobody would describe him without comparing his face to the full moon. The beads of sweat on his face were like pearls, and more fragrant than strong musk.'[30] On that note, Abū Ṭālib said:

> *Pure is he, that by his face rain-giving clouds are sought;*
> *Succour of the orphans, protector of the needy.*

Ibn 'Asākir, Abū Nu'aym and Khaṭīb narrated with a sound [*ḥasan*] chain on the authority of 'Ā'isha 🕮 who said: 'Once I was sitting and spinning thread, and the Prophet 🕮 was mending his shoe. His forehead began to sweat, and light began to shine from the sweat. I started in amazement, and so he 🕮 said: "What makes you start so?" I replied: "Your forehead began to sweat, and the sweat gave off such bright light that if Abū Kabīr al-Hudhalī had seen you, he would have recognised you as more deserving of the poem in which he said:

---

[29] Narrated by Tirmidhī, who declared it to be rigorously authentic.
[30] Narrated by Abū Nu'aym and others.

> *And free of any recrudescence of menses,*
> *Or corruption of nursing, or dangerous illness.*[31]
> *And when you looked at the features of his face,*
> *They shone with the radiance of a shimmering cloud.'"*

Ibn Abī Khaythima said: 'The Prophet ﷺ had a distinctive forehead: if it appeared through his hair, or between the parting of his hair, or at night, or if he turned his face to the people, his forehead would appear as though it were a lighted lamp, shining. They used to say: "He ﷺ is just as his poet Ḥassān ؓ has said:

> *When, in the dark night, his forehead appears*
> *It shines and gleams like a lamp ignited;*
> *So who ever was, or will be, like Aḥmad?*
> *A means to reach the truth; a warner to the heretic."'*

And the *Sunan* of Dāraquṭnī includes the Ḥadīth of Ṭāriq b. ʿAbdullāh al-Muḥāribī, who related that Ẓaʿīna said: 'Do not criticise one another, for I have seen the face of a man who would not degrade you: I have never seen any man whose face was more like the full moon than his,' meaning the face of the Messenger of Allah ﷺ.

HIS BLESSED SWEAT ﷺ AND ITS SWEET FRAGRANCE

Another of his ﷺ attributes was that he would smell fragrant even without using perfume; even so, he often used perfume in order that his community would follow it as a Sunnah, and because perfume was beloved to him. Tirmidhī related that the Prophet ﷺ said: 'Three things of your world are beloved to me: Perfume, women, and the coolness of my eyes is in prayer.' One of the proofs that a sweet fragrance was among his attributes, and that it was the sweetest of fragrances, and that his pure fragrance was sweeter than ambergris and musk, is the Ḥadīth

---

[31] Meaning that the child was not conceived during the end of a menstrual period, and that its mother did not become pregnant again whilst nursing him and so spoil his nursing. (*Sharḥ al-Mawāhib*)

related by Bukhārī, Muslim, and others, on the authority of Anas 🕮, who said: 'I never smelled any ambergris or musk, or anything sweeter than the fragrance of the Messenger of Allah 🕮, and I never touched anything, neither brocade nor silk, softer to touch than the Messenger of Allah 🕮.' The narration of Tirmidhī has it thus: 'Anas said: "I never smelled any musk or perfume sweeter than the fragrance of the sweat of the Messenger of Allah 🕮."'

Muslim also relates from Anas 🕮 that he said: 'The Messenger of Allah 🕮 was radiant in colour, and the beads of his sweat were like pearls. He strode with vigour when he walked. I never touched brocade nor silk softer than the palm of the Messenger of Allah 🕮, nor did I smell musk or ambergris sweeter than the scent of the Messenger of Allah 🕮.' Abū Nuʿaym and Khaṭīb narrate that Āmina, the mother of the Messenger of Allah 🕮, describing when she gave birth, said: '...Then I looked at him, and he was like the full moon, and his scent was like strong musk.'

Muslim narrates on the authority of Jābir b. Samura 🕮, who said: 'I once prayed the midday prayer with the Messenger of Allah 🕮. Afterwards, he left to go home, and I went with him. Two boys met him, and he 🕮 began to wipe their cheeks one after the other. As for me, he wiped my cheek, and I found his hand cool and fragrant, as though he had just taken it from a perfume vendor's vessel.' The *Musnad* of Imam Aḥmad includes the Ḥadīth of Abī Juḥayfa, who said: 'The Prophet 🕮 once made ablutions and prayed the midday prayer. Afterwards, the people stood up and began to take his hand and wipe it on their faces. I took his hand, and placed it on my face, and it was cooler than ice, and more fragrant than musk.'[32]

See, my brother, how these Ḥadīth clearly prove the sweetness of his 🕮 fragrance, a pure, integral, Muḥammadan fragrance, by which Allah 🕮 ennobled him to the height of nobility and honour.

---

[32] The basic form [*aṣl*] of this Ḥadīth was narrated by Bukhārī and Muslim.

The Ṣaḥāba would Perfume Themselves with the Prophet's Sweat ﷺ and seek Blessings from it

Imam Muslim narrated that Anas ﷺ said: 'The Prophet ﷺ came to our house and slept the siesta with us, and began to perspire. My mother—Umm Sulaym bint Milḥān—brought a perfume-bottle and began to decanter the sweat into it. The Prophet ﷺ woke up and said: "O Umm Sulaym, what are you doing?" She said: "We use your sweat as perfume, and it is the finest of perfumes."'

Muslim also narrated that Anas ﷺ said: 'The Prophet ﷺ used to visit Umm Sulaym and sleep in her bed when she was not in it.[33] One day he came and slept in her bed. She then came to the house. It was said to her: "The Prophet ﷺ went to sleep in your room on your bed." So she went in, and his ﷺ sweat had soaked into a part of the sheet. Umm Sulaym opened her purse, and began to soak up the sweat and squeeze it into bottles. The Prophet ﷺ woke up and said: "What are you doing, O Umm Sulaym?" She said: "O Messenger of Allah, we are seeking blessing for our children." He ﷺ said "You are right."'

Muslim narrated from Anas ﷺ on the authority of Umm Sulaym that the Prophet ﷺ used to take his siesta at her house, and she would spread a mat for him to sleep on.[34]

---

[33] She was of his ﷺ unmarriageable kin.

[34] Imam al-Nawawī said, commenting on this Ḥadīth: 'She was unmarriageable kin to him ﷺ, so this Ḥadīth proves the permissibility of visiting unmarriageable kin and sleeping at their houses.' He also said in *Tahdhīb al-Asmā'*: 'Umm Sulaym: It is differed as to what her first name was. Some say Sahla, others Ramla, other Anīsa, others Ramītha, others Ramīṣā'. She was the daughter of Milḥān (or Malḥān), and she was the mother of Anas b. Mālik, the servant of the Messenger of Allah ﷺ—on this there is no difference among the scholars. Umm Sulaym and her sister were aunts to the Messenger of Allah ﷺ by nursing, and she was among the best of the Ṣaḥāba.' So it should not be inferred from this Ḥadīth that he ﷺ was in seclusion with a strange woman, for Umm Sulaym was his unmarriageable kin, his aunt by nursing (breast-feeding).

Indeed, he ﷺ distanced himself from such a suggestion, and repudiated that it should be thought of him: it is narrated by Bukhārī

The Prophet ﷺ would perspire a lot, and she would gather the sweat into perfume bottles. The Prophet ﷺ said: 'O Umm Sulaym, What is this?' She said: 'I mix your sweat with my perfume.' The narration of Aḥmad adds: 'So he prayed for her with a beautiful prayer.'

Umm ʿĀsim, the wife of ʿUtba b. Farqad al-Sulamī said: 'I was one of ʿUtba's four wives, and there was not one woman among us who did not try her best to wear perfume in order to be more fragrant than the others. ʿUtba did not wear perfume, except the oil he would put in his beard, and yet he was the most fragrant of all of us. When he went out, the people would say: "We have never smelt a finer fragrance than ʿUtba's." I said to him one day: "We all try hard to wear nice perfume, but you are more fragrant than all of us. How is this?" ʿUtba replied: "I had a skin complaint in the time of the Messenger of Allah ﷺ, and I went to him ﷺ to complain about it. He told me to undress, so I did so, and stood before him, covering my private parts with my clothes.[35] The Messenger of Allah ﷺ then blew into his hand and rubbed my back and my belly with it. Since that day, this fragrance has stayed with me."'[36]

Abū Yaʿlā and Ṭabarānī narrated the Ḥadīth of Abū Hurayra concerning the story of the man who asked for the Prophet's ﷺ help preparing his daughter for her wedding when he had nothing. The Prophet ﷺ called for a vessel, collected some of his sweat therein, and said: 'Shake this, and let her use it as perfume.'

---

and Muslim on the authority on ʿAlī b. al-Ḥusayn ﷺ that Ṣafiyya ﷺ, the wife of the Prophet ﷺ, said: 'I came to visit the Prophet ﷺ one night when he was on spiritual retreat, and I spoke with him, and then stood to return home. He stood with me to bid me farewell, when two men from the Anṣār passed by. When they saw the Prophet ﷺ, they sped up. The Prophet ﷺ said: "Slow down, she is Ṣafiyya bint Ḥuyayy!" They said "*Subḥān Allah* (Exalted is Allah), O Messenger of Allah!" He ﷺ said: "Satan flows in the Son of Adam like blood; I feared that he would cast evil (in another narration: 'something') into your hearts."' This Ḥadīth legislated for his ﷺ community after him that it is not acceptable for any of them, no matter how high his status or good his character, to be in seclusion with a woman not from his unmarriageable kin.

[35] That is, he covered all his ʿawra.

[36] Narrated by Ṭabarānī in *al-Kabīr* and *al-Ṣaghīr*.

When she put in on, everyone in the city smelled the scent of the perfume, and the family became known as 'the house of the fragrant ones.'[37]

HIS SWEET FRAGRANCE ﷺ WOULD CLING TO EVERYTHING HE TOUCHED AND EVERY WAY HE PASSED BY

Ṭabarānī and Bayhaqī narrated that Wā'il ﷺ said: 'Whenever I used to shake the Messenger of Allah's ﷺ hand, or touch his skin with mine, I would be aware of his touch on my hand afterwards: the scent was more fragrant than musk.'

'Ā'isha ﷺ said: 'The palm of the Messenger of Allah ﷺ was softer than silk, and it was as though he had the hand of a perfume-seller, whether he wore perfume or not. When he shook hands with someone, that person would remark the fragrance for the rest of the day. If he ﷺ patted a child's head, that child would be distinct from other children by the fragrance.'[38]

Anas ﷺ said: 'When the Messenger of Allah ﷺ passed down any of Medina's streets, the people would notice the fragrant scent there, and would say: 'The Messenger of Allah ﷺ has been this way.'[39]

Jābir b. 'Abdullāh ﷺ said: 'One of the attributes of the Messenger of Allah ﷺ was that no one would walk down a street, after he ﷺ had walked down it, without knowing that he had been that way, by the fragrance of his sweat and his sweet scent. Another is that he would never pass by a stone except that it would prostrate before him.'[40]

May Allah show compassion to the one who said:

> *Were a group of riders to follow you,*
> *Your sweet fragrance would be enough to guide them.*

---

[37] *Fatḥ al-Bārī*

[38] Narrated by Abū Nu'aym and Bayhaqī.

[39] Narrated by Abū Ya'lā and Bazzār with a rigorously authentic chain of transmission.

[40] Narrated by Dārimī, Bayhaqī, and Abū Nu'aym. (See *al-Mawāhib*)

The *Musnad* contains the Ḥadīth of Wāʾil Ibn Ḥajar, who said: 'The Prophet was once given a pitcher of water. He drank from it, and then spat into the pitcher, then into the well, and a scent rose from it like the fragrance of musk.'

THE UNIQUE QUALITIES OF HIS SALIVA

Allah bequeathed to His Messenger many unique qualities related to his saliva, including healing powers, the ability to quench thirst, and energy, strength, blessing and increase, and many others. How many ill people did he treat with his noble saliva, curing them instantly!

Bukhārī and Muslim narrate on the authority of Sahl b. Saʿd that the Messenger of Allah said on the day of Khaybar: 'Tomorrow, I will give my standard to a man by whose hand Allah will bring victory; he loves Allah and His Messenger, and Allah and His Messenger love him!' The next day, when the people woke, they all went to the Messenger of Allah hoping that he would give it to them. He said: 'Where is ʿAlī b. Abī Ṭālib?' They said; 'O Messenger of Allah, his eyes are ill.' He said: 'Send him to me.' So he was brought forward—or, in Muslim's narration, Salama said: 'The Messenger of Allah sent me to ʿAlī, and I came leading him, and his eyes were sore'—so the Messenger of Allah spat in his eyes and he was cured, as though he had never had any affliction.'

Ibn Ḥibbān narrates in his *Zawāʾid* that ʿAbdullāh b. Barīda said: 'I heard my father say: "The Messenger of Allah spat on the leg of ʿAmr b. Muʿādh when it was cut off, and he was cured."'

His saliva was also filling for those who partook of it, as in the narration of Bayhaqī in *al-Dalāʾil*, which reports that on the day of ʿĀshūrāʾ, the Prophet would call for the babies of his household, and of his daughter Fāṭima's household, and spit into their mouths, then say to their mothers: 'Do not nurse them until the night.' His saliva would suffice them from needing to be nursed. Ibn ʿAsākir narrates that the Prophet once gave (his grandson) Ḥasan b. ʿAlī his tongue when he was suffering from extreme thirst. Ḥasan sucked it until his thirst was quenched.

Ṭabarānī and Abū Nuʿaym narrate that ʿAmīra bint Masʿūd al-Anṣāriyya and her sisters came to the Prophet ﷺ to pledge allegiance to him. There were five of them. They found him ﷺ eating jerked meat, and so he ﷺ bit off a piece for them. ʿAmīra said: 'Then he gave me the meat, and I divided it between them, and they all ate a piece. From then until the day they met Allah ﷻ, the scent of their breaths never changed.'

HIS CLEANLINESS ﷺ

The Prophet ﷺ was the cleanest of Allah's ﷻ creation, in his body, his clothing, his house, and his social gatherings. His ﷺ noble body was clean and immaculate, as in the Ḥadīth of Hind b. Abī Hāla, in which it is mentioned that his bare skin was bright and shining, meaning that those parts of his body not covered by hair or clothing were the height of beauty and purity.

This is evidence of his ﷺ cleanliness, as is another statement from the same Ḥadīth: 'His neck was as fine as a statue's, pure as silver.' Tirmidhī narrated that Abī al-Ṭufayl said: 'The Messenger of Allah ﷺ was white and handsome, and medium in stature.' Tirmidhī also narrates on the authority of Ibn Abī Juḥayfa that his father said: 'I saw the Prophet ﷺ wearing a red shawl. It was as though his shins were shimmering.' This is because his ﷺ robe fell to his shins, below the knee.

The natural sweet fragrance of his ﷺ sweat is the greatest evidence of the cleanliness of his ﷺ body. Bukhārī and Muslim narrate that Anas ﷺ said: 'I touched neither silk nor brocade softer than the palm of the Messenger of Allah ﷺ, and I never smelled any breath or perfume'—and in one narration 'or any sweat'—'more fragrant than the breath and scent of the Prophet ﷺ.'

Abī Qirṣāfa said: 'My mother, my aunt and I pledged allegiance to the Messenger of Allah ﷺ, and as we were leaving him to go home, my mother and my aunt said to me: "O child, we have never seen the like of this man, nor any face more handsome than his, nor anyone with cleaner clothes, nor softer speech. It was as though we saw light shining from his mouth.'"[41]

So he ﷺ was the cleanest of Allah's creation in both body and clothing. He ﷺ would clean his teeth when leaving and entering his house.

HIS ENJOINING OF CLEANLINESS ﷺ

He ﷺ would enjoin and encourage cleanliness, and discourage uncleanliness. This message came from him in several different forms.

Firstly: He ﷺ clearly stated that cleanliness is one of the principles of Islam. Tirmidhī narrated on the authority of Saʻd ﷺ that the Prophet ﷺ said: 'Allah is Good, and loves goodness.[42] He is Clean, and loves cleanliness.[43] He is Generous,[44] and loves generosity. So keep your courtyards clean, and be not like the Jews.'

Sulaymān b. Ṣurad reported that the Messenger of Allah ﷺ said: 'Clean your teeth, and keep yourselves clean, and perform actions in odd numbers, for Allah is an odd number [*witr*], and loves odd numbers.'[45]

---

[41] In *Majmaʻ al-Zawāʾid,* the author says: '(This Ḥadīth) was narrated by Ṭabarānī, and its chain of transmission includes people unknown to me.

[42] Meaning: Allah is Free of any deficiencies and far removed from any flaws and faults. He loves goodness, which is everything permissible [*ḥalāl*] in origin and execution in regard to the Sacred Law, free from trickery and the like. (*Fayḍ al-Qadīr*)

[43] The great scholar Khafājī said (in summary): 'Allah's being described as 'Clean' in the Ḥadīth, though no one mentions it as one of His Names ﷻ, is considered to be a form of (rhetorical) resemblance, which the earlier scholars also termed 'coupling' (i.e. between 'Clean' and 'cleanliness' etc. [t.]); therefore it should not be objected to. It is also said to mean 'Sacred' (al-Quddūs).'

[44] That is, He is Magnanimous and Bounteous. (*Fayḍ al-Qadīr*)

[45] Narrated by Ibn Abī Shayba and Ṭabarānī. Munāwī said that it is made sound by corroborating reports [*ḥasan li-ghayrihi*].

Khaṭīb and others narrate on the authority of ʿĀʾisha ؉ that the Prophet ﷺ said: 'Islam is clean, so keep yourselves clean—for none will enter Paradise except those who are clean.'

Abū Hurayra ؉ said (quoting the Prophet)[46] ﷺ: 'Keep yourselves clean as well as you are able, for Allah ﷻ has built Islam on cleanliness, and none will enter Paradise save those who are clean.'[47]

Secondly: He ﷺ stressed the importance of maintaining the cleanliness of the body in all its forms:

He ﷺ enjoined bathing, and cautioned against leaving it: Imam Aḥmad narrated on the authority of Jābir ؉ that the Prophet ﷺ said: 'It is incumbent upon every Muslim man to bathe one day out of every seven, and that day is Friday.'[48]

He ﷺ urged the maintenance of the cleanliness of the entire body, and freeing it of dirt, as a part of the religious disposition brought by all Divine Revelations: Muslim narrated on the authority of ʿĀʾisha ؉ that the Prophet ﷺ said: 'Ten aspects of natural disposition [*fiṭra*]:[49] Trimming the moustache and letting the beard grow, using a tooth-stick, cleaning the nose with water, trimming nails, cleaning the knuckles, plucking underarm hair,[50] and shaving the private

---

[46] Ar. *Marfūʿan*

[47] Khafājī (in *Sharḥ al-Shifā*) ascribed the Ḥadīth to Rāfiʿī in *Tārīkh Qazwīn*, and said: 'As we have mentioned, the Ḥadīth has been related from numerous chains which make up for its initial weakness, and so it can be deemed to be no longer weak, but sound [*ḥasan*]. Its meaning is correct and in correspondence with the Sacred Law.'

[48] Also narrated by Nasāʾī and Ibn Ḥibbān.

[49] That is, the religious disposition that Allah has inclined His servants towards. Allah ﷻ says: ﴾Allah's disposition upon which He has placed humanity. There is no change in the Creation of Allah: That is the Upright Religion.﴿ (Qurʾān 30:30) It is one of the matters that all the Prophets brought, and is agreed upon by all Divine Laws.

[50] There is no harm in shaving it rather than plucking it.

parts and cleaning them with water.'[51]

The Prophet 🕮 warned against neglecting this for a long period, as narrated in the *Sunan* of Abū Dāwūd on the authority of Ḥasan 🕮, who said: 'With regard to cutting the moustache, trimming nails, plucking underarm hair and shaving the private parts, the Prophet 🕮 set us a time limit for leaving them of forty nights'—that is, if there was a reason to leave them, or it was for some reason not possible for someone to bathe, cut and clip every week, it was impermissible for them to leave it more than forty nights. If they were to leave it that long, they would be sinful, as the scholars have said.[52]

Thirdly: He 🕮 stressed the importance of washing after eating and drinking. Ḥakīm al-Tirmidhī related on the authority of 'Abdullāh b. Busr that the Prophet 🕮 said: 'Trim your nails, and bury the clippings, and clean your knuckles, and clean your gums after eating, and clean your teeth, and do not come to me with your teeth stained with food, and your breath rank.'[53]

Tirmidhī narrated on the authority of Salmān 🕮 that the Prophet 🕮 said: 'The blessed increase of food lies in ablution before it, and ablution after it.'

The meaning of 'ablution' [*wuḍū*'] here is the lexical meaning, washing the hands, not the *wuḍū*' of the Sacred Law, meaning the obligatory washing of certain limbs. The proof of this is the Ḥadīth narrated by Tirmidhī with a rigorously authentic chain on

---

[51] Ar. *intiqāṣ al-māʾ*, according to Shaykh ʿAlī al-Qārī a synonym for *istinjā*, 'cleaning the private parts with water after answering a call of nature.' (*Sharḥ al-Shifāʾ*)

[52] It is preferred to bury cut nails and hair, because of the narration of Ḥakīm al-Tirmidhī on the authority of ʿĀʾisha 🕮 who said: 'The Prophet 🕮 would enjoin the burial of seven things of the human body: Hair, nails, blood, menses, teeth, foreskin, and the placenta.' Some of this was also narrated by Ṭabarānī in *al-Fatḥ al-Kabīr*.

[53] [This is the Ḥadīth] as mentioned in *al-Jāmiʿ al-Ṣaghīr* with the explanation of Munāwī from his *al-Sharḥ al-Kabīr* for the final expressions ('with your teeth stained with food...'), though he mentions that Ḥakīm has it: '[do not come to me] dry and cracked' and that he isn't aware of any narration containing the words 'stained with...'

the authority of Ibn ʿAbbās ☙ that the Prophet ﷺ was presented with food, and it was said to him: 'Should we not bring you water for *wuḍūʾ*?' He replied: 'I was only ordered to make *wuḍūʾ* when I stand for prayer.'

Fourthly: He ﷺ stressed the importance of clean clothing. Ṭabarānī and Abū Nuʿaym narrate on the authority of ʿUmar b. al-Khaṭṭāb ☙ that the Prophet ﷺ said: 'Of the nobility of the believer in the Sight of Allah is the cleanliness of his clothing, and his contentment with that which is easy,' that is, of the affairs of this world.

Abū Nuʿaym also related on the authority of Jābir ☙ that the Messenger of Allah ﷺ once saw a man whose clothes were dirty, and said: 'Could this man not find anything with which to clean his clothes?'

Here we see the Prophet ﷺ censuring dirty clothes. He did not address the man directly so as not to offend him by confronting him with something he would not like, and to show that the ruling was not personally directed at him, but rather was a censure directed at anyone who leaves his clothes dirty.

He ﷺ would also forbid exposing clothing to dirt, as in the Ḥadīth related by Tirmidhī in his *Shamāʾil* on the authority of Ashʿath b. Salīm, who said: 'I heard from my aunt that my uncle said: "Once, when I was walking in Medina, a man behind me said: 'Lift your loincloth, for it would be cleaner'—and in another narration: 'more pious'[54]—'and longer-lasting.' I realised it was the Messenger of Allah ﷺ, so I said: 'O Messenger of Allah, it is only a grey[55] robe.' The Prophet ﷺ replied: 'Am I not an example for you?' I looked, and saw that the hem of his ﷺ loincloth was half way up his shin."'[56]

---

[54] 'More pious,' meaning avoiding dirt out of fear for Allah ﷻ by distancing oneself from pride and conceit. (*Sharḥ al-Zurqānī*)

[55] Ar. *malḥāʾ*, meaning white mixed with black, according to *al-Ṣiḥāḥ*; and it is said that it means black and white-striped. The meaning of the statement is that it is not the kind of garment worn in gatherings and celebrations; it is a garment for work, not adornment. (*Sharḥ al-Shamāʾil*)

[56] This Ḥadīth guides us to look after what we wear, and protect and take care of it, because neglecting it is waste and squander.

Fifthly: He 🕮 stressed the importance of keeping homes and courtyards clean, as in the above Ḥadīth: 'So keep your courtyards clean, and be not like the Jews.'

Sixthly: He stressed the importance of maintaining the cleanliness of mosques, and made it clear that this is an act of worship, and one of the greatest good deeds.

Abū Dāwūd and Tirmidhī narrate on the authority of Anas 🕮 that the Prophet 🕮 said: 'The rewards of my community were shown to me, even [for] the small obstacle that a man removes from the mosque; and the sins of my community were shown to me, and I did not see a sin graver than a Sūrah or Āyah of the Qur'ān that a man was given, then forgot.'

It is related in Muslim's *Ṣaḥīḥ*, and elsewhere, on the authority of Abū Dharr al-Ghifārī 🕮 that the Prophet 🕮 said: 'My community and its works were shown to me, both good and bad, and I saw amongst the good acts: removing obstacles from the street; and I saw amongst the bad acts: phlegm spat on the floor of the mosque and not buried.'

Maintaining the cleanliness of the mosque, even from a small obstacle, carries with it great reward; and leaving phlegm and dirt in the mosques carries grave recompense. If the believer is commanded to remove phlegm from the mosque, and it is forbidden for him to leave it if he sees it, how could it be permissible for him to spit in the mosque, or cause it to become dirty in any way? This is an even graver sin.

It is incumbent upon the Muslims that they maintain the cleanliness of their mosques, out of fear of punishment, and out of desire for reward!

He 🕮 also stressed the importance of perfuming, cleaning and maintaining mosques. 'Ā'isha 🕮 said: 'The Messenger of Allah 🕮 instructed us to build mosques in our places of residence, and keep them clean and perfumed.'[57]

---

[57] Mundhirī said: 'It was related by Aḥmad and Tirmidhī (who declared it rigorously authentic), and by Abū Dāwūd and Ibn Mājah.'

Samura b. Jundub said: 'The Messenger of Allah 🕮 instructed us to make prayer rooms in our homes, and instructed us to clean them.'[58]

So the Prophet 🕮 enjoined the maintenance of the cleanliness of mosques both public and private, that is those mosques that are built in houses as a place to offer supererogatory and night prayers, and to worship Allah therein, which is a desired Sunnah according to the scholars.

Seventhly: He 🕮 stressed the importance of maintaining the cleanliness of streets and public places, and forbade that they be polluted with dirt and harmful things. He 🕮 declared that this is considered one of the branches of faith, without which it is incomplete.

Bukhārī and Muslim narrate on the authority of Abū Hurayra 🕮 that the Messenger of Allah 🕮 said: 'Faith is seventy-something' —and in another narration 'sixty-something'—'branches. The best of these is saying *There is no god but Allah*, and the lowest is removing obstacles from the street.'

If the believer is not permitted by his faith to leave an obstacle he sees in the street and is able to remove, and which no one else will remove, then it is even more fitting and true that it is impermissible for him to place an obstacle in the street. So reflect, O Muslim, and know that the cleanliness of the roads and streets is part of faith, not merely an extra virtue or something to brag about.

The Prophet 🕮 ordered the removal of harmful obstacles from the street, saying (as narrated by Ibn Ḥibbān on the authority of Abī Barza): 'Remove harmful obstacles from the streets of the Muslims.' He 🕮 also warned those who harmed the Muslims in their streets, as Ṭabarānī narrated with a sound chain on the authority of Ḥudhayfa b. Usayd 🕮, who reported that the Prophet 🕮 said: 'Whosoever harms the Muslims in their streets obliges upon himself their curse.'

---

[58] Narrated by Aḥmad and Tirmidhī, who declared it rigorously authentic. (*Al-Targhīb*)

Ṭabarānī and Bayhaqī narrate on the authority of Abū Hurayra ﷺ that the Prophet ﷺ said: 'Whosoever washes their filth[59] into one of the streets of the Muslims has upon them the curse of Allah, the angels, and all humanity.'

Muslim and others narrate on the authority of Abū Hurayra ﷺ that the Messenger of Allah said: 'Be wary of the two cursed ones.'[60] The people said: 'Who are the two cursed ones, O Messenger of Allah?' He said: 'The one who relieves himself in public streets, or in places of shade,' meaning meeting and gathering places, and the like.

He ﷺ also praised the one who removes harmful obstacles from the street. Bukhārī and Muslim narrate on the authority of Abū Hurayra ﷺ that the Messenger of Allah ﷺ said: 'Once a man was walking in the street, whereupon he found a thorny branch, and moved it, giving thanks to Allah, and so Allah forgave him.' Honour and magnify this noble Prophet ﷺ, who brought happiness and cleanliness to this world, and joy and delight for the next!

Eighthly: The legislation of *wuḍū'* and *ghusl* (washing) that the Messenger of Allah ﷺ brought is the greatest evidence that cleanliness is one of the fundamentals of Islam, and one of the most important principles that the Messenger of Allah ﷺ brought.

They include the removal of impurities, and the effacement of impure incidents, and cleanliness from dirt and filth, and, what is more, the wisdom of the Sacred Law, by their removal of sins and transgressions, as in the Ḥadīth on the authority of Abū Hurayra ﷺ, who reported that the Messenger of Allah ﷺ said: 'When the Muslim'—or 'believing'—'servant makes *wuḍū'*, and washes his face, all the sins he witnesses with his eyes are washed off with the water'—or 'with the final drop of water.'—'When he washes his hands, all the sins his hands have committed are

---

[59] Meaning their dirt and refuse. If all civilisations require the cleanliness of individuals and cities, the faith of the believers and their Islamic civilisation requires from them cleanliness in its most perfect forms.

[60] Or 'the two whose actions cause the people to curse them.' (See Nawawī, *Sharḥ Ṣaḥīḥ Muslim*)

washed away with the water'—or 'with the last drop of the water.' When he washes his feet, all the sins his feet took him to are washed away with the water'—or 'with the last drop of the water'—until he finishes clean of sin.'[61]

There are also a great many health-related wisdoms that derive from the legislation of *wuḍū'* and *ghusl* including renewed vigour and physical vitality, the removal of the traces of bodily secretions, and many others which would require long examination.

Ninthly: The Prophetic Ḥadīth which stress the importance of cleaning the teeth with a tooth-stick [*siwāk*], highlighting its benefits and warning against leaving it, are the clearest evidence that cleanliness and the preservation of physical well-being are Islamic principles.

As for its benefits: Nasā'ī and others on the authority of 'Ā'isha ﵂ that the Messenger of Allah ﷺ said: 'The tooth-stick is purifying for the mouth, and pleasing to the Lord.'

Aḥmad narrated on the authority of Ibn 'Umar ﵃ that the Prophet ﷺ said: 'Use the tooth-stick, for within it is the sweetening of the mouth, and the pleasure of the Lord, Blessed and Exalted is He!'

As for his ﷺ stressing its importance: He ﷺ said: 'If not for my concern for my community, I would have ordered them to use the tooth-stick with every prayer' (That is, I would have made it obligatory for them). Bukhārī narrated it with this wording. Muslim has it: 'at every prayer,' and Nasā'ī, Ibn Mājah and Ibn Ḥibbān have it: 'I would have ordered them to use the tooth-stick when performing ablutions for every prayer.' Aḥmad has it: 'I would have ordered them to use the tooth-stick with every ablution.' Bazzār and Ṭabarānī have it: 'I would have made it obligatory for them to use the tooth-stick for every prayer, just as I made it obligatory for them to perform ablutions.'

---

[61] Ḥāfiẓ al-Mundhirī says in *al-Targhīb*: 'It was narrated by Mālik, Muslim and Tirmidhī, and the washing of the feet is not mentioned in the narration of Mālik and Tirmidhī.'

Jābir 🕌 reported that the Messenger of Allah 🕌 said: 'Two units of prayer after using the tooth-stick is better than seventy units of prayer without using it.'[62]

Because of this, he 🕌 would use the tooth-stick very often. The *Ṣaḥīḥ* collection of Muslim, among others, contains the Ḥadīth on the authority of Shurayḥ b. Hānī, who asked 'Ā'isha 🕌: 'What would be the first thing the Prophet 🕌 did when he entered the house?' She replied: 'Use the tooth-stick.'

Tenthly: He stressed the importance of washing and cleaning in between after eating:

Abū Ayyūb al-Anṣārī 🕌 said: 'The Messenger of Allah 🕌 came out to us and said: "Blessed are those who clean between from my community." [Abū Ayyūb said:] And who are those who clean between, O Messenger of Allah?

'He said: "Those who clean between in their ablutions, and those who clean between when eating. As for cleaning between in ablution: it is rinsing out the mouth and nose, and cleaning between the fingers. As for cleaning between when eating: there is nothing graver upon the two angels than seeing food between their companion's teeth when he stands in prayer."'[63]

HIS BEAUTY AND BEAUTIFICATION 🕌

Allah 🕌 created our Master Muḥammad 🕌 in the most beautiful of human images, and the most perfected of Adamic forms. He 🕌 gathered within him 🕌 the compendium of finery, magnificence, favour and perfection. Allah 🕌 said: ❲He increases the creation of that which He wills. Allah is Able to do all things.❳[64]

So He increases the perfections and beauty of creation as He wills to increase, and He 🕌 increased in the beauty and fairness of the creation of this Noble Prophet 🕌 until he surpassed the

---

[62] Narrated by Abū Nuʿaym with a sound [*ḥasan*] chain, as mentioned by Mundhirī in *al-Targhīb*.

[63] Narrated by Ṭabarānī in *al-Kabīr*, and in a condensed form by Imam Aḥmad, as reported in *al-Targhīb*.

[64] Qur'ān 35:1

peak of fine and noble physical constitution, just as He ﷻ increased the perfection of his ﷺ personal character, until he surpassed the peak of exalted character, as Allah ﷻ said: ❲And indeed, you are on an exalted character.❳[65]

The Ṣaḥāba ﷺ who described him all agreed that neither before nor after him was seen anyone like him ﷺ.

The Commander of the Believers ʿAlī b. Abī Ṭālib said: 'The Messenger of Allah ﷺ was neither short nor tall. His head was large. His hands, his feet, and his joints were prominent. The complexion of his face was red. He had a thin line of hair from his chest to his navel. When he walked, it was as though he was descending from a height. I saw neither before nor after him anyone like him.'[66]

Barāʾ b. ʿĀzib ﷺ said: 'The Prophet ﷺ had the handsomest face and the most excellent character of all people. He was neither excessively tall nor short.'[67] Abū Hurayra ﷺ said: 'I never saw anything fairer than the Messenger of Allah ﷺ; it was as though the sun shone from his face.'[68]

His beautification ﷺ and his enjoining of it: The Prophet ﷺ would beautify himself, and order his companions to beautify themselves. He would affirm this with regard to gatherings and meetings generally, and with regard to Fridays and religious festivals especially. Bayhaqī narrated that the Prophet ﷺ had a cloak that he would wear for the two ʿĪds and Fridays.

Ibn al-Sunnī narrated on the authority of ʿĀʾisha ﷺ that the Prophet ﷺ went out one day to see his brethren, and looked into a jug of water to see his hair and his appearance, and then said: 'Allah is Beautiful, and loves beauty; if one of you goes out to see his brethren, let him prepare himself.'[69]

---

[65] Qurʾān 68:4

[66] Narrated by Imam Aḥmad with this wording; Tirmidhī's similar narration has already been mentioned.

[67] Agreed upon by Bukhārī and Muslim.

[68] Narrated by Tirmidhī.

[69] See Munāwī's commentary on *al-Jāmiʿ al-Ṣaghīr*, vol. 3.

'Beautification'[70] means a person's utilising that which preserves their beauty, and avoiding that which disfigures their personal appearance.

Abū Nuʿaym and Wāqidī narrate on the authority of Jundub b. Makīth that whenever the Prophet ﷺ was visited by a delegation, he would wear his finest clothes, and order his companions to do likewise. Jundub said: 'I saw him when a delegation of Kinda was sent to him, and he was wearing a Yemeni cloak, as were Abū Bakr and ʿUmar.'[71]

The Prophet ﷺ informed us that a fine appearance and beautiful dress are among the sound characteristics of the Prophets. Tirmidhī narrates on the authority of ʿAbdullāh b. Sarjis ﷺ that the Prophet ﷺ said: 'Virtuous conduct and providence are one twenty-fifth of Prophethood.' Mālik's narration in the *Muwaṭṭaʾ* has it: 'Providence, deliberation and good appearance are one twenty-fifth of Prophethood.'[72]

The Prophet ﷺ would chastise those who exposed their physical appearance to disfiguration, as in the chapter in the *Muwaṭṭaʾ* entitled *Concerning the wearing of clothes as a means of beautification*, in which it is narrated that Jābir b. ʿAbdullāh ﷺ said: 'We went out with the Messenger of Allah to the battle of Anmār. As I was sitting under a tree, the Messenger of Allah ﷺ came along. I said: "O Messenger of Allah, come and seek shade." The Messenger of Allah ﷺ sat down. I went to one of the sacks,

---

[70] Ar. *al-tajammul*

[71] See the first volume of *al-Tarātīb*.

[72] 'Good appearance' [*al-samt al-ḥasan*], according to Munāwī, means a fair appearance and bearing. 'Orientation' means 'direction,' which became (in Arabic) a metaphor for beautiful clothing, and an exemplary manner of dress. 'Virtuous conduct' [*al-hadī al-ṣāliḥ*] means upright behaviour and good conduct. 'Providence' [*al-iqtiṣād*, or *al-qaṣd*] means taking the middle position in all affairs between negligence and exaggeration, such as generosity, which is between miserliness and wasteful extravagance; or bravery, which is between cowardliness and recklessness, etc. 'Deliberation' means patience and forbearance in affairs, and not rushing them, so that their consequences can become clear, both good and ill.

and searched in it for something. I found some cucumber,[73] so I sliced it and presented it to the Messenger of Allah ﷺ. He said: "From where did you bring this?" I said: "We brought it with us from town." There was a companion of ours with us, whom we would provide for, who herded the sheep. So, I gave him his provisions at midday, and he turned to go. He was wearing two robes, which were threadbare and ragged. The Messenger of Allah ﷺ looked at him and said: "Does he not have any clothes other than these?" I said: "Yes, O Messenger of Allah, he has two robes in the luggage, which I gave to him." He said: "Call him, and have him wear them." So I called him, and he put them on, and then turned to go. The Messenger of Allah ﷺ said: "What is the matter with him? May his neck be struck, is that not better for him?" The man heard this, and said:"O Messenger of Allah, do you mean in Allah's cause?" (That is, that Allah cause him to die whilst fighting in His cause.)[74] The Messenger of Allah ﷺ said: "In Allah's cause." Later, the man was indeed killed fighting in Allah's cause.'

Mālik narrated that he was informed that ʿUmar b. al-Khaṭṭāb ﷺ said: 'I love to see a reciter (of the Qurʾān) wearing white clothes.' ʿUmar also said: 'If Allah is generous to you, be generous to yourselves; let a man accumulate clothes.' That is, it is good for him to accumulate clothes.

Abū Nuʿaym and Ibn Lāl and others narrate that Ibn ʿUmar said, quoting the Messenger of Allah ﷺ:[75] 'The believer takes his good conduct from Allah; if He is generous to him, he is generous to himself.'[76]

Ḥākim narrated, with his chain of transmission on the authority of Sahl b. al-Ḥanẓaliyya, that the Prophet ﷺ said: 'Beautify your clothes, and prepare your mounts well, so that you stand out[77] amongst the people.'[78]

---

[73] Ar. *qiththāʾ*, a name for cucumber, according to Zurqānī's commentary on the *Muwaṭṭaʾ*.

[74] I.e. Jihād (*Sharḥ al-Zurqānī*)

[75] I.e. *marfūʿan*

[76] See Zurqānī's commentary on the *Muwaṭṭaʾ*.

[77] Literally, 'so that you are as if you are a birthmark or a beauty-spot [*shāma*] amongst the people.'

[78] See *al-Fatḥ al-Kabīr*.

Ṭabarānī and Bayhaqī narrate on the authority of 'Imrān b. Ḥusayn 餐 that the Prophet 餐 said: 'When Allah favours a servant with a blessing, He loves to see the effect of His favour on His servant.'

Bayhaqī narrated on the authority of Abū Hurayra 餐 that the Prophet 餐 said: 'When Allah 餐 favours a servant with a blessing, He loves to see the effect of that blessing, and He dislikes wretchedness and the affectation of wretchedness. He loathes the demanding beggar, and loves the one who is shy, modest and virtuous.'

THE KEENNESS OF HIS BLESSED SIGHT 餐

Allah 餐 said: ❨The sight did not deviate, nor did it transgress.❩[79] Allah 餐 described him 餐, whilst he was present in the Highest of Meeting Places, by saying that his sight did not deviate (i.e. waver or stray), nor transgress (i.e. did not go beyond that which it was beholding manifested before it). This is evidence of the keenness and soundness of his sight, because when vision is overwhelmed by dazzling light, it will either deviate and stray, or will look beyond the thing it is beholding out of fatigue and weakness. None of this happened to the Prophet 餐 because of the keen vision that Allah 餐 gave him.

The unique characteristics of his sight include his ability to see what others could not, as in the narration in the *Sunan* of Tirmidhī, and elsewhere, on the authority of Abū Dharr 餐, that the Prophet 餐 said: 'I see what you all see not, and I hear what you hear not...'

He would see Jibrīl and the blessed angels without their assuming guises: Imam Aḥmad narrates that Ibn Mas'ūd 餐 said: 'The Messenger of Allah 餐 saw Jibrīl in his true form. He had six hundred wings, each wing covering the horizon. Falling from each wing were gems, pearls and sapphires, the amount of which only Allah knows.'

---

[79] Qur'ān 53:17

As for his seeing the angels: One example of this is the relation of Anas ؓ: 'I was sitting with the Prophet ﷺ in a gathering, when a person came along and greeted the Prophet ﷺ and the others, saying: "Peace and mercy of Allah be upon you." The Prophet ﷺ replied: "Upon you be peace and the mercy and blessings of Allah." When the man sat down, he said: "Praise be to Allah in abundance, goodness, and blessed increase, as our Lord loves to be praised, and as is commensurate with Him!" The Prophet ﷺ said to him: "What did you say?" So he repeated it. The Prophet ﷺ said: "By He in whose Hand is my soul, ten angels hastened to write it down, but they didn't know how to write it, so they raised it to the Possessor of Might, and He said: 'Write it as my servant said it.'"'[80] Another example of this is how the Prophet ﷺ witnessed the angels washing the martyr Ḥanẓala ؓ, and how he witnessed Jaʿfar b. Abī Ṭālib ؓ in Paradise flying with the angels, endowed with two wings.

He ﷺ could also see great distances by Divine aid and strength: Bukhārī and Muslim narrate on the authority of Jābir ؓ that the Messenger of Allah ﷺ said: 'When Quraysh did not believe me, I stood in the sanctuary, and Allah showed me the Hallowed House,[81] and I began to tell them of its wonders, all the while looking at it.' So he ﷺ was in Mecca at the sanctuary, seeing the Hallowed House clearly before him.

Allah ﷻ showed him ﷺ the eastern and western extents of the earth: Muslim narrates in his *Ṣaḥīḥ*, as do others, on the authority of Thawbān ؓ that the Messenger of Allah ﷺ said: 'Allah gathered the earth before me and I saw the eastern and western extents of it; and my community's authority will extend over all of that which was gathered before me.' Ṭabarānī narrated on the authority of Ibn ʿUmar ؓ that the Messenger of Allah ﷺ

---

[80] Ḥāfiẓ al-Mundhirī said: 'Aḥmad narrated it, and the people in its chain of transmission are trustworthy. It was also narrated by Nasāʾī and Ibn Ḥibbān in his *Ṣaḥīḥ*, but with the wording "...as our Lord loves and approves."'
[81] In Jerusalem.

said: 'Allah brought the world before me, and I saw what will be therein until the Day of Resurrection, as clearly as I see my own hand.'[82]

He 🕌 could see what was behind him as clearly as he saw what was in front of him: Bukhārī and Muslim narrate (what follows is the wording of Muslim) on the authority of Abū Hurayra 🕌 that the Messenger of Allah 🕌 said: 'Do you see my *qibla* (direction of prayer) here? By Allah, your bows and prostrations are not hidden from me; I see you from behind my back.'

Muslim narrates in his *Ṣaḥīḥ* collection that Abū Hurayra 🕌 said: 'The Messenger of Allah 🕌 led us in prayer one day, and then left, saying: "O so-and-so, do you not pray properly? Should the one who prays not be mindful of how to pray? For he is only praying for his own sake! By Allah, I see what is behind my back just as I see what is in front of me."'

Muslim narrates that Anas 🕌 said: 'The Messenger of Allah 🕌 prayed with us one day. When the prayer was over, he turned his face to us, and said: "O people! I am your Imam, so do not get ahead of me when bowing and prostrating, nor in standing and exiting,[83] for I see you before me and behind me." He then said: "By the one is whose hand is the soul of Muḥammad, if you had seen what I have seen, you would laugh little and weep much." They said: "What have you seen, O Messenger of Allah?" He said: "I have seen Paradise and Hell."'

THE KEENNESS OF HIS NOBLE HEARING 🕌

Allah gave His Messenger our Master Muḥammad 🕌 a special ability to hear, so that he could hear what others could not:

It is narrated on the authority of Abū Dharr 🕌 that the Messenger of Allah 🕌 said: 'I see that which you all see not, and I

---

[82] See Zurqānī's commentary on *al-Mawāhib*, vol. 7.
[83] By giving *salām* at the end of the prayer, or by leaving the mosque after the prayer, in order not to miss a reminder or announcement about something concerning them.

hear that which you hear not. The sky groaned,[84] and it was right that it should groan: there is not within it a space of four fingers except therein is an angel bowing his forehead to Allah in prostration. By Allah, if you knew what I know you would laugh little and weep much, and you would go to the hills and beseech Allah 鷺.'[85]

He 鷺 could hear the door of the heavens open: Ṭabarānī narrated with a sound chain that Ibn 'Abbās 鷺 said: 'The Messenger of Allah 鷺 was on the mountain of Ṣafā with Jibrīl one day, and said: "O Jibrīl, by the One who sent you with the Truth, the family of Muḥammad has not left in its possession a single grain of flour, nor a handful of barley." As soon as he had spoken, he heard a tremendous crash in the heavens which startled him, and he said 鷺: "Has Allah commanded the Resurrection to begin?"

'Jibrīl said: "No, but He has commanded Isrāfīl to come to you with the keys of the earth's treasures, and He has commanded me to make a proposal to you and offer you the like of the mountains of Tihāma in emeralds, sapphires, gold and silver. If you wish, you will be a Prophet-King; and if you wish, you will be a Prophet-Servant." Jibrīl gestured to him to humble himself, so he said: "Nay, I will be a Prophet-Servant," and he repeated it three times, "and if I had said 'a Prophet-King,' the mountains would have come to me as gold."'[86]

He 鷺 could hear the polytheists being punished in their graves: Muslim narrated on the authority of Zayd b. Thābit 鷺, who said: 'One day, the Messenger of Allah 鷺 was in an orchard belonging to Banī al-Najjār, and we were with him. Suddenly, his

---

[84] I.e. a voice came from it because of [the burden of] the multitude of angels therein; the word in Arabic is derived from *al-aṭīṭ*, the groan of a camel.

[85] Narrated by Tirmidhī, Aḥmad, and others.

[86] Ḥāfiẓ al-Mundhirī said: 'It was narrated by Ṭabarānī with a sound [*ḥasan*] chain of transmission, and by Bayhaqī in *al-Zuhd*, and elsewhere.' The like of it is also in *Sharh al-Zurqānī*. Mundhirī also mentions the narration of Ibn Ḥibbān in his *Ṣaḥīḥ*.

mule bucked, and almost threw him, and (we saw that there were) five or six graves there. He ﷺ said: "Who knows the occupants of these graves?" A man said "I do." The Prophet ﷺ said: "When did they die?" The man said: "In (the time of) polytheism." The Prophet ﷺ said: "This community are afflicted in their graves. Were it not that you would not bury your dead, I would have asked Allah to let you hear the punishment of the grave as I hear it.'"

So he ﷺ could hear the torment of those punished in their graves, and he explained that if it were not for his concern that people would not bury each other if they heard the punishment of the grave, he would have called on Allah to let them hear it. However, if they had heard the punishment of the grave, fear and panic would have seized them, and this would have caused them to give up the practice of burying one another out of the fear of hearing it.

He ﷺ could hear the crash of a boulder falling from the precipice of Hell: Abū Saʿīd al-Khudrī ﷺ reported that the Messenger of Allah ﷺ heard a sound which alarmed him, so Jibrīl ﷺ came to him, and the Messenger of Allah ﷺ said: 'What was this sound, O Jibrīl?' He replied: 'It was a boulder, which fell from the precipice of Hell seventy years ago and just now landed at its bottom, and Allah wanted you to hear the sound it made.' After this the Messenger of Allah ﷺ was not seen smiling a full-mouthed smile until Allah ﷻ received him.[87]

He ﷺ heard the torment of those in their graves who had been tale-bearers and backbiters, and those who did not clean and guard themselves from urine: Bukhārī narrated on the authority of Ibn ʿAbbās ﷺ that the Prophet ﷺ passed by one of the walls of Mecca or Medina, and heard the sound of two people being tormented in their graves. The Prophet ﷺ said:

---

[87] Ḥāfiẓ al-Mundhirī ascribed the narration to Ṭabarānī with this wording, and Ḥāfiẓ al-Zurqānī ascribed it to Ibn Abī Shayba with a chain of transmission the narrators of which were trustworthy.

'They are being tormented; yet they are not being tormented for mortal sins.' He then said: 'Rather, one of them would not guard himself from urine, and the other would go about spreading rumours.'

Imam Aḥmad narrated on the authority of Abū Umāma ﷺ that the Prophet ﷺ passed by the graveyard of Baqiʿ al-Gharqad on a very hot day, with people walking behind him. When he heard the sound of their shoes, he realised that they were there, and so he sat down until they were in front of him.

When he passed by Baqiʿ al-Gharqad he came across two graves, in which they had just buried two men. The Prophet ﷺ stopped and said: 'Who have you buried here today?' They said: 'So-and-so and so-and-so.' They said: 'Why do you ask, O Prophet of Allah?' He said: 'As for one of them, he used to not clean himself from urine; and as for the other, he used to go around spreading rumours.' He took a moist palm-leaf, tore it in half, and placed a half on each of the two graves. They said: 'O Prophet of Allah, why did you do that?' He said: 'To lighten it for them.' They said: 'O Messenger of Allah, how long will they be tormented?' He said: 'It is a matter of the unseen, and no one knows it but Allah. Were it not for the separation of your hearts, and the abundance of your conversation, you would hear what I hear.'

PART II
THE ELOQUENCE AND WISDOM OF OUR MASTER MUḤAMMAD ﷺ

HIS NOBLE VOICE ﷺ

THE Prophet's ﷺ voice was at the peak of beauty. Allah ﷻ gifted him with the ability to make himself heard and to cast his voice over long distances and vast areas which no other voice could reach. Tirmidhī narrated that Anas ﷺ said: 'Allah did not send a Prophet except with a beautiful face and a beautiful voice, and your Prophet was the fairest of them in face[88] and voice.'

Bukhārī and Muslim narrate on the authority of Barāʾ b. ʿĀzib ﷺ, who said: 'The Messenger of Allah ﷺ once recited Sūrat al-Tīn in the ʿIshāʾ prayer, and I have never heard a more beautiful voice.' Abū al-Ḥasan b. al-Ḍaḥḥāk narrated that Jubayr b. Muṭʿim ﷺ said: 'The Prophet ﷺ had a beautiful tone of voice.'[89]

---

[88] As for his ﷺ statement in the Ḥadīth of the Night Ascension concerning Yūsuf: 'And then I met a man [meaning Yūsuf ﷺ] who was the most beautiful of Allah's creations, and who surpassed all humanity with his beauty like the full moon surpasses the other celestial bodies,' as in the narration of Bayhaqī, Ṭabarānī, and Ibn ʿĀʾidh: this is interpreted to refer to everyone except the Prophet ﷺ. A proof of this is the precept that the one who speaks is not included in the generality of their speech. An equivalent of this is the statement of the Prophet ﷺ in Muslim's narration: 'And he [Yūsuf] was given half of all beauty.' Ibn al-Munīr said: 'The meaning is that Yūsuf was given half the beauty that was given to our Prophet ﷺ.' See also the comment of Ḥāfiẓ Ibn Ḥajar in *Fatḥ al-Bārī*.

[89] See *Sharḥ al-Mawāhib*.

The aforementioned Ḥadīth of Umm Maʿbad included: 'His speech was sweet.'[90]

His voice would carry further than other voices could carry: Barāʾ b. ʿĀzib 🌙 said: 'The Messenger of Allah 🌙 addressed us so that his voice reached even the maidens in their chambers.'[91] ʿAbd al-Raḥmān b. Muʿādh 🌙 said: 'The Messenger of Allah 🌙 addressed us at Minā, and our hearing was opened so that we could hear what he said whilst we were in our houses. He began to teach them their pilgrimage rites, until he arrived at the stones. He extended his two index fingers and said: "Cast the stones."'[92]

Abū Nuʿaym narrated on the authority of ʿĀʾisha 🌙 that the Messenger of Allah 🌙 sat on the pulpit one Friday and said to the people: 'Sit,' and ʿAbdullāh b. Rawāḥa 🌙 heard him from Banī Ghanm,[93] and so sat down where he was.[94]

Ibn Mājah narrated that Umm Hāniʾ 🌙 said: 'We used to hear the Prophet 🌙 reciting in the middle of the night in the Kaʿba while I was in my bed.' That she could hear this while she was in her house, far from the place of recitation, is evidence that his

---

[90] Ibn al-Athīr said this means his 🌙 voice was soft, like a whisper, and not harsh.

[91] Narrated by Bayhaqī. 'Maidens' here means a young girl who has just begun to reach puberty. It is said that it means a girl who has reached adolescence, but has not yet left her parents, and not yet married. 'Chambers' here means a covered area, used to describe any house in which there is a woman. Barāʾ only specified them with mention because of their distance, and their being secluded in their houses. Their hearing the voice of the Prophet 🌙 while he was in the mosque and they were in their chambers is a sign indicating the strength of his 🌙 voice, and how it reached further than other voices.
(*Sharḥ al-Zurqānī ʿalā al-Mawāhib*)

[92] Narrated by Abū Dāwūd, Nasāʾī and Aḥmad. (*Sharḥ al-Mawāhib*)

[93] A branch of the tribe of Khazraj. (*Sharḥ al-Mawāhib*)

[94] This shows great haste to obey the Prophet's 🌙 commands, although he was not one of those to whom the command was given, because his 🌙 command was directed to those present at the sermon to sit. However, the perfection of good manners necessitated it. See the good conduct of the Ṣaḥāba with him 🌙!

blessed voice carried to places that no other voices could reach. Exalted is He who singled out the Prophet with such magnificent unique qualities and mighty signs!

THE SWEETNESS OF HIS SPEECH

The Messenger of Allah's speech was sweet and beautiful. When he spoke, he captured all hearts, and captivated spirits and minds. When he spoke, light would be emitted from between his teeth.

Ibn 'Abbās said: 'The Messenger of Allah had gaps between his teeth; when he spoke, it appeared as though light was coming from between them.'[95]

Abī Qirṣāfa said: 'My mother, my aunt and I pledged allegiance to the Messenger of Allah, and as we were leaving him to go home, my mother and my aunt said to me: "O child, we have never seen the like of this man, nor any face more handsome than his, nor anyone with cleaner clothes, nor softer speech. It was as though we saw light shining from his mouth."'[96]

THE PURITY AND ELOQUENCE OF HIS SPEECH

The Messenger of Allah was the most eloquent being in speech that Allah created, and the clearest of them in rhetoric. He was given the compendium of speech, and astonishing wisdom, and stern rebuke, and decisive command, and solid judgement, and sound advice, and profound counsel, and irrefutable argument, and conclusive proofs, and manifest evidences.

It is mentioned in the *Musnad* and elsewhere that 'Abdullāh b. 'Umar said: 'The Messenger of Allah came out to us one day as though he was preparing to bid us farewell, and said: "I am Muḥammad, the unlettered Prophet," repeating this three times, "There is no Prophet after me. I have been given the first of

---

[95] Ḥāfiẓ al-Zurqānī ascribed it to Tirmidhī, Dārimī and Ṭabarānī.
[96] In *Majma' al-Zawā'id*, the author says: '(This Ḥadīth) was narrated by Ṭabarānī, and its chain of transmission includes people unknown to me.'

speech and the last of it, and the compendium of it.'" How could he not be the most eloquent of Allah's ﷻ creation, when Allah ﷻ gave him speech that embodied many meanings in simple words?

'Umar ؓ related that the Prophet ﷺ said, whilst on the pulpit, 'O People! I have been given the compendium of speech and its keys, and it has been made concise for me. I have brought it (the Sacred Law) to you white and pure; so do not be confused, and do not let yourselves be harmed by those who are confused.'[97]

Abū Nu'aym narrated in *Tārīkh Aṣbahān* on the authority of Ibn 'Umar ؓ that 'Umar ؓ said: 'O Prophet of Allah, how is it that you are the most eloquent of us, when you never left our presence?' The Prophet ﷺ said: 'The language of Ismā'īl had vanished, so Jibrīl brought it to me and I retained it.'[98]

Ḥāfiẓ al-Zurqānī said:

> Indeed, the Messenger of Allah ﷺ surpassed this, for he would speak to everyone with their own language, with extensive eloquence, i.e. extensive in his ﷺ knowledge of all the languages of the Arabs, and their pure dialects, as is narrated in the *Musnad* and elsewhere on the authority of Ka'b b. 'Āṣim al-Ash'arī ؓ, who said: 'I heard the Messenger of Allah ﷺ say: It is not righteousness to fast when travelling" in the dialect of some of the people of Yemen.'"[99]

---

[97] Ḥāfiẓ Ibn Kathīr related the Ḥadīth in full, ascribed to Abū Ya'lā, and then said: 'Ibn Abī Ḥātim also narrated it, and it has other narrations which strengthen it.'

[98] Ḥāfiẓ al-Zurqānī said: 'Abū Nu'aym narrated it in *Tārīkh Aṣbahān* with a weak [ḍa'īf] chain of transmission, as did Ibn 'Asākir and Abū Aḥmad al-Ghaṭarīf, with the wording "The language of Ismā'īl had vanished, so Jibrīl came to me with it, and so I memorised it." Zubayr b. Bikār narrated with a good [jayyid] chain of transmission on the authority of the Commander of the Believers 'Alī ؓ, quoting the Messenger of Allah ﷺ: 'The first person whose tongue Allah opened to pure Arabic was Ismā'īl.' (*Sharḥ al-Zurqānī*)

[99] The Ḥadīth in its original form is in Bukhārī and Muslim. (Their dialect replaced the Arabic definite article *al* with *am*, and the Prophet ﷺ spoke to them accordingly. [t])

Another example of this is the report of 'Aṭiyya b. 'Urwa al-Sa'dī, that the Prophet 鄒 said about something which was said to him: 'The higher hand is the one that gives, and the lower hand is the one that takes.'[100] 'Aṭiyya said: 'The Messenger of Allah spoke to us in our language,' i.e. the language of Banī Sa'd, which replaced the Arabic letter 'ayn with the letter nūn.[101]

HIS WAY OF SPEAKING 鄒

The Prophet 鄒 would speak clearly and precisely, so that if the one listening desired to count his words, he would be able to do so, because of their clarity and eloquence. Our lady 'Ā'isha 鄒 said: 'The Messenger of Allah 鄒 did not used to draw out his speech as you all do; he would speak so that that if someone wished to count his words, they would be able to.'[102]

Abū Dāwūd narrates that 'Ā'isha 鄒 said: 'His 鄒 speech was concise, so everyone who heard it understood it.' He also narrated on the authority of Jābir 鄒, who said: 'In his 鄒 speech was elegance, or composure.'

Bukhārī and Muslim narrate on the authority of Anas 鄒 that when the Prophet 鄒 spoke, he would repeat his words three times[103] so as to be understood, and when he came to a group of

---

[100] Using the words *munṭiya* and *munṭāh*, instead of the usual *mu'ṭiya* and *mu'ṭāh*. [t]

[101] This Ḥadīth is related in full in *Sharḥ al-Mawāhib*, ascribed to Ibn 'Abd al-Barr and Ḥākim. Ḥāfiẓ al-Qasṭalānī said: 'This was one of his 鄒 unique characteristics: he would speak to everyone in their own language, according to the differing Arabic dialects, and their different word formation and ways of speaking.'

[102] Narrated by Bukhārī and Muslim. The relation of Ismā'īlī adds: 'The speech of the Messenger of Allah 鄒 was clear, so that hearts understood it.'

[103] One of the wisdoms of this is that the first saying is to cause people to listen, the second is to alert, and the third is to command; three repetitions is the limit of responsibility and clarity, for the one who does not understand after that will not understand even if the repetition is increased.

people he would greet them three times, and would speak with succinctness, without jesting or triviality. He disliked prattling and vain chatter.

The Prophet 🕮 disliked exaggerated speech and the pretension of eloquence, as is narrated in the *Sunan* of Abū Dāwūd and Tirmidhī with a good [*jayyid*] chain of transmission, on the authority of Ibn 'Umar 🕮, that the Messenger of Allah 🕮 said: 'Allah 🕮 despises the exaggerator from amongst men: the one who wags his tongue like the cow wags hers.'[104]

When he 🕮 spoke, he would neither offend nor would he bore: Muslim narrated on the authority of Jābir b. Samura 🕮, who said: 'I used to pray with the Prophet 🕮, and his prayer was moderate, as was his sermon.'

Abū Dāwūd narrated on the authority of Jābir b. Samura 🕮 that the Messenger of Allah 🕮 would not elongate the Friday sermon; rather, it would be a few light words.

Imam Aḥmad and Abū Dāwūd narrated that Ḥakīm b. Ḥazzām 🕮 said: 'I saw a Friday prayer with the Messenger of Allah 🕮. He stood leaning on a staff—or a bow—and praised Allah and glorified Him, with words that were light, pleasant, and full of blessed increase.'

His 🕮 state when delivering sermons: The Prophet's 🕮 state would change when he gave public counsel, in respect to his concern and his gravity, and this would be visible on his face 🕮. Muslim narrated on the authority of Jābir 🕮 that when the Messenger of Allah 🕮 gave sermons, his wrath would intensify, and his voice would raise, and his eyes would redden, as though he were warning an army, saying '(The enemy) is coming!'[105]

Ṭabarānī and Bazzār narrated on the authority of Jābir 🕮 that whenever revelation came to the Prophet 🕮, or he preached, one would say, 'He is the warner of a people to whom has come

---

[104] In *al-Nihāya*, the author says: 'This is the one who prattles in his speech, and over-emphasises with his tongue, and wraps it around his speech, the way a cow wraps the cud around its tongue.'

[105] Literally, 'coming to you, morning and evening!' (An Arabic idiom. [t])

punishment!' After the state had passed from him, one would see him as the brightest-faced of all people, and the cheeriest of them, and the most joyous of them.[106]

Imam Aḥmad narrated on the authority of Zubayr b. al-ʿAwwām ﷺ, who said: 'The Messenger of Allah ﷺ delivered to us a sermon, and reminded us of the Days of Allah, until it was visible on his face, as though he were warning a people to whom the affair would come the next day. If he had recently been with Jibrīl, he would not smile openly until the state had left him.'

The strength of his ﷺ admonition and reminding, and its effect on the Ṣaḥāba: When the Prophet ﷺ gave admonition, it would affect the hearts of those who listened, and it would soothe their souls, until they would shed tears and their hearts would tremble and be humbled, and their state would become clearly visible.

Ḥanẓala b. Rabīʿ said: 'I met Abū Bakr al-Ṣiddīq, and he said to me: "How are you, Ḥanẓala?" I replied: "Ḥanẓala is a hypocrite." He said to me: "What are you saying?!" I said to him: "When we are with the Messenger of Allah ﷺ, and he reminds us of Hell and Paradise, it is as though we see them with our own eyes; but when we leave him, our wives, children and agriculture distract us, and we forget much...'''

Tirmidhī narrated on the authority of ʿIrbāḍ b. Sāriya ﷺ, who said: 'The Messenger of Allah ﷺ admonished us with a sermon from which our hearts cowered, and our eyes wept.'

In narrations other than Tirmidhī's: 'The Messenger of Allah admonished us with a sermon from which our skin burned, and our eyes wept, and our heart cowered. We said: "It is as though this is a farewell sermon, O Messenger of Allah. What covenant would you make with us?" He said: "That you are mindful of Allah and that you follow my Sunnah and the Sunnah of the rightly-guided Caliphs who come after me. Cling firmly to this, for every innovation is misguidance."'[107]

---

[106] See *Jāmiʿ al-ʿUlūm wal-Ḥikām.*
[107] See volume three of *al-Maṭālib al-ʿĀliya.*

Usayd b. Ḥuḍayr said: 'While I am in three states, I am of the people of Paradise: When I recite the Qur'ān or hear it, when I hear the admonition of the Messenger of Allah ﷺ, and when I witness a funeral.'

His ﷺ sermons and admonition affected even inanimate objects, as is related in the *Musnad*—and its origin is narrated by Muslim—on the authority of Ibn 'Umar ﷺ, who said: 'One day, the Messenger of Allah ﷺ recited this Āyah on the pulpit: ❨And they have not accorded to Allah His due; yet the entire earth is in His Grasp on the Day of Resurrection, and the heavens are rolled up in His Right Hand. Sublime is He, and Exalted from all that they associate!❩[108] The Messenger of Allah ﷺ then said, whilst gesturing with his hand, moving it back and forth: "The Lord exalts Himself thus: *I am the Compeller, I am the Supreme, I am the Sovereign Lord, I am the Majestic, I am the Generous.*" The pulpit began to shake under the Messenger of Allah ﷺ, until we said "it will collapse under him! Will it fall with the Messenger of Allah ﷺ?"[109] So the pulpit trembled, affected by his admonition and reminding ﷺ. Woe betide those hearts that do not tremble with his admonitions ﷺ!

He ﷺ alerted preachers to their responsibility to the Lord of the Worlds: The position of preaching, admonishing and reminding is an important, crucial position. Because of this, the Prophet ﷺ would alert preachers to the importance of sincere intention when admonishing, and that behind it is a responsibility to the Lord of the Worlds.

Ibn Abī Dunyā and Bayhaqī narrated a *mursal* Ḥadīth[110] with a good [*jayyid*] chain of transmission[111] on the authority of Mālik b. Dīnār, on the authority of Ḥasan ﷺ, that the Messenger of Allah ﷺ said: 'No servant of Allah gives a sermon except that Allah will ask them on the Day of Resurrection what they intended by it.'

The narrator said:

---

[108] Qur'ān 39:67

[109] As in the narration of Muslim.

[110] I.e. a Ḥadīth related from a Tābi'ī without specifying which Ṣaḥābī they heard it from. (*Al-Ta'rīfāt*) [t]

[111] *Al-Targhīb wal-Tarhīb* 1:125

Whenever Mālik b. Dīnār would relate this Ḥadīth, he would weep and say: 'You think that I am glad to speak to you, but I know that Allah 🕮 will ask me on the Day of Judgement concerning it: "What did you intend by it?" I will say: "You are witness over my heart; if I did not know that it was more beloved to You, I would never have read it in front of two people."'

He 🕮 would warn against affecting speech in order to captivate men's hearts: Abū Dāwūd narrated on the authority of Abū Hurayra 🕮 that the Messenger of Allah 🕮 said: 'Whoever speaks with excess speech in order to captivate the hearts of men:'—or 'of people:'—'Allah will not accept their repentance on the Day of Resurrection, nor their ransom.'[112]

HIS PRAISE OF ELOQUENCE 🕮
AND HIS DISLIKE OF UNGRAMMATICAL SPEECH

Abū Hurayra 🕮 said: 'We said: "O Messenger of Allah, we have never seen anyone more eloquent than you." He said: "Allah Almighty did not make me ungrammatical in speech;[113] He chose for me the best of speech: His Book, the Qur'ān."'[114]

It is related in *al-Mustadrak* on the authority of ʿAlī b. al-Ḥusayn 🕮 that ʿAbbās 🕮 came to the Messenger of Allah 🕮 wearing two robes, and with two braids, and he was white-skinned. When he saw him, he smiled. ʿAbbās said: 'O Messenger of Allah, why do you smile, may Allah make you ever smile?' He [the Messenger of Allah 🕮] said: 'The beauty of the Prophet's uncle 🕮 pleases me.' Abbās said: 'What beauty?' He [the Messenger of Allah 🕮] said: 'The tongue.'[115]

---

[112] The author of *al-Nihāya* says that the word *ṣarf* here could mean 'repentance' or 'voluntary work,' and the word *ʿadl* here could mean 'ransom' or 'obligatory act.'

[113] I.e. 'rather, he made my speech pure Arabic speech.'

[114] The author of *al-Jāmiʿ al-Ṣaghīr* ascribed the Ḥadīth and its commentary to Shīrāzī in *al-Alqāb* and to Daylamī in *al-Firdaws*.

[115] Ḥāfiẓ al-Zurqānī said: 'It is a *mursal* Ḥadīth.'

The narration of 'Askarī has it: 'And what is beauty in a man? He [the Messenger of Allah ﷺ] said: "The eloquence of his tongue."'[116] The scholars of the previous generations ﷺ compiled volumes in which they collected the compendium of his speech ﷺ.

We will mention forty Ḥadīth of this compendium, that perhaps Allah ﷺ might ascribe for us the reward mentioned in the Ḥadīth narrated by Ibn al-Najjār on the authority of Abū Saʿīd ﷺ, in which the Prophet ﷺ said: 'Whoever preserves for my community forty Ḥadīth from my Sunnah, I will include him in my intercession on the Day of Resurrection.'

Ibn ʿAdī narrates on the authority of Ibn ʿAbbās ﷺ that the Prophet ﷺ said: 'Whoever preserves for my community forty Ḥadīth from the Sunnah, I will be for them an intercessor and a witness on the Day of Resurrection.'[117]

---

[116] Narrated by Qaḍāʿī and Khaṭīb. Daylamī narrated a Ḥadīth on the authority of Jābir ﷺ, quoting the Prophet ﷺ: 'Beauty is correct speech, and perfection is good action with sincerity.' 'Askarī narrated on the authority of Ibn ʿUmar ﷺ that ʿUmar ﷺ passed by a group of people practising archery, and said: 'You have shot badly.' They said: 'We are learning.' (But they said it with ungrammatical Arabic [t]). 'Umar said: 'Your fault in your grammar is graver to me than your fault in your archery. I heard the Messenger of Allah say: "May Allah forgive a person who rectified his tongue."' (*Sharḥ al-Mawāhib*)

[117] Imam al-Nawawī said: 'All of this Ḥadīth's chains of transmission are weak.' Ibn ʿAsākir said: 'The Ḥadīth is related from ʿAlī, ʿUmar, Anas, Ibn ʿAbbās, Ibn Masʿūd, Muʿādh, Abū Umāma, Abū al-Dardāʾ, and Abū Saʿīd, all by chains of transmission which are disputable, and not able to be considered rigorously authentic. However, its many different narrations strengthen it, and the best of its chains is the relation of Muʿādh, though it is weak.' (*Sharḥ Fayḍ al-Qadīr*). See also the eminent scholar Ibn Ḥajar al-Makkī's note in his commentary on Nawawī's *Forty Ḥadīth*. If we assume it is weak (despite its many chains of transmission), the majority of scholars are of the opinion that a weak Ḥadīth can be acted upon if it is related to virtuous acts, as is included in our commentary on the *Bayqūniyya*.

FORTY ḤADĪTH
ILLUSTRATING HIS ELOQUENCE AND WISDOM ﷺ

Ḥadīth No. 1

His ﷺ counsel to Ibn ʿAbbās ؓ, in which he clarified how a believer should be with Allah ﷻ.

Tirmidhī narrated on the authority of Ibn ʿAbbās ؓ, who said: 'I was riding behind the Prophet ﷺ one day, and he said to me: "O son! I will teach you some words: Watch over Allah, and He will watch over you. Watch over Allah, and you will find Him in front of you. If you ask, ask Allah. If you seek aid, seek the aid of Allah. Know that if all the people were to come together to benefit you, they would not benefit you except by that which Allah had ordained for you; and if they came together to harm you, they would not harm you except with that which Allah had ordained for you. The pens have been lifted, and the pages have dried."'

Imam Aḥmad's narration adds: 'Draw near to Allah in times of ease, and He will remember you in times of difficulty. Know that patience in the face of what you dislike is tremendous good, and victory comes through patience, and deliverance comes with distress, and ease comes with hardship.'

Ḥadīth No. 2

His ﷺ counsel to Ibn ʿUmar ؓ.

Tirmidhī narrated that Ibn ʿUmar ؓ said: 'The Messenger of Allah ﷺ took hold of my shoulder[118] and said: "Be in this world as though you are a stranger, or a wayfarer; and count yourself amongst those who are in their graves."' The narrations of Nasāʾī and Aḥmad add: 'Worship Allah as though you see Him.'

In this counsel is a clarification of the stages of the journey to the King of Kings. These three stages comprise all of the stations of the seekers, and the ranks of those who have arrived, and we have undertaken, by way of commenting on this Ḥadīth, an extensive and valuable study, which we will mention later, if Allah wills it.[119]

---

[118] Or 'my shoulders.'

[119] In vol. 2 of *Our Master Muhammad, The Messenger of Allah* ﷺ (2009). [p]

69

Ḥadīth No. 3

The Prophet ﷺ clarifies the action that makes the Muslim beloved to Allah, and to the people.

Ibn Mājah narrated on the authority of Sahl b. Saʿd al-Sāʿidī ﷺ that a man came to the Prophet ﷺ and said: 'O Messenger of Allah! Direct me to an action that, if I perform it, Allah will love me, and the people will love me.'

He ﷺ said: 'Abstain from this world, and Allah will love you; abstain from what is in the hands of the people, and the people will love you.'[120]

Ḥadīth No. 4

The Prophet ﷺ counsels that a person should not be a drain on others, greedy for what they possess; and that they should give their all to every prayer, for it might be their final prayer.

Saʿd b. Abī Waqqāṣ ﷺ reported that once a man came to the Prophet ﷺ and said: 'O Messenger of Allah, counsel me.'

He said ﷺ: 'Despair of what is in the hands of people, and beware of greed, for it is the constant poverty. Offer your prayers as though you are preparing to die, and beware of laxity in this.'[121]

Ḥadīth No. 5

The Prophet ﷺ enjoins hastening to perform righteous acts, and the absence of procrastination and laziness concerning them, before one is prevented from them by preoccupations and obstacles.

---

[120] Ibn Abī Dunyā narrated it on the authority of Shaykh Ibrāhīm b. Adham ﷺ, as a *muḍal* Ḥadīth (i.e. a Ḥadīth which has two consecutive unnamed narrators in its chain (*Sharḥ Nukhbat al-Fikr*) [t]), as mentioned by Mundhirī in *al-Targhīb*.

[121] Ḥāfiẓ al-Mundhirī said: 'It was narrated by Ḥākim and Bayhaqī in *al-Zuhd*, and Ḥākim said (and the wording is his) "Its chain is rigorously authentic [*Ṣaḥīḥ*]," and Ṭabarānī narrated it on the authority of Ibn ʿUmar.'

Abū Hurayra 🐾 reported that the Messenger of Allah 🐾 said: 'Hasten to act before the occurrence of seven:[122] You are not waiting except for the obscurity of poverty, or the corruption of wealth, or denigrating illness, or confused senility,[123] or sudden death, or the Antichrist—an evil which lies in wait, or the Hour—for the Hour is more wretched, and more bitter still.'[124]

Ḥadīth No. 6

The Prophet 🐾 forbids that a person be an opportunist; rather, they should always be beneficent, following the way of truth.

Ḥudhayfa 🐾 reported that the Messenger of Allah 🐾 said: 'Do not be opportunists,[125] saying: "If people are good, we are good; and if the people are wicked, we are wicked." Resolve to be good if the people are good; and if they are bad, do not yourselves be wicked.'[126]

Ḥadīth No. 7

The Prophet 🐾 enjoins honesty, and elucidates its good consequences, and warns against lying, and elucidates its bad consequences.

Ibn Masʿūd 🐾 reported that the Messenger of Allah 🐾 said: 'Be truthful, for honesty leads to righteousness, and righteousness leads to Paradise. A man continues to be honest, and to pursue honesty, until he is written before Allah as one with great faith.[127]

---

[122] I.e. get ahead of the occurrence of any of these seven things, by being concerned and occupied with righteous deeds. (*Fayḍ al-Qadīr*)

[123] I.e. the addled speech that comes in years of ill-health, of feeble-mindedness and raving.

[124] Narrated by Tirmidhī, who declared it sound, and Ḥākim, who considered it rigorously authentic, as in Mundhirī's *Targhīb*, and *Fayḍ al-Qadīr*.

[125] This means a person with no opinion of their own; they follow everyone else's opinion. It is said that it refers to someone who says to everyone 'I am with you.' (*Al-Nihāya*)

[126] Narrated by Tirmidhī, who declared it sound, as in *al-Targhīb*, and elsewhere.

[127] Ar. *Ṣiddīq*

Beware of lying, for lying leads to iniquity, and iniquity leads to Hell. A servant continues to lie, and to pursue lies, until he is written before Allah as a liar.'[128]

The Prophet ﷺ enjoined honesty: honesty in speech, so that it is in accordance with the reality of the Sacred Law; honesty in actions, with sincere devotion to Allah ﷻ; honesty in states, by keeping Allah ﷻ in mind throughout them.

He ﷺ then stated that the realisation of honesty causes the one who attains it to reach righteousness. Righteousness means abundance of good, here meaning the goodness of faith, and the realisation of the greatest elements of faith:

Allah ﷻ says: ❨Rather, righteousness is he who believes in Allah, and the Last Day, and the angels, and the Scripture, and the Prophets; and gives his wealth, out of love for Him,[129] to kinsfolk, and orphans, and the needy, and wayfarers, and beggars, and to set slaves free; and performs the prayer, and pays the poor-due; and those who fulfil their covenants when they make them; and those who are patient through trial and tribulation, and at the time of adversity. Such are those who are truthful. Such are the God-fearing.❩[130]

Consider His ﷻ words ❨Such are those who are truthful❩, after He has enumerated the branches of righteousness; compare this to the Prophetic Ḥadīth we are currently considering, and you will understand the meaning.

He ﷺ also stated that whosoever realises righteousness will, by means of it, reach Paradise. He ﷺ then warned against lying, in word, deed and state, and informed us that it leads the one who commits it to iniquity [fujūr], which means in origin something exceeding its boundary. In this case, the meaning is that lying causes the one who commits it to exceed the boundaries of the Sacred Law, which Allah ﷻ has placed, and restricted them to. This iniquity inevitably leads to Hell.

---

[128] Narrated by Bukhārī, Muslim, Abū Dāwūd, and Tirmidhī, who declared it rigorously authentic, and the wording is his, as in *al-Targhīb* and elsewhere.

[129] Or 'despite his love for it (i.e., wealth).'

[130] Qur'ān 2:177

All speech, actions, states, and ranks are connected, and each of them leads to another. They all have their effects, and they all have their consequences, whether good, or evil.

Ḥadīth No. 8
The excellence of love based on faith, and its effect.

Ibn Mas'ūd 鱗 related that a man came to the Messenger of Allah 鱗 and said: 'O Messenger of Allah, what is your opinion of a man who loves a people, but is not among them?' i.e., who is unable to match their deeds. The Messenger of Allah 鱗 said: 'A person is with those whom they love.'[131]

Tirmidhī narrated that Anas 鱗 said: 'I saw the companions of the Messenger of Allah 鱗 rejoice in something more strongly than I had ever seen them rejoice before. A man said: "O Messenger of Allah, what of a man who loves another because of the good deeds he performs, but he does not perform the same?" The Messenger of Allah 鱗 replied: "A person is with those whom they love."'[132]

Ḥadīth No. 9
The Prophet 鱗 warns against holding low opinions, and explains the obligations of the Muslim towards his brother.

Abū Hurayra 鱗 reported that the Messenger of Allah 鱗 said: 'Beware of conjecture, for conjecture is the falsest of speech. Do not probe into the affairs of others. Do not spy on one another. Do not compete with one another. Do not envy one another. Do not despise one another. Do not be at odds with one another.

'Be—O servants of Allah—brothers, as Allah has commanded you. The Muslim is a brother to the Muslim: he does not oppress him, nor does he cheat him, nor does he belittle him. Piety is here, piety is here, piety is here'—and he pointed to his breast three times. It is evil enough for a person to belittle his Muslim brother. All of a Muslim is sacred to another: his blood, his wealth, and his dignity.'[133]

---

[131] Narrated by Bukhārī and Muslim.

[132] See Ḥāfiẓ al-Mundhirī's *Targhīb*.

[133] Ḥāfiẓ al-Mundhirī said: 'It was narrated by Mālik, Bukhārī and Muslim, and the wording is his (i.e. Muslim's [t]), and it is the most

Muslim's narration adds: 'Allah ﷻ does not look at your physical forms, nor your wealth; He looks at your hearts, and your deeds.'

Ḥadīth No. 10

The Prophet ﷺ counsels the believer to concern himself with that which will benefit his religion and his worldly life, seeking Allah's aid in this, and encourages him to work, and warns him against indolence and laziness.

Muslim narrated on the authority of Abū Hurayra ﷺ that the Messenger of Allah ﷺ said: 'The strong believer is better and more beloved to Allah than the weak believer; and there is goodness in both of them. Concern yourself with that which is beneficial, and seek Allah's aid, and be not indolent. If something afflicts you, do not say "if only I had done such-and-such; rather, say: "Allah decrees, and does as He wills," for *if only* provides an opening for the works of Satan.'

Ḥadīth No. 11

The Prophet ﷺ enjoins consciousness of Allah in private and in public.

Muʿādh ﷺ reported that the Messenger of Allah ﷺ said: 'Be conscious of Allah wherever you are, and follow the sin with a good deed; it will erase it. Treat people with good manners.'[134]

Ṭabarānī narrated, with a chain of transmission the men of which were trustworthy, on the authority of Abū Salama, that Muʿādh ﷺ said: 'O Messenger of Allah, counsel me.' He [the Messenger of Allah ﷺ] said: 'Worship Allah as though you see him, and number yourself amongst the dead. Make remembrance of Allah as every stone, and every tree. If you commit a sin, perform a good deed after it: [if it was] in secret, then secretly, and [if it was] in public, then in public.'[135]

---

complete of his narrations.' The meaning of Mundhirī's statement 'and it is the most complete of his narrations' is that it is the most complete after combining the different narrations together, as will become clear if one revises *Ṣaḥīḥ Muslim*.

[134] Narrated by Tirmidhī, who said: 'It is a sound, rigorously authentic Ḥadīth.'

[135] Reported in *al-Targhīb*, and the author commented: 'Abū Salama did not meet Muʿādh.'

Ḥadīth No.12

The Prophet 🌸 enjoins the good treatment of parents and the avoidance of womanizing.

Ibn 'Umar 🌸 reported that the Messenger of Allah 🌸 said: 'Treat your parents well, and your children will treat you well. Be chaste, and your women will be chaste.'[136]

Ḥadīth No. 13

The Prophet 🌸 reveals the attributes that will cause the one who possesses them to enter under Allah's 🌸 shade.

Abū Hurayra 🌸 reported that he heard the Messenger of Allah 🌸 say: 'There are seven people to whom Allah will grant His shade on the day when there is no shade but His: A just leader, a young man who grows up worshipping Allah 🌸, a man whose heart is attached to the mosques, two men who love each other for the sake of Allah, who came together upon that, and left one another upon it, and a man who is called upon by a woman of noble lineage and beauty, and says *I fear Allah*, and a man who gives charity in secret, so that his left hand does not know what his right hand has given, and a man who remembers Allah in seclusion, and his eyes shed tears.'[137]

Ḥadīth No. 14

The Prophet 🌸 warns against a person's speaking words without first scrutinising them.

Abū Hurayra 🌸 reported that he heard the Messenger of Allah 🌸 say: 'The servant says something without scrutinising it,[138] for which he falls into Hell the distance between the sunrise and the sunset.'[139]

---

[136] Ḥāfiẓ al-Mundhirī said: 'It was narrated by Ṭabarānī with a sound chain, and he and others also narrated it from a report of 'Ā'isha 🌸.'

[137] Narrated by Bukhārī and Muslim, and others. The Prophet 🌸 mentioned, in many Ḥadīth, a large group of people whom to Allah will grant His shade, and these Ḥadīth have been gathered by some of the scholars of Ḥadīth, so consult them if you wish.

[138] Ḥāfiẓ al-Mundhirī says: 'This means without considering whether it is good or evil.'

[139] Narrated by Bukhārī and Muslim.

Tirmidhī has it: 'A man says something in which he sees no harm, for which he falls for seventy years.'[140] Ḥakim's narration has it: 'A man says something which he does not imagine will go as far as it does, for which he falls for seventy years in Hell.' Bayhaqī's narration has it: 'The Messenger of Allah ﷺ said: "A servant says something, only in order to amuse the company, for which he falls a distance further than what lies between the heavens and the earth. A man may trip over his tongue worse than he trips over his feet."'

Abū al-Shaykh narrated with a sound chain on the authority of Anas ﷺ that the Messenger of Allah ﷺ said: 'It might be that a man from amongst you speaks a word, by which he amuses people, and because of it falls further than the sky. Perhaps a man from amongst you speaks a word, by which he amuses his companions, and so Allah becomes angry with him because of it, and is not satisfied with him until he enters Hell.'[141]

Ḥadīth No. 15

The Prophet ﷺ describes the states of people in this world, and their consequences in the hereafter.

Abū Kabsha al-Anmārī ﷺ related that he heard the Messenger of Allah ﷺ say: 'I swear upon three things, and I tell you this, so remember it: No money is diminished that is spent on charity. No servant is oppressed, and bears it patiently, except that Allah increases their rank. No servant opens the door of begging,[142] except that Allah opens upon them the door of poverty.

'I tell you this, so remember it: This world is only for four people: A servant to whom Allah grants wealth, and knowledge, and so he is conscious of his Lord concerning it, and maintains his family ties by means of it, and recognises that Allah has a right over it. This is the finest of ranks. And a servant to whom Allah grants knowledge, but not wealth, and he says with

---

[140] Literally 'seventy autumns.'

[141] See all of these narrations in Mundhirī's *Targhīb*.

[142] I.e. begging for people's wealth without real cause. As for the one who has real cause, they should ask according to their need, if they find no way to meet their need by working, or the like.

sincerity: "If I had wealth, I would have done the works of so-and-so,"[143] he is judged by his intention, and the reward of these two is the same.

'And a servant to whom Allah grants wealth, but not knowledge, who squanders his wealth without knowledge, and is not conscious of his Lord concerning it, and does not maintain his family ties by means of it, and does not recognise Allah's right over it. This is the lowest of ranks.

'And a servant to whom Allah grants neither wealth, nor knowledge, who says: "If I had wealth, I would have done the works of so-and-so." He is judged according to his intention,[144] and the sin of these two is the same.'[145]

Ḥadīth No. 16

The Prophet ﷺ informs us of the different kinds of good deeds, and their effects.

Abū Umāma ﷺ reported that the Messenger of Allah ﷺ said: 'Kind deeds guard against the ruin of evil; and secret charity assuages the Lord's anger; and maintaining ties of kinship increases the life-span.'[146]

The relation of Umm Salama ﷺ adds: 'Every kindness is a charity. The people of kindness in this world are the people of kindness in the hereafter; and the people of cruelty in this world are the people of cruelty in the hereafter. The first people to enter Paradise will be the people of kindness.'[147]

---

[143] I.e. I would have given charity, and done good works, as the wealthy, pious, generous person did.

[144] This means that he intended that if he had wealth, he would have squandered it, and sinned, and done just as the other did, i.e. by wasting it on himself and his wickedness. He is judged according to his intention, and so that sin is ascribed to him.

[145] Narrated by Tirmidhī and Ibn Mājah. Tirmidhī declared it sound, and rigorously authentic [*ḥasan ṣaḥīḥ*].

[146] This is Ṭabarānī's narration in *al-Kabīr*, with a sound chain.

[147] This addendum is Ṭabarānī's narration in *al-Awsaṭ*. It was also narrated by Mundhirī in the form '*it is narrated that...*'

Ḥadīth No. 17

The Prophet ﷺ informs us of the obligation to love him more than all creation.

Anas ؓ related that the Messenger of Allah ﷺ said: 'None of you believes until I am more beloved to them then their father, and their son, and all people.'[148]

Ḥadīth No. 18

The Prophet ﷺ informs us of the characteristics by means of which the believer may taste the sweetness of faith.

Anas ؓ reported that the Prophet ﷺ said: '[There are] three things that if a person has them, he finds with them the sweetness of faith: He to whom Allah and His Messenger are more beloved than anything else; and he who loves a servant only for the sake of Allah; and he who hates to return to disbelief after Allah has saved him from it like he would hate to be cast into fire.'

Another narration has it: '[There are] three things that if a person has them, he finds the sweetness and flavour of faith: that Allah and His Messenger are more beloved to him than anything else; and that he loves for Allah's sake and hates for Allah's sake; and that a great fire's being lit, and his being cast into it, is more beloved to him than that he associate anything with Allah.'[149]

Ḥadīth No. 19

Concerning the Muslims' rights over one another.

Abū Hurayra ؓ reported that the Messenger of Allah ﷺ said: 'The rights of a Muslim over a Muslim are six.' It was said: 'What are they, O Messenger of Allah?' He ﷺ said: 'If you meet him, greet him with *salām*. If he calls you, answer him. If he asks your advice, advise him. If he sneezes and praises Allah, tell him "Allah have mercy on you." If he falls sick, visit him. If he dies, follow his funeral procession.'[150]

---

[148] Narrated by Bukhārī and Muslim.

[149] Narrated by Bukhārī, Muslim, Tirmidhī and Nasā'ī.

[150] Narrated by Bukhārī with the wording 'five' (rather than 'six' [t]), and by Muslim with this wording.

Ḥadīth No. 20

A warning against envy and hatred, which was the disease that ruined the nations of old.

Zubayr b. al-ʿAwwām 🕌 reported that the Messenger of Allah 🕌 said: 'The disease of the nations that came before you has pervaded you: envy and hatred. Hatred is the shearer, not of hair, but of religion. By He in whose Hand is Muḥammad's soul, you will not enter Paradise unless you believe; and you will not believe unless you love one another. Shall I not tell you of something which, if you do it, you will love one another?' The people said 'Tell us, O Messenger of Allah!' He said: 'Spread greetings of peace amongst you.'[151]

Ḥadīth No. 21

The rights and etiquettes of the street.

Saʿīd 🕌 reported that the Messenger of Allah 🕌 said: 'Beware of sitting in the streets.' The people said: 'O Messenger of Allah, we might have no option but to sit there.'[152] He said: 'If you must sit, then observe the rights of the street.' They said: 'O Messenger of Allah, what is the right of the street?' He said: 'Lowering the gaze, preventing harm, returning greetings, and commanding good and forbidding evil.'[153]

Abū Dāwūd's narration adds: 'And giving directions.' Ṭabarānī adds: 'And helping those in trouble.'

Ḥadīth No. 22

He who fears Allah 🕌 rushes to salvation from His punishment by obeying Him.

Abū Hurayra 🕌 related that the Messenger of Allah 🕌 said: 'He who fears, presses on;[154] and he who presses on, reaches home.

---

[151] Narrated by Tirmidhī and Aḥmad. Bazzār narrated it with a sound chain, as mentioned in Mundhirī's *Targhīb*, and in *Majmaʿ al-Zawāʾid*. The core of the Ḥadīth is in *Ṣaḥīḥ Muslim*, and elsewhere.

[152] I.e. they might be forced to sit in the streets to discuss an important matter.

[153] Narrated by Bukhārī and Muslim.

[154] The great scholar Munāwī said that the meaning of the word in Arabic [*adlaja*] is to travel during night's first hours, and that *dallaja*

Allah's merchandise is valuable indeed; Allah's merchandise is Paradise.'[155]

Ḥadīth No. 23

The excellence of aiding a Muslim, and sheltering him, and facilitating and helping him; and the excellence of seeking knowledge, and gathering to recite and study the Book of Allah ﷻ.

Abū Hurayra ﷺ reported that the Messenger of Allah ﷺ said: 'Whoever relieves the worldly distress of a believer, Allah will relieve for them the distress of the Day of Resurrection. 'Whoever gives shelter to a Muslim, Allah will shelter them in this world and the next. Whoever eases a person in difficulty, Allah will give them ease in this world and the next. Allah is engaged in helping a servant as long as the servant is engaged in helping his brother.

'Whoever travels a road in search of knowledge, Allah will make for them a road to Paradise. No group of people gather together in one of Allah's houses, reciting the Book of Allah and studying it together, except that tranquillity descends upon them, and mercy covers them, and the angels surround them, and Allah makes mention of them to those who are with Him. Whoever's deeds slow them down will not be sped up by their lineage.'[156]

Ḥadīth No. 24

The responsibilities of a servant on the Day of Resurrection.

Abū Barza al-Aslamī ﷺ reported that the Messenger of Allah ﷺ said: 'A servant's steps will not cease on the Day of Resurrection until he has been asked concerning four: His life and by what

---

means to travel during the latter part of the night. The meaning is that the one who walks in the desert until nightfall is driven by his fear of desert predators, and of becoming lost, so he does not sleep there, but rather presses on until he reaches the safety of home. There is a lesson in this for those seeking and journeying to Allah.

[155] Narrated by Tirmidhī, who said: 'It is a sound, singularly-narrated Ḥadīth [*hasan gharīb*].' Ḥākim also narrated it, and declared it rigorously authentic, and Dhahabī concurred.

[156] Narrated by Muslim and the authors of the *Sunan*.

means he exhausted it, his knowledge and how he acted upon it, his wealth and how he earned and spent it, and his body and by what means he wore it out.'[157]

Bazzār, Bayhaqī and Ṭabarānī narrated, with a rigorously authenticated chain of transmission[158] on the authority of Muʿādh b. Jabal 🕮 that the Messenger of Allah 🕮 said: 'A servant's steps will not cease on the Day of Resurrection until he has been asked concerning four things: His life and by what means he exhausted it, his youth and by what means he wore it out, his wealth and how he earned it and spent it, and his knowledge and how he acted upon it.'

Ḥadīth No. 25

The Prophet's 🕮 sermon, in which he enjoined the adherence to the Book of Allah 🕮, and seeking guidance by following his 🕮 way.

Jābir 🕮 said: 'When the Messenger of Allah preached, his eyes would redden, and his voice would rise, and his wrath would become severe, as though he were warning an army. He would say: "The truest of speech is the Book of Allah, and the best of guidance is the guidance of Muḥammad. The most wicked of matters are those which are innovated. Every innovation is heresy, and every heresy is misguidance, and every misguidance is in Hell.

"'The Hour will come to you suddenly; the Hour and I have been sent like this;[159] the Hour might come upon you at any moment! I am closer to every believer than themselves; he who (dies and) leaves wealth, it is for his family. He who leaves debt, or dependents, it is my responsibility. I am the protector of the believers."'[160]

---

[157] Narrated by Tirmidhī, who said: 'A sound, rigorously authentic Ḥadīth.'

[158] As reported in several places in Mundhirī's *Targhīb*.

[159] (And he 🕮 put his first and middle fingers together.) (*Ṣaḥīḥ Muslim*) [t]

[160] Narrated by Imam Aḥmad, Muslim, Nasā'ī and Abū Dāwūd. (*Al-Jāmiʿ al-Ṣaghīr wa Sharḥuh al-Kabīr*)

Ḥadīth No. 26

The Prophet's 🕮 sermon at the first Friday prayer he prayed in Medina.[161]

'All praise is due to Allah. I praise Him, seek His aid, and ask His forgiveness, and His guidance. I believe in Him. I do not deny Him; I direct my enmity at those who deny Him. I testify that there is no god but Allah, alone without partner, and that Muḥammad is His servant and Messenger, whom He has sent with guidance, and the way of truth, and light, and counsel, at a time between Messengers, when knowledge was slight, and the people were misguided, and time was at its end, and the Hour was near, and the end was nigh. Whosoever obeys Allah and His Messenger has found guidance. Whosoever disobeys them has wandered, erred, and strayed deep into misguidance.

'I advise you to be mindful of Allah, for the finest advice one Muslim can give another is to focus him on the hereafter, and instruct him to be mindful of Allah. Beware that which Allah Himself warns you of; there is no finer advice, nor better reminder, than that. It is a source of piety for those who act upon it with fear and dread. It is a sincere source of aid for what you hope to find in the hereafter.

'Whosoever rectifies that which is between them and Allah, privately and openly, intending nothing by it except Allah's 🕮 pleasure, will find it a reminder for them when their time comes, and a treasure for them after death, when a person will be in dire need of that which they have sent ahead, and will long to distance themselves from all else besides it. Allah warns you of Himself; and Allah is Kind to the servants. He it is whose word is true, His promise fulfilled; in this there is no doubt, for He 🕮 says: ⟨The judgements I render do not change; and I am not unjust to the servants.⟩[162]

---

[161] Ḥāfiẓ Ibn Jarīr al-Ṭabarī said: 'Yūnus b. ʿAbd al-Aʿlā told me that Ibn Wahb told him on the authority of Saʿīd b. ʿAbd al-Raḥmān al-Jamḥī that he was informed concerning the Prophet's 🕮 sermon at the first Friday prayer he prayed in Medina to (the tribe of) Banī Sālim b. ʿAmr b. ʿAwf 🕮, that he said... (and then quoted the sermon as above).'
[162] Qurʾān 50:29

'Be mindful of Allah now and always, secretly and openly, for whosoever is mindful of Allah, He covers over their sins, and magnifies their reward. Whosoever is mindful of Allah triumphs with magnificence. Being mindful of Allah guards against His rancour, His punishment, and His wrath. Being mindful of Allah illuminates faces, and raises ranks.

'Make the most of what you have, and do not sell Allah short. Allah has taught you His Book, and showed you His Way; that He might manifest His knowledge of the truthful, and the liars. Do good, as Allah has done good to you. Take His enemies as your enemies, and strive in Allah's way as He merits. He has chosen you, and called you Muslims, that those who perish might perish in the midst of clarity; and that those who live might live in the midst of clarity. There is no strength but Allah's strength, so make much mention of Allah, and work for that which comes after death; for whosoever rectifies that which is between them and Allah, Allah will suffice them that which is between them and humanity. This is because Allah has power over humanity, and they have no power over Him. He owns humanity, and they do not own Him. Allah is Great. There is no strength except the strength of Allah, the Exalted, the Mighty.'

Ḥāfiẓ Ibn Kathīr said:

> This is how Ibn Jarīr narrated it, and the Companion who narrated it is not named.[163] Bayhaqī mentioned in the chapter concerning the Messenger of Allah's 🕮 first sermon in Medina...

Ibn Kathīr then quoted Bayhaqī's chain of transmission up to 'Abd al-Raḥmān b. 'Awf, who said that the first sermon that the Messenger of Allah 🕮 preached in Medina began with his standing, praising and magnifying Allah as He merits, and then saying: 'O People! Send good works ahead of you. Know with certainty that one of you will be struck down, and leave his flock without a shepherd, and then his Lord will say to him, without

---

[163] I.e. it is *mursal.*

any interpreter, or veil between them: "Did my Messenger not come to you and deliver to you the message? Did I not give you wealth, and favour you? What have you sent ahead of yourself?"

'He (the servant) will look right and left, and see nothing, then he will look in front of him and see nothing but Hell. Whosoever is able to protect his face from the fire, even with half a date, let him do so; and whoever does not find even this, let them do so with a kind word, for with it, a good deed is rewarded from tenfold up to seven hundred-fold. Peace, and the mercy and blessings of Allah be upon you,[164] and upon the Messenger of Allah.'

The Messenger of Allah 🕮 then preached another sermon, saying: 'Praise is due to Allah. I praise Him and seek His aid. We take refuge in Allah from the evil of our souls, and the sins of our deeds. Whomsoever Allah guides cannot be sent astray. Whomsoever Allah sends astray cannot be guided. I testify that there is no god but Allah, alone without partner.

'The best of speech is the Book of Allah; successful are those in whose hearts Allah beautifies His Book, and those whom He enters into Islam after disbelief, and those who prefer Allah's Book to the speech of people. It is the best of speech, and the most lasting. Love those who love Allah; love Allah with all your hearts. Do not tire of Allah's speech, and His remembrance; do not let your hearts become hardened to it.

'Whomsoever Allah chooses and elects, He appoints for them the best of works, and the best of people, and that which is virtuous of speech, and the best of all that humanity have been given, of permissible and impermissible things. Worship Allah, and do not associate anything with Him. Fear Him as He should be feared, and be true to Allah in that which your mouths utter. Love one another through the Grace of Allah. Allah hates that His treaty be broken. Peace, and the mercy and blessings of Allah be upon you.'

Ibn Kathīr said, after relating this:

---

[164] 'Upon you' is an addition from the *Sīra* of Ibn Hishām.

This chain of transmission also does not name the Companion who related it,[165] but it is strengthened by that which was mentioned before it, although the wording differs.'[166]

Ḥadīth No.27

The Prophet's ﷺ sermon in which he urged the importance of repentance, and a servant's relationship with his Lord; and warned against the danger of leaving the Friday prayer.

Jābir ؓ narrated that the Messenger of Allah ﷺ gave a sermon, saying: 'O People! Repent to your Lord, before you die, and rush to perform good deeds before you are busy. Maintain the tie between yourselves and your Lord, by making much remembrance of Him, and giving much charity, secretly and in open, and you will be given provision, victory, and comfort. Know that Allah has made the Friday prayer incumbent upon you in this, my place, and on this, my day, in this, my month, from this, my year, onward until the Day of Resurrection.

'Whoever leaves it, whether in my lifetime or after me, whether his leader is just or tyrannical—and leaves it out of disdain for it and rejection of it—Allah will not make them whole, and will not bless them. They will have no prayer, nor Zakāt, nor pilgrimage, nor fast, nor righteousness, until they repent. Whoever repents, Allah will turn to them in forgiveness.'[167]

Ḥadīth No. 28

The Prophet's ﷺ sermon in which he mentioned several warnings and reminders.

Tirmidhī narrated that Abū Saʿīd al-Khudrī ؓ said: 'The Messenger of Allah ﷺ prayed the afternoon prayer with us one day, and then stood to deliver a sermon. He did not leave anything that would come to pass until the Hour except that he

---

[165] I.e. it is *mursal.*

[166] See *al-Bidāya wal-Nihāya.*

[167] The author of *al-Targhīb* said: 'It was narrated by Ibn Mājah; and Ṭabarānī narrated it in *al-Awsaṭ* on the authority of Abī Saʿīd al-Khudrī in a more concise form.'

informed us of it; some of us remembered it, and some of us forgot it. Part of what he said was: "The life of this world is a sweet crop, and Allah has appointed you as vice-regents in it, and He is watching what you do. Beware of this world, and beware of women.

"'Let no man allow his fear of people to prevent him speaking the truth if he knows it. A flag will be assigned to every traitor on the Day of Resurrection according to the magnitude of his treachery; and there is no treachery graver than a leader who betrays his group: his flag will be planted in his backside.

"'The children of Adam were created in many different ranks: some of them are born believers, live as believers, and die believers; some of them are born believers, live as believers, and die disbelievers; some of them are born disbelievers, live as disbelievers, and die as believers; and some of them are born disbelievers, live as disbelievers, and die disbelievers. Some of them anger slowly, and calm down quickly. Some of them anger quickly, and calm down quickly, one with the other. Some of them calm slowly, and anger quickly. The best one them is the one who is slow to anger, and quick to calm down. The worst of them is the one who is quick to anger, and slow to calm down. Some of them gratify agreeably, and request agreeably. Some of them gratify begrudgingly, and request agreeably, one with the other. Some of them gratify begrudgingly, and request disagreeably.

"'The best of them is the one who gratifies agreeably and requests agreeably, and the worst of them is the one who gratifies begrudgingly, and requests disagreeably. Anger is a burning coal in the child of Adam's heart. Have you seen the redness of a person's eyes, and the swelling of their veins? Whoever feels these things, let them cleave to the earth.'"

Abū Saʿīd said: 'We began to look at the sun, to see if any of the day remained. The Messenger of Allah ﷺ said: "Nothing more remains of this world of its allotted time, except the equivalent of that which remains of the allotted time of this day."'

Imam Aḥmad narrated it, with the addition: 'You complete seventy nations, of which you are the finest and most noble in Allah's ﷺ sight.'

Ḥadīth No. 29

The Prophet's 🕌 sermon in which he mentioned the might of Allah 🕌, His eternal self-subsistence, and His equity with His creation.

Imam Muslim narrated that Abū Mūsā al-Ash'arī 🕌 said: 'The Messenger of Allah 🕌 told us five things, saying: "Allah 🕌 does not sleep, and it is not fitting for Him that He should sleep. He lowers equity and raises it. The work of the night is raised to Him before the work of the day; and the work of the day is raised to Him before the work of the night. His veil is light; if it was revealed, the rays of His Countenance would burn any of His creation whom He looked upon."'

Ḥadīth No. 30

The Prophet's 🕌 sermon in which he encouraged shyness before Allah 🕌 as He merits.

It is narrated on the authority of 'Ā'isha 🕌 that the Messenger of Allah 🕌 said, on the pulpit, surrounded by people: 'O People! Be shy before Allah, as He merits!' A man said: 'O Messenger of Allah, we are indeed shy before Allah!' He 🕌 replied: 'Whosoever would be shy, let them not spend a single night without thinking of their death, and let them protect the stomach, and what it contains,[168] and protect the head, and what it contains,[169] and let them remember death, and decay, and let them forsake the allure of this world.'[170]

This Ḥadīth is supported by the narration of Tirmidhī and others on the authority of Ibn Mas'ūd 🕌, who said: 'The Messenger of Allah 🕌 said: "Be shy before Allah, as He merits." We said: "O Prophet of Allah, we are indeed shy before Allah, praise be to Him!" He 🕌 said: "Not so: shyness before Allah, as He merits, is to protect the head and that which it contains, and to protect the stomach and that which it contains, and to remember

---

[168] I.e. make sure that what the stomach contains of food and drink, and passion, is entirely permissible.

[169] I.e. make sure that what the head contains of visual and aural senses, and mental, intellectual and conversational ability, and the like, is devoted to that which Allah 🕌 has legislated and approved.

[170] Narrated by Ṭabarānī in *al-Awsaṭ*.

death and decay, and that whosoever desires the hereafter forsakes this world. The one who does all this is shy before Allah as He merits.'"

Ḥadīth No. 31

The Prophet's 🕌 sermon in which he described the Awliyā' of Allah 🕌, and mentioned the gravity of mortal sins.

It is narrated by 'Ubayd b. 'Umayr al-Laythī, on the authority of his father, that the Messenger of Allah 🕌 said in the Farewell Pilgrimage: 'The Awliyā' of Allah[171] are those who pray, and those who maintain the five prayers that Allah has prescribed for them, and fast Ramaḍān hoping for reward, and pay Zakāt gladly, and avoid the mortal sins Allah has prohibited.'

A man from amongst his companions said: 'O Messenger of Allah, how many are the mortal sins?' He said: 'Nine, the gravest of which is associating partners with Allah, [then] killing a believer unjustly, fleeing the battlefield, slandering a chaste woman, witchcraft, usurping the wealth of an orphan, consuming usury, disobeying Muslim parents, and exposing the Sacred Precinct, your *qibla* in life and death, to harm. No man will die, having avoided these mortal sins, and having prayed, and paid Zakāt, except that he will accompany Muḥammad 🕌 in the heart of Paradise, the doors of which are adorned with gold.'[172]

Ḥadīth No. 32

The Prophet's 🕌 sermon in which he warned against oppression, greed and obscenity.

'Abdullāh b. 'Umar 🕌 said: 'The Messenger of Allah 🕌 delivered to us a sermon, saying: "Beware of oppression, for oppression is the darkness of the Day of Resurrection. Beware of obscenity and depravity. Beware of greed, for those who came before you were only ruined by greed: it ordered them with alienation,[173] so they broke their ties; it ordered them with stinginess, so they were stingy; it ordered them with iniquity, so they were iniquitous."

---

[171] 'Friends of Allah,' or 'saints'. [t]

[172] Ḥāfiẓ al-Mundhirī said: 'It was narrated by Ṭabarānī in *al-Kabīr* with a sound [*ḥasan*] chain of transmission.'

[173] I.e. to cut family ties and deny mercy to others.

'A man stood, and said: "O Messenger of Allah, which Islam is best?" He ﷺ said: "That the Muslims are safe from your tongue, and your hand." That man (or another man) said: "O Messenger of Allah, which migration is best?" He said: "That you avoid what your Lord dislikes."'[174]

Ḥadīth No. 33

The Prophet's ﷺ sermon in which he warned against harming the Muslims, and seeking out their faults.

Tirmidhī narrated on the authority of Ibn 'Umar ﷺ that the Prophet ﷺ climbed the pulpit, and called with a loud voice, saying: 'O you who have entered Islam with your tongues, but faith has not entered you hearts! Do not harm the Muslims, and do not seek out their faults (i.e. their sins and mistakes). Whoever seeks out the faults of his Muslim brother, Allah will seek out his faults; if Allah seeks out a person's faults, He will reveal them, even if it is (secluded) deep in his saddle-bag.'

Ibn 'Umar ﷺ looked at the Ka'ba one day, and said: 'How mighty you are, and how mighty is your sanctity! But the believer is more sacred to Allah than you!'[175]

Ḥadīth No. 34

The Prophet's ﷺ sermon in which he warned his community against competing for this world whilst forgetting their religion.

Bukhārī and Muslim narrate, on the authority of 'Uqba b. 'Āmir ﷺ that the Prophet ﷺ came out one day, and prayed for the people of Uḥud his prayer for the dead, and then went to the pulpit and said: 'I will precede you, and I am a witness over you. By Allah, I am looking at my pool[176] at this moment.

---

[174] Mundhirī said in *al-Targhīb*: 'It was narrated by Abū Dāwūd in a concise form, and by Ḥākim—and the wording is his—who declared it rigorously authentic [*ṣaḥīḥ*] according to the criteria of Muslim.'

[175] The author of *al-Targhīb* said: 'Ibn Ḥibbān narrated it in his *Ṣaḥīḥ*, with the wording: "O you who have entered Islam with your tongues, but faith has not entered you hearts! Do not harm the Muslims, and do not revile them, and do not search for their mistakes..."'

[176] In paradise. [t]

'I have been given the keys to the treasures of the earth (or 'the keys of the earth'), and by Allah, I do not fear for you that you will associate partners with Allah after me, but I fear that you will compete for it (the world).'

Another narration reports that the Messenger of Allah ﷺ prayed for the martyrs of Uḥud eight years after the battle, as though he were bidding farewell to both the living and the dead. He then climbed the pulpit and said: 'I will proceed ahead of all of you, and I am a witness over you. Your meeting place is the pool, and I am looking at it now, as I stand. I do not fear for you that you will associate partners with Allah, but I fear that you will compete for this worldly life.' Another narration has it: '...but I fear that you will compete for this worldly life, and fight with one another, and perish as those before you perished.'

Ḥadīth No. 35

The Prophet's ﷺ sermon in which he urged the importance of preparing for the hereafter.

Ibn 'Umar ﷺ reported that the Prophet ﷺ gave a sermon one day, saying: 'The life of this world is a contemporary spectacle, which the righteous and the wicked alike consume. The hereafter is a true destiny, ruled by an Omnipotent King. Goodness in its entirety is in Paradise, and evil in its entirety is in Hell, so strive to act, conscious of Allah, and know that your works will be displayed to you: whosoever performs an atom's weight of good shall see it, and whosoever performs an atom's weight of evil shall see it.'[177]

Ḥadīth No. 36

The Prophet's ﷺ sermon in which he warned against omitting the sending of benedictions upon him ﷺ when he is mentioned; and against negligence in the month of Ramaḍān; and against the neglect of parents generally, and especially when they reach old age.

---

[177] It was narrated by Shāfiʿī ﷺ, and the like of it was narrated by Abū Nuʿaym in *al-Ḥilya*, on the authority of Shaddād b. Aws with a chain going back to the Prophet ﷺ [*marfūʿan*], as in *al-Mishkāt*, *al-Mawāhib*, and elsewhere.

Ka'b b. 'Ujra 🕌 said: 'The Messenger of Allah 🕌 said: "Gather around the pulpit," so we gathered around it. When he 🕌 climbed the first step, he said: "Āmīn." When he climbed the second step, he said: "Āmīn." When he climbed the third step, he said: "Āmīn." Later, when he came down, we said: "O Messenger of Allah, we have heard from you today something we had never heard before."

'He 🕌 said: "Jibrīl 🕌 came to me, and said: 'Whoever lives through Ramaḍān, and is not forgiven, may they be distanced!' I said 'Āmīn.' When I climbed the second step, he said: 'In whoever's presence you are mentioned, and he does not send benedictions upon you, let him be distanced!' I said 'Āmīn.' When I climbed the third, he said: 'Whoever has parents who reach old age, or one of them does, and they do not cause him to enter Paradise, may he be distanced!' I said 'Āmīn.'"' Ḥākim narrated it, and said: 'Its chain is rigorously authentic.' Ibn Ḥibbān narrated it in his *Ṣaḥīḥ* with the following wording:

'Ḥasan b. Mālik b. al-Huwayrith narrated on the authority of his father, who narrated on the authority of his grandfather 🕌, who said that the Messenger of Allah 🕌 climbed the pulpit. When he reached the first step, he said: "Āmīn." He then climbed another, saying "Āmīn," and then climbed a third, saying "Āmīn." He then said: "Jibrīl 🕌 came to me and said 'O Muḥammad! Whoever lives through Ramaḍān, and is not forgiven, may Allah distance them!' I said 'Āmīn.'

He then said: 'Whoever reaches adulthood with one or both of his parents alive, and then enters the fire, may Allah distance them!' I said 'Āmīn.' Then he said: 'Whoever fails to send benedictions on you, when you are mentioned in their presence, may Allah distance them!' I said 'Āmīn.'"'

Ibn Khuzayma also narrated it, as did Ibn Ḥibbān in his *Ṣaḥīḥ*, with the wording: 'Abū Hurayra 🕌 reported that the Prophet 🕌 climbed the pulpit, and said: "Āmīn, Āmīn, Āmīn." It was said: "O Messenger of Allah, why did you climb the pulpit, saying 'Āmīn, Āmīn, Āmīn'?" He 🕌 said: "Jibrīl 🕌 came to me, and said: 'Whoever lives through Ramaḍān, and is not forgiven, may Allah distance them! Say "Āmīn!"' I said 'Āmīn' ...'" and the rest of the Ḥadīth followed.

Ḥadīth No. 37

The Prophet's ﷺ sermon, in which he warned against making false claims concerning knowledge and proficiency in Qur'ānic recitation.

Ibn 'Abbās ﷺ reported that the Messenger of Allah ﷺ woke one night in Mecca, and said: 'O Allah, have I delivered the message?' three times. 'Umar b. al-Khaṭṭāb got up, and said: 'By Allah, yes; and you have inspired, and striven, and counselled.' He ﷺ said: 'Faith will be manifested, until it casts disbelief back to the place from whence it came, and the oceans will be traversed in the cause of Islam. A time will come when people will study the Qur'ān, gaining knowledge of it, and reciting it, and then they will say: "We have read, and learned; who is better than us?"' He ﷺ said: 'Is there any good in such people?' The people said: 'O Messenger of Allah, who are they?' He ﷺ said: 'They are from amongst you (i.e. from this community), and they are the fuel of the Hellfire.'[178]

This Ḥadīth is attested to by the narration, on the authority of 'Umar b. al-Khaṭṭāb ﷺ, that the Messenger of Allah ﷺ said: 'Islam will be manifested until merchants spread throughout the ocean, and steeds rush into battle in Allah's cause. Then, a people will arise who will recite the Qur'ān, and say: "Who is superior to us in their recitation? Who is more knowledgeable than us? Who has a deeper understanding than ours?"' He ﷺ then said to his companions: 'Is there any good in such people?' They said: 'Allah and His Messenger know better.' He ﷺ said: 'They are from this community, and they are the fuel of the Hellfire.'[179]

---

[178] Ḥāfiẓ al-Mundhirī said: 'It was narrated by Ṭabarānī in *al-Kabīr*, and its chain is sound, Allah willing.'

[179] Ḥāfiẓ al-Mundhirī said: 'It was narrated by Ṭabarānī, in *al-Awsaṭ* and by Bazzār with an unblemished chain of transmission, and also by Abū Ya'lā, Bazzār and Ṭabarānī on the authority of 'Abbās b. 'Abd al-Muṭṭalib ﷺ.'

Ḥadīth No. 38

The Prophet's ﷺ sermon, in which he informed us of the people's condition at the Gathering.

Ibn ʿAbbās ؓ said: 'I heard the Messenger of Allah ﷺ give a sermon on the pulpit, in which he said: "You will all meet Allah barefoot, naked and uncircumcised."' (One narration has it: '...and on foot.')

Another narration has it that Ibn ʿAbbās ؓ said: 'The Messenger of Allah ﷺ addressed us, saying: "O People! You will be gathered before Allah ﷻ, barefoot, naked, and uncircumcised. ❰As We began the first creation, so shall We repeat it. A promise binding upon Us; We will perform it.❱[180] Truly, the first of creation to be clothed will be Ibrāhīm ﷺ. Truly, men from my community will be brought forward, and will be taken to the left, and I will say 'My Lord, they are my companions!' He will say: 'You do not know what they did after you.' I will say as the pious servant said: ❰I was a witness over them while I dwelt among them...❱ until His word ❰...the Mighty, the Wise.❱[181] It will be said to me: 'They did not cease to turn on their heels after you departed from them,' and so I will say: 'Away with them! Away with them!'"'[182]

Ḥadīth No. 39

The Prophet's ﷺ sermon in which he enjoined the propagation and dissemination of his sayings, and prayed that the faces of those who did so would be made radiant.

Jubayr b. Muṭʿim ؓ said: 'I heard the Messenger of Allah ﷺ at al-Khayf (in Minā) say:[183] "May Allah invigorate the servant who hears my words, commits them to memory, and passes them on to those who did not hear them, for many a person has carried knowledge to one who is wiser than he. There are three things, for the sake of which the heart of a believer will never hold

---

[180] Qur'ān 21:104
[181] Qur'ān 5:117-118
[182] Narrated by Bukhārī, Muslim, Tirmidhī, and others.
[183] Ṭabarānī narrated in *al-Awsaṭ* that Anas ؓ said: 'The Messenger of Allah ﷺ gave us a sermon in the mosque of al-Khayf, in Minā...' (Mundhirī, *al-Targhīb*)

rancour: Acting sincerely for the sake of Allah 🪬, giving counsel to the leaders of the Muslims, and cleaving to their group; for their prayers protect those under their authority.'"[184]

The *Ṣaḥīḥ* of Ibn Ḥibbān adds: 'Whoever's intention is this world, Allah will scatter his affairs, and will show him his poverty, and nothing of this world will come to him, except that which is written for him. Whoever's intention is the hereafter, Allah will bring unity to his affairs, and will place wealth in his heart, and the world will come to him despite itself.'[185]

Ḥadīth No. 40
The Prophet's counsel 🪬, which encompassed wisdom and manners.

Abī Dharr 🪬 said: 'I said, "O Messenger of Allah, counsel me." He said: "I counsel you to be conscious of Allah, for it will beautify your entire affair." (In another narration: "For it is the head of the entire affair.") I said; "O Messenger of Allah, give me more." He 🪬 said: "Recite the Qur'ān, and make remembrance of Allah 🪬, for it is remarked of you in the heavens, and is a light for you on earth." I said: "O Messenger of Allah, give me more." He said: "Be silent often, for it casts Satan out, and aids you in your religious affairs." I said: "Give me more." He said: "Beware of much laughter, for it kills the heart, and takes the light of the face." I said: "Give me more." He said: "Speak the truth, even if it is bitter." I said: "Give me more." He said: "Do not fear to face criticism in Allah's cause." I said: "Give me more." He said: "Let what you know about yourself prevent you from (finding fault) in others."'[186]

---

[184] Ḥāfiẓ al-Mundhirī said in *al-Targhīb*: 'It was narrated by Aḥmad, Ibn Mājah, and Ṭabarānī, in *al-Kabīr*, in condensed and extended forms, except that he said "...their prayers *surround* those under their authority." All of them narrated it from Muḥammad b. Isḥāq, from 'Abd al-Salām, from Zuhrī, from Muḥammad b. Jubayr b. Muṭ'im, on the authority of his father. Aḥmad has another chain from Ṣāliḥ b. Kaysān, from Zuhrī, and their chains are sound.'

[185] See *al-Targhīb*, vol. 1.

[186] Narrated by Imam Aḥmad, Ṭabarānī, Ibn Ḥibbān in his *Ṣaḥīḥ*, and Ḥākim (and the wording is his), who said: 'Its chain is rigorously authentic.' (*Al-Targhīb*)

The narration in Ibn Ḥibbān's *Ṣaḥīḥ* adds, after his 🕮 words 'beware of much laughter:' 'I said: "O Messenger of Allah, give me more." He 🕮 said: "Perform Jihād, for it is the monasticism of my community." I said: "O Messenger of Allah, give me more." He said: "Love the poor, and sit with them." I said: "O Messenger of Allah, give me more." He said: "Look at those who are lower than you,[187] and do not look at those who are higher than you, for it will better facilitate your not taking Allah's blessings upon you lightly." I said: "O Messenger of Allah, give me more." He said: "Speak the truth, even if it is bitter." I said: "O Messenger of Allah, give me more." He 🕮 said: "Let that which you know about yourself prevent you from the people,[188] and do not take issue with what they do,[189] it is enough of a defect that you should recognise in people that which you ignore in yourself."'

Ṭabarānī's narration has it: '"It is enough of a fault in a person that he has three attributes: he recognises in people that which he ignores in himself, and he is ashamed of them for that which he is also guilty of, and he harms his companions." The Messenger of Allah 🕮 then beat his hand on my (Abū Dharr's) chest, and said: "O Abū Dharr, there is no intelligence like being prepared, and no piety like abstinence,[190] and there is no honour like good conduct."'

Ḥadīth No. 41

The Prophet 🕮 illustrates some of his noble virtues.

Imam Muslim and Tirmidhī narrated on the authority of Abū Hurayra 🕮 that the Messenger of Allah 🕮 said: 'I have been preferred over the Prophets by six matters: I have been given the compendium of speech, and I have been given victory by dread, and the spoils of war have been made permissible for me, and the

---

[187] I.e. in worldly affairs.

[188] I.e. let the faults that you know you have prevent you from speaking about others and their deeds, for it is doubtful that you are free of defects like the defects of other people, or uglier than that, whether you recognise it or not. (*Sharḥ al-Munāwī*)

[189] I.e. do not be angry with them for what they do to you. (*Sharḥ al-Munāwī ʿalā al-Jāmiʿ al-Ṣaghīr*)

[190] I.e. from that which troubles the heart concerning its permissibility or impermissibility.

earth has been made for me a place of worship, and pure, and I have been sent to all humanity, and I have been made the Seal of the Prophets.'

He ﷺ often spoke of the favour Allah ﷻ granted him by giving him the compendium of speech, meaning the ability to speak succinctly and simply, yet with great depth of meaning.

Bukhārī and Muslim narrated on the authority of Abū Hurayra ؓ that the Messenger of Allah ﷺ said: 'I was sent with the compendium of speech, and given victory by dread. Once, when I was sleeping, I saw myself being given the keys to the treasures of the earth, which were placed in my hand.'

Abū Yaʻlā narrated in his *Musnad* on the authority of ʻUmar ؓ, quoting the Messenger of Allah ﷺ: 'I have been given the compendium of speech, and speech has been made succinct for me,' as was mentioned earlier among the Ḥadīth related to this issue.

PART III
THE EXALTED STATUS OF OUR MASTER MUHAMMAD ﷺ

THE SUPERIORITY OF HIS INTELLECT ﷺ
ABOVE ALL OTHERS

THE intellect is a divine gift which Allah ﷻ has bestowed upon human beings, and by which he has ennobled them above all other living creatures. The intellect is the means by which intelligent beings recognise beauty and ugliness, and perfection and deficiency, and the means by which they distinguish the greater good, and the worse evil.[191]

The intellect of our Master Muḥammad ﷺ, the Messenger of Allah, reached a level of superiority and perfection not reached by anyone but he, by Allah's grace and favour over him ﷺ.

Allah ﷻ said: ﴾Nūn. By the pen, and by that which they write, by the grace of your Lord, you are not mad.﴿[192] i.e., you are at the highest level of intellectual brilliance and distinction, for Allah ﷻ has sworn by His word ﴾Nūn﴿, which is abundant divine assistance, and by the original, comprehensive pen, and by that which the recorders write in the highest of stations, the scratches of whose pens the Messenger of Allah ﷺ heard, and by that which is written by all the pens derived from the original one.

---

[191] Imam al-Ghazālī ﷺ described the echelons of intellect, and the means by which they are traversed if the veils and partitions are lifted, the details of which may be found in his writings.

[192] Qur'ān 68:1-2

With this mighty oath, Allah ﷻ bore witness to the extensiveness of the intellect of this noble Messenger ﷺ, and declared that there was no trace of madness in him, and that he was the possessor of nothing less than a perfect intellect, and superior breadth of knowledge. How should his intellect not be above all intellects, when Allah ﷻ has blessed him, and favoured him, and chosen him for the final, comprehensive prophetic message, and the revelation of the Qur'ān, in which all knowledge is encompassed? Such a blessing cannot be borne except by one whom Allah ﷻ has distinguished with the most complete and superior of intellects. For this reason, He said: ❨By the grace of your Lord, you are not mad.❩ i.e., by virtue of your Lord's blessing you with Prophethood and revelation, and the Qur'ān, which comprises the entirety of knowledge and wisdom, you are not mad. This negates what the Prophet's ﷺ enemies fabricated about him, and decisively confirms the superiority of his intellect and wisdom.

How can it be conceived that the one who received revelation of the Qur'ān, which comprises the entirety of knowledge and learning, and received revelation of the highest wisdom, above all others, could have had the slightest hint of imbalance, or imperfection? The Sūrah continues: ❨And for you will be endless reward❩ i.e., because of your patience in the face of their slander, your reward will be without end; ❨And you are on an exalted character.❩

The Prophet ﷺ is the most intellectually complete of Allah's creation, as Ibn 'Abbās ؓ said: 'The best of humanity, and the most intelligent, is your Prophet, Muḥammad ﷺ.'

The upright Tābi'ī, Wahb b. Munabbih, from whom Bukhārī, Muslim and others narrated Ḥadīth, said: 'I read seventy-one scriptures [from previous revelations], and found in all of them that Allah ﷻ did not give to any of humanity, from the world's beginning, to its end, intellects comparable to Muḥammad's ﷺ intellect, except as a single grain of sand compared to all the sand in the world; and that Muḥammad ﷺ is the most intelligent, and soundest in judgement, of all humanity.'[193]

---

[193] *Sharḥ al-Mawāhib.*

A complete intellect is the basis from which praiseworthy characteristics and talents develop, and the means by which virtues arise, and vices are avoided. It delivers it possessor to untold goodness and grace, as is narrated in the story of Khālid b. al-Walīd's conversion to Islam, when he came to see the Messenger of Allah 🕊, and greeted him as a Prophet. Khālid said: 'He returned my greeting, with a smile. I said: "I testify that there is no god but Allah, and that you are the Messenger of Allah."'

He 🕊 said to him: 'Come,' and so he went forward. The Messenger of Allah 🕊 said: 'Praise be to Allah, who has guided you! I had seen you possessed intellect, and I did not expect it to guide you except to goodness...'

Ṭabarānī narrated, on the authority of Qurra b. Hubayra 🕊, that he went to the Prophet 🕊 and said: 'We used to have gods and goddesses, whom we worshipped and prayed to instead of Allah 🕊; but they did not answer us. We asked of them; but they did not give to us, so we came to you, and Allah guided us through you, and now we worship Allah.' The Messenger of Allah 🕊 said: 'Success indeed belongs to him who has been granted sagacity.' Qurra said: 'O Messenger of Allah, grant me to wear two or your garments, which you have worn,' and so he gave them to him. At the place of standing, on 'Arafat, the Messenger of Allah 🕊 said: 'Repeat your words for me,' so he repeated them. The Messenger of Allah 🕊 said: 'He who is granted sagacity has found success,' i.e. [who is granted] a sound intellect, which guides to Islam, and to carrying out commandments, and avoiding the unlawful. Allah 🕊 said: ❨Only those of sagacity pay heed.❩[194]

This is a clarification from the Prophet 🕊 that a sound intellect necessitates that its possessor adheres to the Islamic religion, because it is a sound, perfect religion, which is the utmost goal of the sound intellect, as is related from the Prophet 🕊: 'The peak of the intellect, after faith in Allah, is modesty, and good conduct.'[195]

---

[194] Qur'ān 13:19
[195] Narrated by the author of *al-Firdaws*, on the authority of Anas 🕊. Nasā'ī declared its chain of transmission to be weak [*ḍa'īf*]. (*Fayḍ al-Qadīr*)

This is because Islam is the religion of wisdom, and irrevocable logic. Allah ﷻ said: ❨We have revealed it, an Arabic Qur'ān, so that you might comprehend❩,[196] i.e. comprehend its meanings, commands and prohibitions, and so come to know with certainty that it commands you only with that which is good for you, and forbids you only that which is bad for you.

Ibn Mas'ūd ؓ said: 'If you hear Allah say: ❨O you who believe!❩, listen attentively, for all who listen to this religion, and understand, perceive, and comprehend it, will inevitably surrender to it, and accept it.'

An innately intelligent Bedouin man came to the Messenger of Allah ﷺ, who explained to him Islam's commandments and prohibitions. The Bedouin went out and declared his Islam, and his tribe said to him: 'How did you know he was the Messenger of Allah?' The Bedouin said: 'Muḥammad ﷺ did not give any commandments that provoked the intellect to say: "It would be better if he prohibited that;" nor any prohibitions that provoked the intellect to say: 'It would be better if he commanded that.'"

'Abd al-Muṭṭalib[197] intellectually rationalised the existence of the hereafter, when he said one day: 'There is no vicious oppressor except that Allah took retribution from him before he died.' It was said to him 'So-and-so was oppressive and wicked.' He replied: 'Allah took retribution from him on such-and-such a day.' Someone else was mentioned, and he said: 'Allah took retribution from him on such-and-such a day.' It was said: 'So-and-so was oppressive and wicked, and nothing afflicted him.' He thought at length, and then said: 'Therefore, there must be a final day, in which Allah will take retribution from him.' Allah ﷻ alerted the people of sagacity to this when He said: ❨Or do those who commit sins suppose that We will make them as those who believe, and do good works, equal in life and death? Dire is the judgement that they make! Allah created the heavens and the earth in truth, that every soul may be rewarded according to what it has earned; and they will not be wronged.❩[198]

---

[196] Qur'ān 12:2
[197] Who lived before the time of Islam. [t]
[198] Qur'ān 45:21-22

In this regard, Allah 鑿 said, informing us of what the disbelievers will say on the Day of Resurrection: ⟨And they say: 'If we had only listened, and used our intelligence, we would not be amongst the dwellers of the flames'⟩,[199] meaning: if they had paid heed to this religion, they would have known and comprehended its commandments, its meanings and its wisdoms, and its rulings; but they were blind and deaf to it.

Ḥasan al-Baṣrī 鑿 said, attributing it to the Prophet 鑿,[200] 'When Allah created the intellect, He said to it: "Come forward," so it came forward. Then He said to it: "Go back," so it went back. Then He said: "I have not created anything more beloved to Me than you; through you I take, and through you I give."'

The most beloved of intellects to Allah is the intellect of our Master Muḥammad 鑿, because it is the soundest, broadest, and most complete of intellects. The perfection of his 鑿 intellect and the breadth of his mind are manifest in all of his affairs, and works, and sayings, and states. We will mention a few of examples of this, which amount to no more than a single drop from his ocean 鑿.

Firstly: The way he 鑿 confronted a world in which ignorance had spread throughout all of its realms and peoples, both Arab and non-Arab, until their intellects had wandered astray, and they had become ignorant of their religion, and had begun worshipping idols and stones which their own hands had fashioned. One of them might have made a small structure out of dates or date-paste, and worshipped it for a while, before becoming hungry and eating it!

Confronting this stony, perverted mentality and changing it into a sound, refined mentality was a grave task, requiring an outstanding intellect, a sound mind, strong rhetoric, eloquent speech, overwhelming evidence, convincing arguments, endurance, forbearance, and broad knowledge of the varieties and methodologies of argumentation.

There is no doubt that all of this was by the instruction of the Wisest of the wise, by revelation from the Lord of the Worlds, for

---

[199] Qur'ān 67:10
[200] Without mentioning which companion he heard it from [*mursal*].

He ﷻ is the One who showed him the way to preach, and showed him its different methods, and clarified for him its approaches, in order that he could follow them, as Allah ﷻ said: ❨Call to the way of your Lord with wisdom, and good counsel; and reason with them in the way that is best. Your Lord is well aware of those who stray from His path; and He is well aware of those who are guided.❩[201]

However, divine teachings and inspirations necessitate a considerable, enlightened intellect to be granted by Allah, in order to bear them, and to apply them, and place them in their correct contexts, for people differ in their status:

There are those who, if wisdom is presented to them, they submit to it, and accept it.

There are those who are controlled by unbridled passions, who need to be counselled and informed of the evil that they are doing, and the consequences of their actions.

There are those whose hearts have been overwhelmed by corrupt religious beliefs, who are in need of something to remove these doubts from their hearts by means of convincing arguments, and sound reasoning.

For this reason, Allah made the forms of preaching diverse, because every style has its context, its effect, and its place. From this, it is known with certainty that the sharpest of all intellectuals was our Master Muḥammad ﷺ.

Secondly: Whoever considers the manner in which the Prophet ﷺ reasoned with the idolaters, and the evidences he presented to the Jews, and the Christians, and the way he convinced them, and dumbfounded them with his reasoning, and frustrated their arguments, will be struck by the shining rays of his unmatched insight, and will be convinced that he ﷺ possessed the most complete, the most eminent, the broadest, and the finest of intellects.

---

[201] Qur'ān 16:125

Ḥusayn Abū 'Imrān worshipped seven earthly idols, believing them to be gods. He was renowned in Quraysh, and one day they came to him, and said: 'Speak to this man,' meaning Muḥammad ﷺ, 'for he speaks of our gods, repudiating them.' They went with him, and sat down near the Prophet's ﷺ door. He ﷺ said: 'Make room for the elder,' meaning Ḥusayn. Ḥusayn said: 'What is this that we have heard about you mentioning our gods with scorn?' 'O Ḥusayn,' he ﷺ said, 'how many gods do you worship?' 'Seven on earth,' he replied, 'and one in the heavens.'

The Prophet ﷺ said: 'If hardship afflicts you, upon whom do you call?' 'I call the one in the heavens,' said Ḥusayn. The Prophet ﷺ said: 'If your wealth is exhausted, upon whom do you call?' 'I call the one in the heavens,' said Ḥusayn. The Prophet ﷺ said: 'And He alone answers you, yet you associate these partners with Him? Have you thanked Him sufficiently; or do you fear that you will be overwhelmed?' 'Neither one of these,' said Ḥusayn. 'O Ḥusayn,' said the Prophet ﷺ, 'Enter Islam, and be saved.' 'I have my tribe, and my family,' said Ḥusayn. 'What should I say?'

The Prophet ﷺ replied: 'Say: "O Allah, I seek your guidance, that my affair might be rectified; increase me in knowledge that will benefit me."' Ḥusayn repeated it, and before he stood up, he had embraced Islam. His son 'Imrān approached him and kissed his head, hands and feet. When the Prophet ﷺ saw this, he began to weep, and said: 'I weep for what 'Imrān has done: Ḥusayn (his father) entered as a disbeliever, and 'Imrān did not approach him, or look in his direction; when he embraced Islam, he gave him his right. Such tenderness has moved me greatly.' When Ḥusayn wanted to leave, the Prophet ﷺ said to his companions: 'Stand, all of you, and see him to his house,' out of respect for him. When he exited the threshold of the door, and the people of Quraysh saw that he had entered Islam, they said: 'He has changed his religion!' and withdrew from him.[202]

Consider the way the Prophet ﷺ reasoned with the man who came to him asking for permission to fornicate, as narrated in the *Musnad*: The Prophet ﷺ said to the man: 'Would you find it acceptable for people to fornicate with your mother?' The man

---

[202] The author of *al-Iṣāba* ascribed the Ḥadīth to Ibn Khuzayma, with his chain of transmission.

said no. The Prophet 🕋 said: 'Other people hate this, too.' He 🕋 continued: 'Would you find it acceptable for people to fornicate with your sister?' The man said no. The Prophet 🕋 said: 'Other people hate this, too.' He 🕋 then said: 'Would you find it acceptable for people to fornicate with your daughter?' the man said no. The Prophet 🕋 said: 'Other people hate this, too.' The man said: 'O Messenger of Allah, I charge you to witness that I have repented of fornication.'

Behold the subtlety and delicacy of this reasoning, and the strength of its impact on the soul!

Thirdly: The masterful way he 🕋 united the hearts of his people, who had been at odds with each other, and the way he resolved the disputes between them, and distanced them from enmity and hatred, especially in the midst of clashes, tribalism and bigotry. All of this proves the breadth of his 🕋 intellect, and the eminence of his discernment. Consider the story of the placing of the Black Stone, over which the Arab tribes argued and competed, until they were on the verge of conflict, from which they were only saved by his 🕋 decisive reasoning, so that they were all pleased. This was before his 🕋 mission, when he was only thirty five years old.

When they rebuilt the Ka'ba, the people of Quraysh contended with each other concerning the lifting of the Stone, each tribe competing for the honour of lifting it, and placing it. There was much bickering between them, until they decided to charge the next person who entered through the door of Banī Shayba to make the decision; and the Prophet 🕋 was the next person to enter. They explained to him the situation. He 🕋 called for a sheet, and it was brought to him. He placed the Black Stone in the middle of the sheet, and called every subdivision from the Arab tribes to take hold of the edge of the sheet. They all lifted it together, and when they reached the Stone's resting place, the Prophet 🕋 picked it up, and placed it himself.[203] Look how the Messenger of Allah 🕋 guided them to compromise, in order to settle their dispute.

---

[203] This story was narrated by Abū Dāwūd al-Ṭayālisī, Ibn Rāhuwayh, and others. (*Sharḥ al-Mawāhib*, vol. 1)

Fourthly: One of the greatest evidences of the superiority of his noble intellect 🌸 and great sagacity is the alert way he dealt with those who declared enmity against him, and the way he guarded against them, and caused their schemes to backfire.

This can be ascertained from studying his encounters with them; here, we will present a modest selection of examples:

1—His 🌸 caution against their schemes and ruses: Zayd b. Thābit 🌸 said: 'I was brought to the Prophet 🌸 when he came to Medina, and it was said to him 🌸: "This man is from Banī al-Najjār, and he has learned seventeen Sūrahs." I recited them for him, and it pleased him. He said to me: "Learn the writing of the Jews (i.e. their script and their language), for I do not trust them with my Book." I did as he asked, and half a month had not passed before I had mastered it. I used to write to them for him, and when they wrote to him, I would read for him 🌸.'[204]

The author of *al-Iṣāba* said: 'We narrated in the *Musnad* of 'Abd b. Ḥumayd, as narrated by Thābit b. 'Ubayd, on the authority on Zayd b. Thābit, who said: 'The Prophet 🌸 said to me: "I write to peoples, and fear that they will augment, or subtract, so learn Syriac." I learned it in seventeen days.'

Maqrīzī's *Khiṭaṭ* includes:

> Syriac is an ancient script, with a basis in the Sunnah, for Abū Bakr 'Abdullāh b. Abī Dāwūd narrated in his *al-Maṣāḥif*, on the authority of Zayd b. Thābit, who said: 'The Messenger of Allah 🌸 said: "Writings come to me that I do not wish for everyone to read; are you able to learn the script of Hebrew?" (or, he said "Syriac") I said yes, and learned it in seventeen days.'

---

[204] Ḥāfiẓ [Ibn Ḥajar al-'Asqalānī], in *al-Iṣāba*, ascribed it to Bukhārī as a narration of *ta'līq* (i.e. one in which he mentioned the chain of transmission whilst not mentioning one or more narrators on his end of the chain (*Sharḥ Alfiyyat al-Ḥadīth*)[t]), and to Baghawī and Abū Ya'lā with fully connected chains.

The Prophet 鑾 ordered Zayd b. Thābit to learn Hebrew, that he might correspond with the Jews in their own language, and that he might be free of any ruses they might include in their writings, and for other reasons.

A proverb of this nature has it: 'Whoever learns the language of a people is safe from their scheming.'

2—His 鑾 commission of scouts to ascertain the enemy's numbers and preparations, and the means he employed to determine this: Abū Dāwūd al-Ṭayālisī, Ibn Rāhuwayh, and others narrate that on the day of Badr, the Prophet 鑾 sent ʿAlī 鑾, Zubayr, and Saʿd b. Mālik in a delegation to the wells of Badr, in order to gain information about the enemy, and their numbers and preparations. They found a group fetching water for Quraysh, among which were a slave of Banī al-Ḥujjāj, and a slave of Banī al-ʿĀṣ. They asked them about the numbers of the idolaters, and they answered that the number was substantial. They took them to the Messenger of Allah 鑾, who was praying. When he finished, he said to the two slaves: 'Tell me about Quraysh.'

They said: 'They are behind the dune you see on the far side.' 'What are their numbers?' he 鑾 asked. They replied that they were substantial in number. 'How many are there?' he 鑾 asked. They said: 'We do not know.' 'How many (camels) do they slaughter a day?' he asked. 'Sometimes nine; sometimes ten,' they replied. He 鑾 said to his companions: 'The people (i.e. the enemy) are between nine hundred and one thousand,' and so it proved.[205]

3—His 鑾 commission of people to discover news about the enemy secretly: An example of this is the day of the battle of the Confederates (al-Aḥzāb), when he 鑾 sent Ḥudhayfa, saying: 'O Ḥudhayfa, go to the people, and see what they do; and do nothing until you return to us.' Another narration has it: 'Go and bring me news of the people; and do nothing until you return to me.'[206]

---

[205] See *Sharḥ al-Mawāhib*.
[206] The author of *Sharḥ al-Mawāhib*, and others, ascribe it to Ibn Isḥāq.

4—His 🕌 commissioning people to spread sedition within the ranks of the enemy, and his selecting the appropriate man to enter their ranks, deceive them, and break their unity: An example of this is what he 🕌 did on the day of the battle of the Confederates, when Nuʿaym b. Masʿūd al-Ashjaʿī 🕌 came to him, and said: 'I have embraced Islam, but my people do not know it; so command me as you will.' The Prophet 🕌 said: 'Among us, you are only one man, so leave us, if you can, for war is nothing but deception. Go, and break the solidarity of the enemy, and have at them with all your cunning.'

He left, and went to Banī Qurayẓa, who were a Jewish faction to whom he was a confidant, and said to them: 'You know my regard for you, and the special relationship between us.' They said: 'You speak true; you are not suspicious in our sight.' 'Quraysh and Ghaṭafān[207] are not like you,' he said. 'The city is your city; it holds your wealth, your sons, and your women. You are unable to withdraw from it to anywhere else. They have come to wage war against Muḥammad and his companions, and you have aided them in this.

'Their city, and their wealth, and their women are elsewhere: if they see an opportunity, they will take it; if not, they will return to their city, leaving you alone to deal with him (i.e. Muḥammad 🕌 and his companions), in your city. You will have no hope if you are left to face him alone. Do not fight with them until you take hostages from their nobles, who will remain in your possession as a sign of their trustworthiness, so that you may with them fight Muḥammad, until you finish him.' They said to Nuʿaym: 'You have given us sound advice.'

Nuʿaym b. Masʿūd then went to Quraysh, and said to Abū Sufyān, and those with him: 'You know my regard for you, and my enmity towards Muḥammad. A matter has come to my knowledge that I feel I must tell you of, as advice for you, so keep it to yourselves. They said: 'We will.' Nuʿaym said: 'The Jews have regretted their actions, and sent Muḥammad this message: "We regret what we have done. Will it please you if we take noblemen

---

[207] They had come from Mecca, and gathered on the outskirts of Medina, in order to wage war against the Prophet 🕌 and his companions. The Jews of Banī Qurayẓa, who lived in Medina, had joined them in this.

from Quraysh and Ghaṭafān, and strike their necks, and then join you against the rest of them, until we have eradicated them?" He [Muḥammad ﷺ] answered them: "Yes." If the Jews come to you seeking hostages,' Nuʿaym said, 'do not give them a single man.'

Nuʿaym then went to Ghaṭafān, and said: 'You are my origin, and my family, and the most beloved of people to me; and I do not believe you distrust me (i.e. I am trustworthy in your sight).' They said: 'You speak true; you are not suspicious in our sight.' 'In that case,' Nuʿaym said, 'keep secret what I am about to tell you.' They said; 'We will,' and Nuʿaym told them the same thing he had told Quraysh.

Allah decreed for His Messenger ﷺ that Abū Sufyān and the heads of Ghaṭafān sent to the Jews of Banī Qurayẓa a delegation of the two tribes, which contained ʿAkrima. They said: 'We are not in our homes, and the camels and horses are exhausted, so prepare for battle, that we might put an end to Muḥammad, and be rid of him.'

The Jews of Banī Qurayẓa sent a reply to them, saying: 'Today is the Sabbath, and we do not work on it. Some of us once worked on it, and were afflicted with that which you are not unaware (i.e. they were transformed into beasts). We will not fight with you until you give us some of your men, to be in our possession as a security, until we have put an end to Muḥammad; for we fear that, if the battle becomes severe upon you, you will return home, and leave us with the man [Muḥammad ﷺ], and we will have no hope of defeating him.' 'By Allah,' said Quraysh and Ghaṭafān, 'that which Nuʿaym told us of was true.' They sent a message to Banī Qurayẓa, saying: 'By Allah, we will not fight with you unless you give us hostages,' and they refused to do so.

Allah disappointed them, and sent upon them winds on a severely cold night, and so their fires went out, and their lodgings were destroyed.

5—His ﷺ concealment and disguise of matters from his enemies: The Prophet ﷺ used to disguise and conceal military affairs from his enemies, so they would not become aware of them, and prepare to defend against them, or gather more forces. Because of this, lives were spared.

Bukhārī and Muslim narrate that Kaʻb b. Mālik 🕊 said: 'The Messenger of Allah 🕊 never intended to fight a battle except that he feigned otherwise, until that battle came (the battle of Tabūk), which he fought in severe heat, after a long journey, against a considerable number. He revealed to the Muslims that they should prepare their battle gear, and told them the course he wanted to take, and did not feign as if to take another course.'

The Prophet 🕊 also confused his enemies on the night of the migration, when they came to his house to kill him 🕊, and he ordered ʻAlī 🕊 to sleep in his bed, and cover himself with his 🕊 robe.

6—He 🕊 used methods of provoking dread, and intimidation:

The Prophet 🕊 utilised methods of provoking dread and fear in his enemies, in order to weaken their effectiveness, and prevent their evil and harm, and the villainy of their souls.

It is related that when the Prophet 🕊 set out to conquer Mecca, and arrived at Ẓahrān, he ordered his companions to light ten thousand fires, so that Quraysh could see them, and be struck by dread because of their abundance. When Abū Sufyān and those with him saw them from afar, they said: 'It is like the fires of ʻArafat!' (i.e. in their great number) This cast fear into their hearts.

The Prophet 🕊 also ordered his uncle ʻAbbās to sit with Abū Sufyān on the road by the narrow mountain pass, in order that he would see the Muslim armies passing by, in their regiments. They began to pass by, regiment after regiment, until Abū Sufyān said to ʻAbbās: 'Who are these regiments, O ʻAbbās?' ʻAbbās began to tell him about the regiments, one by one. This was one of the incidents that provoked Abū Sufyān to compromise, and surrender, until he finally embraced Islam.

7—His 🕊 selection of competent, courageous warriors to fight fierce battles:

The Prophet 🕊 would select the most highly qualified men to enter fierce battles, according to the most fitting preparations. Afterwards, the subtlety of his reasoning 🕊 and his accuracy in selecting that particular man would become clear to the Ṣaḥāba.

On the day of Khaybar, he ﷺ said: 'Tomorrow, I will give the standard to a man whom Allah and His Messenger love, and by whose hand Allah will bring victory.' The next day, the people rushed to the Messenger of Allah ﷺ, all hoping to be given the standard. He ﷺ said: 'Where is ʿAlī b. Abī Ṭālib?' They said: 'O Messenger of Allah, he complains of an ailment in his eyes.' He was sent for, and brought forward, red-eyed. The Prophet ﷺ spat into his eyes, and prayed for him, saying: 'O Allah, remove this heat and cold from him!' He was cured instantly, as though there had never been any problem.

The narrations of Bayhaqī and Ṭabarānī add: ʿAlī ﷺ said: 'I have not had sore eyes, nor a headache, since the Messenger of Allah ﷺ gave me the standard on the day of Khaybar.'

Yūnus' narration on the authority of Ibn Isḥāq adds: ʿAlī ﷺ would wear thick robes in severe heat, and not complain of the heat; and wear light clothes in extreme cold, and not complain of the cold. He was asked the reason for this, and replied that it was because of the Prophet's ﷺ prayer for him on the day of Khaybar.

On the day of Uḥud, when the battle became fierce, the Prophet ﷺ said: 'Who will take up this sword as it merits?' Men approached him, including Zubayr b. al-ʿAwwām, and asked him three times, but were all refused, until Abū Dujāna Samāk b. Kharasha approached, and said: 'What does it merit, O Messenger of Allah?' He ﷺ said: 'That the face of the enemy be struck with it, until it bends.'

He was a brave man, who would strut around at times of war. When the Prophet ﷺ saw him strutting, he said ﷺ: 'This is a gait that Allah hates, except on occasions such as this.'

Zubayr said: 'By Allah, I was watching what Abū Dujāna was doing, and following him. He took a red bandana of his, and wrapped his head with it. The Anṣār (Helpers) said: "Come out, O bandana of death!" He came out, saying:

> *I am he whose friend has made with him a pact*
> *At the foot of the mountain, by the palm-tree,*
> *That I will not spend my time in the back rows;*
> *I will strike with the sword of Allah, and the Messenger.'*

He did not encounter any of the idolaters except that he slew them. Zubayr said: 'There was a man amongst the idolaters who did not leave a single wounded man except that he killed him. The two began to approach one another, and I prayed that Allah would bring them together. They met, and each rained a blow on the other. The idolater struck Abū Dujāna, who parried the blow with his shield. His sword stuck in the shield. Abū Dujāna struck him, and killed him. I then saw him raise the sword above the head of Hind bint 'Utba, and then lower it, and say: "I hold the sword of the Messenger of Allah 🕌 in too high esteem to use it to strike a woman."'[208]

8—His 🕌 selection of intelligent, sagacious envoys to be sent to rulers and kings, to spread the message, and advance wise, reasoned arguments: This is apparent from the skilful way they presented their case, and their oratorical prowess when meeting with rulers and kings.

The Messenger of Allah 🕌 sent 'Alā' b. al-Ḥaḍramī to Mundhir b. Sāwā, with a written message inviting him to embrace Islam. When he met him, he [al-Ḥaḍramī] said: 'O Mundhir, you are a man of great sagacity, so do not allow yourself to be humiliated in the hereafter. This Zoroastrianism is an evil religion, which does not befit the nobility of the Arabs. It is not a characteristic of the people of scripture that they marry those whom it is shameful to marry,[209] or that they eat that which it is dishonourable to eat, or that they worship, in this world, the same fire that will consume them in the hereafter.

'You are not a senseless man, nor a simpleton. Ask yourself, if a person never lies about this worldly life, is it appropriate to doubt him? If a person is never disloyal, is it appropriate to suspect him? If a person never fails to keep his word, is it appropriate to mistrust him? If it is so, then here we have an unlettered Prophet of whom, by Allah, no intelligent person can say: "If only he had prohibited that which he has enjoined, and enjoined that which he has permitted," or: "If only his mercy

---

[208] See *Sharḥ al-Mawāhib*.
[209] I.e. adulterous marriage, a practice of ancient Zoroastrianism. [t]

were greater, or his requital less." In all of these respects, he is in line with the expectations of those of intellect, and the mind of those of discernment.'

Mundhir said to him: 'I have considered that which I am upon (Zoroastrianism), and have found it to be of this world, not the hereafter. I have considered your religion, and found it to be correct both for the hereafter, and this world. What is there to prevent me from accepting a religion in which there is contentment in life, and repose in death? Yesterday, I was astounded by those who accepted it; today, I am astounded by any who would refuse it. Part of extolling a message is to extol the Messenger; I will consider the matter.'[210]

The Messenger of Allah 🪷 also sent Muhājir b. Abī Umayya al-Makhzūmī, the brother of Umm Salama, the mother of the believers, to Ḥārith b. 'Abd Kulāl, one of the kings of Ḥumayr. When Muhājir met Ḥārith, he said: 'O Ḥārith, you were the first of those to whom the Prophet showed himself, and you neglected him. You are one of the most powerful kings; yet, when you consider the supremacy of kings, consider also the One who will conquer all kings. If your day pleases you, fear tomorrow; for there were kings before you, whose traces are gone, and whose legends remain. They lived long, and expected much; but prepared little. Some of them were taken by death, and some of them were consumed by misfortune and affliction.

'I call you to the Lord who, if you desire guidance, will not withhold it from you; and if He desires anything for you, no one can prevent Him from it. I call you to the unlettered Prophet: there is nothing finer than that which he enjoins; and nothing fouler than that which he prohibits. Know that you have a Lord, Who brings death to the living, and life to the dead, and knows the treachery of the eyes, and what the heart conceals.'[211]

---

[210] The meaning of Mundhir's statement 'I will consider the matter' is that he would consider whether he would go and visit the Messenger of Allah 🪷, or write to him, not that he would consider whether to embrace Islam or not; his words 'today, I am astounded by any who would refuse it' show that he considered Islam to be the true religion. (*Sharḥ al-Mawāhib*, and elsewhere)

[211] *Al-Rawḍ al-Unuf*

9—His 卌 **social conduct and diplomacy, and his ability to accommodate many different kinds of people amicably, winning them over to the truth, with benevolent conduct and gentle speech:** It is narrated on the authority of Abū Hurayra 卌 that the Prophet 卌 said: 'The height of intellect, after faith in Allah, is winning people's hearts.'[212]

He used to be sociable with fools and simpletons, in order to ward off their calamities, and evils, and in order to attract their hearts towards righteousness and guidance:

It is narrated in the *Ṣaḥīḥ* on the authority of 'Ā'isha 卌 that a man asked permission to see the Prophet 卌, and when he saw him, he said: 'The worst brother of the tribe, and[213] the worst son of the tribe!' When he sat, the Prophet 卌 smiled at him, and was jovial with him. One narration adds: When he entered, he spoke with him gently. When the man left, 'Ā'isha 卌 said: 'O Messenger of Allah, when you saw the man, you said such-and-such about him; then you smiled with him, and treated him jovially.'

He 卌 said: 'O 'Ā'isha, when did you think me obscene? The worst of people in rank in Allah's sight on the Day of Resurrection are those whom the people left, out of fear of their evil.' Another narration has it: 'out of fear of their obscenity,' i.e. out of fear of their obscene words and deeds. When the man, who was considered a simpleton, came in, the Prophet 卌 did not greet him with coarseness and harshness; rather, he spoke to him gently, and was sociable with him.

For this reason, the scholars say that this Ḥadīth is a basis for sociability. They made a distinction between praiseworthy sociability, and blameworthy sycophancy:

---

[212] Narrated by Bayhaqī and Bazzār, with a weak chain of transmission, as stated in *Fayḍ al-Qadīr* and *Sharḥ al-Mawāhib*. 'Asqalānī ascribes it, in *Fatḥ al-Bārī*, to Bazzār with the wording: 'The height of intellect, after faith in Allah, is sociability with people.' Sakhāwī revised this, concluding that Bazzār's wording is actually 'winning people's hearts.' (*Sharḥ al-Mawāhib*)

[213] One narration has 'or' instead of 'and,' indicating the narrator's uncertainty about which expression was used (i.e. 'brother' or 'son' [t]).

Sociability is sacrificing a worldly matter in order to rectify the affairs of this world, or the hereafter, or both of them. This includes gentle speech, avoiding harshness in speech, kindness when teaching the uneducated, compassion when correcting the actions of the wicked, without treating them harshly as long as they do not reveal their deeds openly, or rebuking them with blows, in order that they desist from performing such deeds.

Imam al-Qasṭalānī said: 'This is permissible, and it is possible that it is recommended.' Ḥāfiẓ al-Zurqānī said: 'It may be recommended, or obligatory.'

Daylamī narrates in *al-Firdaws* on the authority of ʿĀ'isha ﷺ quoting the Messenger of Allah ﷺ: 'Allah has commanded me to treat people sociably, as He has commanded me to fulfil the obligatory.' Ibn ʿAdī and Ṭabarānī narrate on the authority of Jābir ﷺ, also quoting the Messenger of Allah ﷺ: 'Treating people sociably is charity.'[214]

Sycophancy is sacrificing a religious matter in order to rectify a worldly one, and it is blameworthy. Allah ﷻ absolved His Prophet ﷺ from it, saying: ﴿They wish that you would compromise (out of sycophancy), that they might compromise.﴾[215] The Prophet ﷺ would be sociable, not sycophantic.

ʿAmr b. al-ʿĀṣ ﷺ said: 'The Messenger of Allah ﷺ would tackle the evil of the people, and by means of it bring them together...' as narrated in full by Tirmidhī and others.

Fifthly: One of the greatest indications of his noble, perfect intellect ﷺ, and its superiority, is the breadth of his knowledge. Allah ﷻ bestowed him richly with great knowledge, and showed him His signs, and aided him with clear proofs, and validated him with miracles, and vouchsafed for him all manner of divine revelation. No one could have borne this, except one whom Allah ﷻ had singled out with a mighty heart, and a vast intellect: the greatest Master ﷺ.

---

[214] Both of these Ḥadīth have some weakness in their chains of transmission. (*Sharḥ al-Munāwī*)

[215] Qur'ān 68:9

It should be known, in this regard, that all the matters and affairs, and guidance and learning, and details and concepts, brought by the Messenger of Allah 🕌 fulfil the expectations of the wise, and the sagacious, and are the utmost goal of the people of intellect and discernment.[216] This is clear from several aspects:

1 – The basis for legal responsibility is the intellect, to the extent that if the intellect is lost, responsibility is lifted. This is clear in view of the intellect's acceptance of the proofs that lead to adherence to the obligations of responsibility. If the sacred commandments that the Prophet 🕌 brought had been contrary to the conclusions of the sound intellect, the intrinsic necessity of legal responsibility for the intellectually sound would have been inappropriate.

2 – If his 🕌 commandments, prohibitions and judgements were illogical, responsibility to them would be impossible to meet, because it would necessitate faith in that which the intellect could not possibly have faith.

3 – If anything that the Prophet 🕌 brought was illogical, the disbelievers of his time would have been the first to take him up on this, because they were especially eager to repudiate that which he 🕌 brought. They would even resort to inventing lies against him, and against his law, sometimes calling him a magician, sometimes calling him insane, and sometimes calling him a liar. They would refer to the Qur'ān as magic, and poetry, and other contradictory speech; for how can magic and poetry spring from madness?

If his 🕌 judgements were illogical, the first thing they would have said was: 'This does not make sense,' or 'this is illogical,' or the like, and they would not have needed to resort to contradictory statements about magic and poetry, and the like.

---

[216] As was shown by 'Alā' b. al-Ḥaḍramī 🕌 to Mundhir b. Sāwā, when the Messenger of Allah 🕌 sent him with his letter, and Mundhir accepted it, as we have seen.

4 – All of the wise and intelligent people of his 🪷 time bore witness to the truth of what he brought, and to its logic and wisdom, and for this reason they submitted, and embraced Islam. We have seen how Mundhir b. Sāwā said: 'What is there to prevent me from accepting a religion in which there is contentment in life?'

Ja'far b. Abī Ṭālib 🪷 said to Najāshī:[217] 'We were a people of ignorance, worshipping idols, and eating carrion, and performing obscenities, and neglecting ties of kinship, and mistreating neighbours, the strong of us consuming the weak. Then, Allah sent to us a Messenger from among us, whose lineage, honesty, trustworthiness and virtue we knew, and he called us to declare the oneness of Allah 🪷, and worship Him, and to leave the stones and idols which we and our forefathers worshipped in His lieu. He ordered us to speak the truth, and keep our trusts, and maintain our ties of kinship, and respect our neighbours' rights, and leave sin and bloodshed. He forbade us iniquity, and false testimony, and consuming the property of the orphan.'

Upon hearing this, Najāshī said: 'Welcome to you, and to he from whom you have come. I testify that he is the Messenger of Allah, and that he is the one whom we find in the Gospel, and that he is the Messenger foretold by 'Īsā,[218] the Son of Maryam. By Allah, if it were not for my position as king, I would go to this Prophet, and carry his shoes for him.'[219]

Aktham b. Ṣayfī sent a group of his people to the Prophet 🪷 when he heard of his coming. They went to the Prophet 🪷, and said to him: 'We are envoys of Aktham b. Ṣayfī, who asks: Who are you, and what are you, and what have you brought?' He 🪷 said: 'As for who I am: I am Muḥammad b. 'Abdullāh. As for what I am: I am Allah's servant and Messenger. I have brought you the word of Allah 🪷: ❨Allah commands justice, kindness, and aiding kith and kin; and He forbids obscenity, evil and transgression. He admonishes you, that you might take heed.❩'[220]

---

[217] The Negus.

[218] Jesus Christ 🪷.

[219] Narrated by Aḥmad. Ṭabarānī's narration has it: 'I would go to him, and kiss his 🪷 feet.'

[220] Qur'ān 16:90

'Repeat this statement for us,' they said, so he 🙻 repeated it, until they memorised it. They went to Aktham, and said: 'He did not bring up his lineage, so we asked him about it. We found him to be of pure lineage, and noble. He addressed us with some words, and we heard them.' When Aktham heard them, he said: 'I see him enjoining good conduct, and forbidding bad conduct: so be leaders in this, and do not lag behind.'[221]

Everything that the Messenger of Allah 🙻 brought is logical, and wise, and because of this, the people of sagacity and discernment submitted to it.

It is not possible that there could be logical flaws or impossibilities in that which the Messenger of Allah 🙻 brought; rather, it contains wonders of exalted wisdom, which human intellects cannot encompass, or penetrate, due to the weakness of the intellect in achieving this, just as eyesight is too weak to look directly at the sun, and encompass its light: the eyes only see enough of sunlight to establish its existence beyond doubt; they cannot encompass it in its totality.

The Muḥammadan law is the ruling of Allah 🙻, and the ruling of Allah 🙻 issues from His knowledge and wisdom. How could the knowledge of a created being encompass all of that?

THE BREADTH OF HIS KNOWLEDGE 🙻
AND HIS ABUNDANT LEARNING
WHICH NO ONE COULD ENCOMPASS BUT ALLAH 🙻
WHO BESTOWED IT UPON HIM 🙻

The Messenger of Allah 🙻 was endowed with broad knowledge, and deep understanding. Allah 🙻 showered him with an abundance of beneficial learning, and a profusion of lofty erudition. Allah 🙻 acknowledged the breadth of his 🙻 knowledge, and announced the magnitude of his refinement,

---

[221] Ḥāfiẓ Ibn Kathīr said: 'It was narrated by Abū Yaʿlā in *Maʿrifat al-Ṣaḥāba*.'

saying: ⟨Allah revealed to you Scripture, and wisdom, and taught you that which you knew not. The grace of Allah upon you has been great.⟩[222]

He 🌿 is the most knowledgeable of Allah's creation, and the most well acquainted of them with Allah 🌿, as is related in the *Ṣaḥīḥ* of Bukhārī and Muslim, that he 🌿 said: 'The most god-fearing of you, and the most knowledgeable of you concerning Allah, is me.' The narration of Aṣīlī has it: 'I am the most knowledgeable of you concerning Allah.'

Whoever ponders Allah's 🌿 instruction of His Messengers and Prophets, as mentioned in the noble Qur'ān, will plainly deduce that our Master Muḥammad 🌿 was taught by Allah 🌿 knowledge that was greater, more abundant, broader and more extensive. This is because Allah 🌿 said: ⟨And (He) taught you that which you knew not⟩, using the term ⟨that which⟩, the implication of which is comprehensiveness and encompassment, in order that it would include all the knowledge that Allah 🌿 taught His Messengers and Prophets, and also encompass all the other learning that Allah 🌿 bestowed upon him 🌿.

Ḥāfiẓ Abū Bakr b. 'Ā'idh narrated that Ibn 'Abbās 🌿 said: 'When the Prophet 🌿 was born, Riḍwān, custodian of Paradise, said in his ear: "Rejoice, O Muḥammad, for no prophet has any knowledge except that it has been given to you, and so you are the most knowledgeable of them, and the most bold-hearted.'[223]

It is narrated in the *Ṣaḥīḥ* of Bukhārī and Muslim (and the following wording is Muslim's) that Anas 🌿 said: 'The people asked the Prophet of Allah 🌿, until they had asked him copious amount of questions. One day, he came out and climbed the

---

[222] Qur'ān 4:113

[223] 'Allāmah al-Qasṭalānī narrated it in *al-Mawāhib*, transmitting it from Shaykh Badruddīn al-Zarkashī. Ḥāfiẓ al-Zurqānī said: 'It was reported by Ibn 'Abbās without mentioning that the Prophet 🌿 said it [*arsala*]. This kind of narration [*mursal*] from a Ṣaḥābī is originally connected to the Prophet 🌿, and it is considered as though he 🌿 said it [*al-rafʿ*], for there is no possibility it was a personal opinion.' (Because it contained knowledge of the unseen that only the Prophet 🌿 could have related. [t])

pulpit, and said: "Ask me: you will not ask anything except that I will answer it for you.'" In one narration, he said: '...except that I will inform you concerning it, as long as I stand here.'

'When the people heard this, they fell silent, and were fearful that they were in the midst of a grave matter. I began to look right and left, and saw that every man was hiding his face in his robe, and weeping. A man from the mosque whom the people used to insult, ascribing him to other than his father, began the questioning, saying: "O Prophet of Allah, who is my father?" He said: "Your father is Ḥudhāfa." Umar b. al-Khaṭṭāb 🕮 then began, saying: "We are pleased with Allah as our Lord, and Islam as our religion, and Muḥammad as our Messenger," seeking refuge from evil tribulation.

The Messenger of Allah 🕮 said: "I have never seen good and evil the like of which I have seen this day: Paradise and Hell were shown to me, and I saw them in front of this wall.'"

Consider his 🕮 statement: 'You will not ask anything except that I will answer it for you.'

Despite all of this, Allah 🕮 commanded the Prophet 🕮 to ask Him always for an increase in knowledge, saying: ❨And say: 'My Lord! Increase me in knowledge.'❩[224] Allah 🕮 did not command His Messenger 🕮 to ask for an increase in anything except in knowledge.

For this reason, the Prophet 🕮 consistently prayed night and day for increased knowledge. When he woke up at night, he would say: 'There is no god but You. O Allah, I extol Your glory, and Your praise! O Allah, I seek Your forgiveness for my sin, and ask Your mercy. O Allah, increase me in knowledge, and do not cause my heart to stray after You have guided me. Grant me mercy from Yourself, for You give generously.'[225]

Tirmidhī and Ibn Mājah narrate with a sound [ḥasan] chain of transmission on the authority of Abū Hurayra 🕮 that the Prophet 🕮 supplicated, saying: 'O Allah, benefit me with what You have taught me, and teach me that which will benefit me, and increase me in knowledge. Praise be to Allah, no matter the circumstance! I seek refuge in Allah from the state of the denizens of Hell.'

---

[224] Qur'ān 20:114
[225] Narrated in Muslim's *Ṣaḥīḥ*, and elsewhere.

It is also narrated that he ﷺ was always in a state of increase in his knowledge and divine learning. Divine emanations and openings would constantly visit him ﷺ, as is narrated in Muslim's *Ṣaḥīḥ* on the authority of 'Iyāḍ b. Ḥimār al-Majāshi'ī, who reported that the Messenger of Allah ﷺ said: 'My Lord has commanded me to teach you that which you know not, of that which He has taught me today...'

Every day, Allah ﷻ showered him ﷺ with knowledge and learning, and commanded him to teach the people some of that knowledge, in accordance with what they needed, and what they could bear, and what they were ready for, in accordance with Allah's instructions. After all this, there is no one from among Allah's creation who is capable of encompassing the breadth of the Messenger of Allah's ﷺ knowledge, or its varieties or its types: no one can encompass this except Allah ﷻ, who bestowed it all upon him ﷺ.

I will mention some aspects of the evidences that prove the breadth of his ﷺ knowledge and his abundant learning, in order that those who are unaware of it might learn, and those who are heedless might become attentive; and that those who are true believers might find their faith in this noble Messenger ﷺ increase.

THE FIRST PROOF:
THE GATHERING OF THE QUR'ĀN IN HIS NOBLE BREAST ﷺ

The noble Qur'ān, which Allah ﷻ has revealed to him ﷺ, and gathered in his noble breast, and taught him, and explained to him, and commanded him to explain to the people, and revealed its deep realities to him, and its secrets, and illuminations, and its exoteric and esoteric significations. Allah ﷻ said:

❴Read: In the name of your Lord, who created: created humanity from a clot. Read: and your Lord is most generous, who teaches by the pen: teaches humanity that which they knew not.❵[226]

---

[226] Qur'ān 96:1-5

These five verses marked the beginning of the revelation of the Qurʾān to the Prophet 🕮, which Jibrīl 🕮 brought to him on the night of his prophecy.

It is narrated in the *Ṣaḥīḥ* of Bukhārī and Muslim on the authority of ʿĀʾisha 🕮 who said: 'The first revelation to visit the Messenger of Allah came in the form of visions in his sleep. He would not see a vision except that it came with the clarity of the sunrise. Then, solitude became beloved to him, and he so would go alone to the cave of Ḥirāʾ and worship there for many nights, taking provisions with him. The truth came to him when he was in the cave of Ḥirāʾ. The angel came to him, and said: "Read!" He said: "I cannot read."'

The Prophet 🕮 said: 'So he took hold of me, and embraced me, until he had reached the limit of my endurance, and then released me, and said: "Read." I said: "I cannot read." So he took hold of me, and embraced me again, until he had reached the limit of my endurance, and then released me, and said: "Read." I said: "I cannot read." He took hold of me and embraced me a third time, and then released me, and said: ❰Read: In the name of your Lord, who created: created humanity from a clot. Read: and your Lord is most generous, who teaches by the pen: teaches humanity that which they knew not.❱[227]...'

Jibrīl 🕮 brought the noble Qurʾān to the Messenger of Allah 🕮, and told him to read, so he said 'I cannot read,' because he was raised illiterate, never learning to read and write. Jibrīl 🕮 repeated his instruction 'read' three times, and followed each one with a powerful embrace, in order to impart to him that which Allah 🕮 had inspired in him of meanings, secrets and illuminations, bound together with his body, heart and soul. He then said to him ❰Read: In the name of your Lord❱, meaning: 'you are able to read by virtue of your Lord's name, not by virtue of your learning or your education, because you have no prior learning or instruction.' By means of this, the Messenger of Allah 🕮 became a learned orator, reciting the word of Allah 🕮, after living forty years without bringing a single verse to his people. This is a clear proof that Muḥammad 🕮 is the Messenger of Allah, speaking by inspiration from Allah 🕮.

---

[227] Ibid.

Allah ﷻ said: ⟨Say: 'If Allah willed, I should not have recited it to you, nor would He have made it known to you: for I dwelt amongst you a whole lifetime before it. Do you not comprehend?'⟩[228]

This means that whoever seeks to comprehend the matter of our Master Muḥammad ﷺ will be convinced that he is truly the Messenger of Allah, for there is no other plausible explanation. His affair is not a case of genius, or of intellectual brilliance and intelligence; rather, his affair is simply that he is a Messenger, inspired by Allah ﷻ.

More than this, Allah ﷻ showed the falsehood of the contentions of those who denied the Prophethood of our Master Muḥammad ﷺ, who claimed that the guidance and knowledge that he brought were the result of education and judiciousness, or the result of intellectual brilliance, or genius. All of these claims are refuted by the fact that he ﷺ was illiterate, never having learned to read or write, or listened to a teacher. Allah ﷻ said: ⟨And you were not a reader of any scripture before it, nor did you write it with your right hand—for then, those who follow falsehood might have doubted.⟩[229]

When the Prophet's ﷺ enemies accused him of having listened to one of the non-Arab slaves, and bringing what he brought from him, Allah ﷻ replied to them, saying: ⟨And We know that they say: 'It is only a human being who teaches him⟩, referring to a non-Arab slave-boy owned by one of the Quraysh. Allah then said: ⟨The tongue of the one to whom they refer is outlandish; and this is eloquent Arabic speech!⟩[230]

This means that the slave from whom they claimed the Messenger ﷺ was taking spoke a foreign tongue, and had no eloquence; yet the Messenger of Allah ﷺ brought them this eloquent Arabic Qur'ān. How could it be imagined that this eloquent Arabic Qur'ān could have come from this foreign man, who had no eloquence?

The Messenger of Allah ﷺ did not compose this Qur'ān himself, nor did he take it from another created being, because of

---

[228] Qur'ān 10:16
[229] Qur'ān 29:48
[230] Qur'ān 16:103

their inability to bring the like of it; it came from the Lord of the worlds. Allah 🕮 said: ❴The Most Merciful has made known the Qur'ān. He created humanity, and taught them eloquent speech.❵[231] The first human being whom the Most Merciful taught the Qur'ān was the Master of the sons of Adam, Muḥammad 🕮. From him, the rest of humanity received the Qur'ān, and learned it.

He 🕮 was also the first person whom Allah 🕮 taught how to speak eloquently about the meanings of the Qur'ān. Allah 🕮 taught His Messenger 🕮 the Qur'ān: how to recite it, its meanings, its wisdoms, its secrets, its signs, and its unique attributes. Allah said: ❴We shall cause you to read, so you shall not forget.❵[232]

And He said: ❴Move not your tongue with it, seeking to hasten it; it is upon Us to gather it and to read it. And when We read it, follow its reading; then, it is upon Us to explain it.❵[233] This means: 'It is upon Us, O Muḥammad 🕮, to gather for you the Qur'ān in your breast, and it is upon Us to make its recitation firm on your tongue; so do not hasten the Qur'ān before its inspiration is completed, in order to grasp it quickly, because you fear it will slip away from you.'

Allah 🕮 is the One who gathered the Qur'ān in his 🕮 breast, and made him recite it with his tongue, and undertook to explain it to him, saying: ❴It is upon Us to explain it❵, i.e. to explain its meanings, rulings, and commands and prohibitions:

This includes Allah's teaching the Prophet 🕮 the unique qualities of the Qur'ānic lexis, as indicated in the Ḥadīth narrated by Abū Dāwūd and Tirmidhī from Thawrī, from Abū Isḥāq, from Muhallab b. Abī Ṣufra, who said: 'I was told, by the one who heard him say it, that the Messenger of Allah 🕮 said: "If you are plotted against by night (or in one narration 'if you await the enemy by night'), say: "❴Ḥā Mīm❵, they will not gain victory."'[234]

---

[231] Qur'ān 55:1-4

[232] Qur'ān 87:6

[233] Qur'ān 75:16-19

[234] He 🕮 said this to them before one of the battles. Ḥāfiẓ Ibn Kathīr said: 'The chain of transmission is rigorously authentic [ṣaḥīḥ]. Abū ʿUbayd preferred to narrate it: "Say: '❴Ḥā Mīm❵' and they will not gain victory"

It also includes the Prophet's 🕮 knowledge of the unique characteristics of the Qur'ānic verses, as is narrated concerning the final verses of Sūrat al-Baqara by Tirmidhī, on the authority of Nuʿmān b. Bashīr, that the Prophet 🕮 said: 'Allah wrote scriptures a thousand years before He created the heavens and the earth, from which He revealed the two verses that close Sūrat al-Baqara. If they are recited in a house for three nights, Satan cannot approach it.'[235]

It also includes what is reported about the unique characteristics of the first ten verses of Sūrat al-Kahf, and its last ten verses, that they are a source of protection from the Antichrist. Aḥmad narrates in his *Musnad* on the authority of Abū Dardāʾ 🕮 that the Prophet 🕮 said: 'Whoever memorises the first ten verses of Sūrat al-Kahf will be protected from the Antichrist.'[236] Imam Aḥmad also narrates on the authority of Abū Dardāʾ that the Prophet 🕮 said: 'Whoever recites the final ten verses of Sūrat al-Kahf will be protected from the temptations of the Antichrist.'[237]

Ḥāfiẓ Ḍiyāʾ al-Maqdisī narrates in his *Mukhtāra* on the authority of ʿAlī b. al-Ḥusayn 🕮, on the authority of his father 🕮, from ʿAlī 🕮, quoting the Prophet 🕮: 'Whoever recites Sūrat al-Kahf on Friday is protected from every tribulation for eight days, and if the Antichrist emerges, they will be protected from him.'[238]

(i.e. "if you say this, they will not gain victory").' This is a proof that ﴾Ḥā Mīm﴿ is a source of protection.

[235] Tirmidhī said: '(It is) a singularly-narrated Ḥadīth [*gharīb*].' Ḥākim narrated it in *al-Mustadrak*, saying: 'It is rigorously authentic according to the stipulations of Muslim, but Bukhārī and Muslim did not narrate it.'

[236] Ḥāfiẓ Ibn Kathīr said: 'It was narrated by Muslim, Abū Dāwūd, Nasāʾī, and Tirmidhī from the Ḥadīth of Qatāda. Tirmidhī's wording is: "Whoever memorises the first three verses of Sūrat al-Kahf...," and he said: "It is a sound, rigorously authentic Ḥadīth."'

[237] Ibn Kathīr said: 'Muslim and Nasāʾī also narrated it from the Ḥadīth of Qatāda, and Nasāʾī's wording is: "Whoever reads ten verses from al-Kahf..."'

[238] See *Tafsīr Ibn Kathīr*. The origin of the Ḥadīth is in the *Musnad*, and elsewhere.

The like of this is also related about the first verses of Sūrat Yā Sīn. Ibn Isḥāq and others narrated that when the idolaters lay in wait for the Prophet 🕌 on the night of the emigration, he came out before them carrying a handful of dust, which he began to throw at their heads, reciting: ❨Yā Sīn. By the wise Qur'ān...❩, until he arrived at Allah's word: ❨And We have placed before them a barrier, and behind them a barrier, and so have covered them, so they see not.❩[239] The Messenger of Allah 🕌 went on his way, and they spent the night waiting by his door. Each of them then began to brush the dust from their heads. Allah 🕌 cast a barrier between them and His Messenger 🕌, so they did not see him when he went past them. This subject is vast, and there is no space here to go into great detail concerning it.

It also includes his 🕌 knowledge of the unique characteristics of the chapters of the Qur'ān, as is evidenced by what is reported concerning Sūrat Yā Sīn, and its being the heart of the Qur'ān, and its possessing many unique characteristics; and concerning Sūrat al-Dukhān, and that whoever recites it in the evening is forgiven his sins before morning; and Sūrat Tabārak,[240] and that it protects from the torment of the grave; and Sūrat al-Baqara and its blessings; and the chapters of refuge sought,[241] and the protection they afford their reciter; and other characteristics confirmed in prophetic Ḥadīth.[242] All of this proves to us that the Prophet 🕌 had great knowledge of the unique characteristics of the letters, verses and chapters of the Qur'ān. Glory be to the All-Knowing Opener, who endowed the Prophet 🕌 with this knowledge!

It also includes his 🕌 knowledge of the secret indications of the noble Qur'ān, beyond the apparent meanings. This is attested to by the narration of Imam Aḥmad in his *Musnad*, on the authority of Ibn ʿAbbās 🕌, who said: 'When the chapter

---

[239] Qur'ān 36:1-9

[240] Sūrat al-Mulk

[241] Chapters 113 and 114

[242] We have mentioned some of these in our book *Tilāwat al-Qurʾān al-Majīd* ('The Recitation of the Glorious Qur'ān').

⟨When Allah's succour and the conquest come...⟩[243] was revealed, the Prophet ﷺ knew that his passing was approaching.' Another narration, also on the authority of Ibn 'Abbās ﷺ, has it: 'When the chapter ⟨When Allah's succour and the conquest come...⟩ was revealed, the Messenger of Allah ﷺ said: "My passing is imminent."[244] He passed away that year.'

Imam Aḥmad narrated (and the origin of the Ḥadīth is in *Ṣaḥīḥ Muslim*) on the authority of 'Ā'isha ﷺ who said: 'Towards the end of his affair, the Messenger of Allah ﷺ would frequently say: "I extol Allah's glory, and His praise! I seek Allah's forgiveness, and repent to him," and he ﷺ said: "My Lord has informed me that I will see a sign in my community, and has commanded me that, upon my seeing it, I should extol His praise, and seek His forgiveness, for He is ever-ready to accept repentance; and I have now seen it:" and he recited: ⟨When Allah's succour and the conquest come...⟩ to the end of the chapter.'

The depth of the Prophet's ﷺ knowledge of the meaning and unique characteristics of the noble Qur'ān, and its deep realities, signs, and indications, and its secrets and significances, cannot be comprehended or encompassed except by Allah ﷻ, who endowed him ﷺ with it.

Allah ﷻ said: ⟨We have not left anything out of the Scripture.⟩[245] He ﷻ also said: ⟨And We sent down to you the Scripture, as an explanation of all things, and a source of guidance, mercy, and glad tidings to those who submit.⟩[246]

It is narrated on the authority of Ibn Mas'ūd ﷺ that the Prophet ﷺ said: 'The Qur'ān was revealed to me in seven modes, each mode (in another narration: 'each verse') with an outer and an inner, and each mode has a limit, and each limit has an explanation.'[247]

---

[243] Qur'ān 110:1

[244] Literally: 'My soul has announced its death to me.'

[245] Qur'ān 6:38

[246] Qur'ān 16:89

[247] Narrated by Ṭabarānī on the authority of Ibn Mas'ūd, and by Baghawī on the authority of Ḥasan and Ibn Mas'ūd, ascribed by them to the Prophet ﷺ, as mentioned in *Fayḍ al-Qadīr 'alā al-Jāmi' al-Ṣaghīr*. 'Allāmah Zarkashī ascribed it in *al-Burhān* to the *Ṣaḥīḥ* of Ibn Ḥibbān. The meaning of 'every mode has a limit' is that every mode has a boundary in the

The *Sunan* of Tirmidhī, and others, includes the Ḥadīth of our Master ʿAlī 🕮, in which the Prophet 🕮 said about the Qurʾān: 'It is Allah's firm rope, and it is the wise remembrance, and it is the straight path, and desires cannot pervert it, and tongues cannot obscure it, and those of discernment will never tire of it, and it will never wear out through repetition, and its wonders will never cease...'

Ibn Abī Ḥātim narrated on the authority of Ibn ʿAbbās 🕮: 'The Qurʾān is multifaceted and varied, and full of outer and inner meanings; its wonders never cease, and its limit is never reached.' Ibn Masʿūd said: 'Whoever desires the knowledge of the first and the last, let them recite the Qurʾān.'[248]

The noble Qurʾān is an ocean of knowledge and wisdom, which Allah 🕮 gathered for His Messenger 🕮, with its meanings and realities. The cousin and son-in-law of Allah's Messenger 🕮, the Commander of the Faithful, ʿAlī 🕮, said: 'If I spoke to you about Sūrat al-Fātiḥa, I would over-burden (the like of) seventy camels.' What, then, of the knowledge of our Master Muḥammad 🕮, and his understanding of the Qurʾān? Everything that the scholars know, and the Muḥammadan successors have spoken, amounts only to drops from the Prophet's 🕮 ocean, and flames engendered from his light, and emanations from his 🕮 secrets.

The knowledgeable scholars have done much research into the sciences derived from the noble Qurʾān; yet they have not arrived to a thorough examination of its roots. Each of them has spoken only in accordance with his knowledge, and the understanding he has been given; but the ocean of Qurʾānic meanings and secrets is without end.

It is related in *al-Itqān*, and elsewhere, that Qāḍī Abū Bakr b. al-ʿArabī 🕮 said, in *Qānūn al-Taʾwīl*:

---

meaning that Allah intended by it. The meaning of 'every limit has an explanation' means that every meaning or ruling that seems obscure has an explanation by means of which its meaning and intent can be ascertained. The 'outer' means that of which the meaning is apparent; the 'inner' means that of which the meaning is concealed.
(*Shurūḥ al-Munāwī ʿalā al-Jāmiʿ al-Ṣaghīr*)

[248] Saʿīd b. Manṣūr narrated on the authority of Ibn Masʿūd 🕮 that he said: 'Whoever desires knowledge, let him recite the Qurʾān, for within it is an account of the first and the last.' (*Al-Itqān*)

The Qur'ānic sciences number seventy-seven thousand, four hundred and fifty, according to the number of words in the Qur'ān multiplied by four: for each word has an outer and inner meaning, and a limit and an explanation. This is general, without considering their composition, or the connectors between them: for no one could enumerate or have knowledge of this except Allah ﷻ.

'Allāmah Rāghib said:

Just as Allah ﷻ sealed the Prophethood of all Prophets with our Prophet Muḥammad ﷺ, and sealed their laws with his law in respect to both abrogation and completion, he made the book that was revealed to him ﷺ encompass all the fruits of the books He revealed to them, as He indicated with His word: ❨A Messenger from Allah, reciting purified pages, containing corrected scriptures.❩[249] He made one of the miracles of this Book that, despite its small size, it contains manifold meaning, so that the human mind cannot encompass it, and worldly devices cannot exhaust it, as Allah indicated with His word: ❨If all that existed on earth of trees were pens, and the ocean, with seven more oceans to aid it (were ink), the words of Allah could not be exhausted.❩[250]

'Allāmah Zarkashī said in *al-Burhān*:

The noble Qur'ān contains the knowledge of the first and the last, and there is nothing that cannot be extrapolated from it by whomever Allah ﷻ gives sound discernment. One of them even discovered reference to the life-span of the Prophet ﷺ, of sixty-three years, in Allah's ﷻ word in Sūrat al-Munāfiqīn: ❨And Allah grants respite to no soul when its time comes❩,[251] because it comes at the end of the sixty-third chapter.

---

[249] Qur'ān 98:2-3
[250] Qur'ān 31:27
[251] Qur'ān 63:11

This is not the place for an examination of the sciences of the Qur'ān, and its meaning and indication; we have mentioned a modest example of them in order to illustrate the breadth the knowledge of our Master, the Messenger of Allah ﷺ, and his Qur'ānic learning, which cannot be encompassed by anyone but Allah ﷻ, who bestowed it upon him.

THE SECOND PROOF:
THE WISDOM THAT ALLAH REVEALED TO HIM ﷺ

Another evidence of the breadth of the Prophet's ﷺ learning and knowledge is the wisdom that Allah ﷻ revealed to him. Allah said: ❨Allah revealed to you Scripture, and wisdom.❩[252] And He ﷻ said: ❨And remember that which is recited in your households of the revelations of Allah, and wisdom. Allah is Subtle, Aware.❩[253]

This wisdom is the Sunnah of his ﷺ actions, words, states and tacit approval, as was set down by Imam al-Shāfiʿī ﷺ in several places in his writings.

It is also the opinion of a great many of the Tābiʿīn, such as Ḥasan al-Baṣrī, Qatāda, Muqātil b. Ḥayyān, and others, as Ḥāfiẓ Ibn Kathīr transmitted from them, explaining Allah's word: ❨Allah revealed to you Scripture, and wisdom.❩ The Prophetic Sunnah was called 'wisdom' because wisdom is comprised of sound speech and upright action, placed in their appropriate places. There is no doubt that his ﷺ speech, actions, states, and tacit approvals were all the very essence of wisdom.

Allah ﷻ also referred to the Prophetic Sunnah as 'the Balance' when He said: ❨Allah it is who has revealed the Scripture with truth, and the Balance. How can you know? Perhaps the Hour is near.❩[254] The 'Balance' associated with the Scripture here is the Muḥammadan Wisdom, the Prophetic Sunnah, which is associated with the Scripture in His word ❨Allah revealed to you Scripture, and wisdom❩: for parts of the Qur'ān explain other parts.

---

[252] Qur'ān 4:113
[253] Qur'ān 33:34
[254] Qur'ān 42:17

The Prophetic Sunnah, comprised of his ﷺ speech, actions, states and tacit approvals, is called 'the Balance' because it is the scale by which speech, actions, and states are measured. All of humanity must compare their speech, actions and states to his ﷺ Sunnah: that which matched the balance is sound and correct, and accepted and successful; that which is contrary to the balance of the Sunnah is obnoxious, and rejected, as is narrated by Muslim, on the authority of 'Ā'isha ﵂ that the Prophet ﷺ said: 'Every action that is not in accordance with our manner is rejected.'

Allah's word ﴾Allah revealed to you Scripture, and wisdom﴿ has been considered by many of the rightly-guided scholars as evidence that the Sunnah was revealed by inspiration from Allah ﷻ, as is also indicated by His word: ﴾And he speaks not from caprice; it is nothing save inspiration, inspired.﴿[255] 'Speech' is more general than 'recitation;' and Allah ﷻ did not say: 'And he recites not,' or 'And he reads not from caprice,' so that it could be said that this is referring specifically to the noble Qur'ān; rather, he said: ﴾And he speaks not from caprice.﴿ This means that Muḥammad, the Messenger of Allah ﷺ does not enunciate the Qur'ān, nor any other speech, from caprice; ﴾it is nothing﴿, i.e. his speech is nothing ﴾save inspiration, inspired﴿, which Allah revealed to him by one of the means of inspiration.

Abū Dāwūd and Tirmidhī narrated on the authority of Miqdād ﵁ that the Messenger of Allah ﷺ said: 'Truly, I have been given the Scripture, and the like of it besides it.' The meaning of 'the like of it besides it' is the Sunnah, as a great many of scholars have mentioned. Allah ﷻ gave His Messenger ﷺ the Prophetic Sunnah, just as He gave him the Scripture, which is the glorious Qur'ān. Bayhaqī narrated in *al-Madkhal* with his chain of transmission, on the authority of Ḥassān b. 'Aṭiyya, who said: 'Jibrīl ﵟ used to reveal to the Messenger of Allah ﷺ the Sunnah, just as he would reveal to him the Qur'ān; he would teach it to him as he taught him the Qur'ān.'[256]

---

[255] Qur'ān 53:3-4

[256] See *Sharḥ al-Ṭarīqat al-Muḥammadiyya* by the great Gnostic, Shaykh Nābulsī ﵟ.

The scholars have also adduced, as proof of this, the narration found in the *Ṣaḥīḥ* collections of Bukhārī and Muslim, and elsewhere (and the wording here is Bukhārī's), on the authority of Abū Saʿīd al-Khudrī 🕌, that the Messenger of Allah 🕌 said: 'The thing that I fear most for all of you is that which Allah grants you from the treasures of the earth.' (Another narration has it: 'The thing that I fear most for all of you is that which is granted to you of the splendour and delight of this worldly life.') A man said: 'Does goodness bring evil?' Abū Saʿīd said: 'The Prophet 🕌 was silent, until I was certain that he was receiving revelation. Then, the Messenger of Allah 🕌 began to wipe his forehead.[257] He said: "Who was the questioner?" The man said: "It was I." He 🕌 said: "Goodness does not bring aught but goodness'[258]—or, in one narration: 'Goodness does not bring evil.'

'"This wealth is green, and sweet. Everything that spring produces either kills by distending the stomach, or comes close to killing;[259] except for those creatures who eat greenery, until, when their haunches widen, they face the sun, ruminate, evacuate their bowels, and return to their grazing. This wealth is sweet. Whoever takes it rightfully, and uses it rightfully, it is the best of support; whoever takes us unrightfully is like the one who eats and is never satisfied.'"

Many scholars use this Ḥadīth as evidence that the prophetic Ḥadīth was revealed by divine inspiration from Allah 🕌. They also substantiate this with the Ḥadīth, narrated by Bukhārī and

---

[257] I.e. wiping away sweat, as is mentioned in the narration of Dāraquṭnī, which was his 🕌 custom when revelation came to him, and his blessed forehead would drip with sweat. Because of this, the Ṣaḥāba would know that it was revelation.

[258] In Dāraquṭnī's narration, he 🕌 repeated it three times.

[259] Another narration has it: 'Some of that which spring produces kills by distending the stomach, or comes close to killing.' The Messenger of Allah 🕌 was drawing an example of the one who chases after the world, and its wealth, and is blinded by it from his religion and his hereafter, and so amasses and withholds it, and does not recognise Allah's right to it, until he becomes proud, and wicked; and an example of the one who takes this wealth rightfully, and uses it rightfully, and fulfils the responsibilities that are incumbent upon him, and is not distracted by it from his religion, or blinded from his hereafter. The best of men is he!

others, in which Ya'lā b. Umayya 🌸 said to 'Umar b. al-Khaṭṭāb 🌸: 'Show me the Prophet 🌸 state when he is receiving revelation.' He replied: 'When the Prophet 🌸 was in al-Ji'rāna, with a group of his companions, a man came and said: "O Messenger of Allah, what do you say about a man who performed 'Umra[260] whilst wearing perfume?" The Prophet 🌸 was quiet for a moment, and then revelation came to him.

"Umar gestured to Ya'lā, who approached. The Messenger of Allah 🌸 was covered by a robe to shade him, so Ya'lā put his head inside [the robe]. The Messenger of Allah 🌸 was red-faced, and murmuring. Then, it was lifted from him, and he said: "Where is the one who asked about 'Umra?" The man was brought forward. The Prophet 🌸 said: "Clean off the perfume that you are wearing three times, and take off the robe, and then perform your 'Umra as you would perform Ḥajj."'

THE THIRD PROOF:
HIS KNOWLEDGE 🌸 OF THE UNSEEN

Another evidence of the breadth of the Prophet's 🌸 learning is his disclosure of the unseen. Part of his 🌸 knowledge is the disclosure of the unseen that Allah 🌸 favoured him with. Allah 🌸 said: ❨(He is) the Knower of the unseen, and He discloses His secret to none, save those Messengers whom He has chosen, and then He sends a guard to go before them, and another to go behind.❩[261] He 🌸 also said: ❨When the Prophet confided a matter to one of his wives, and when she divulged it, and Allah made it known to him, he informed (her of) part thereof, and passed over part. When he told her, she said: 'Who told you this?' He said: 'The Knower, the Aware, has told me!'❩[262]

The Prophet's 🌸 knowledge of the unseen is of many different forms; we will mention some of them:

---

[260] The lesser pilgrimage. [t]
[261] Qur'ān 72:26-27
[262] Qur'ān 66:3

Firstly: His ﷺ knowledge of everything from the beginning of creation until the people of Paradise enter Paradise, and the people of Hell enter Hell, as is attested to by the Ḥadīth narrated by Bukhārī on the authority of 'Umar b. al-Khaṭṭāb ؓ, who said: 'The Messenger of Allah ﷺ stood before us, and informed us of everything from the beginning of creation until the people of Paradise enter Paradise, and the people of Hell enter Hell. Some of us remembered it, and some of us forgot it.'[263]

Bukhārī and Muslim narrate that Ḥudhayfa ؓ said: 'The Messenger of Allah ﷺ stood before us, and did not leave anything until the Hour except that he made mention of it; some of us retained knowledge of it, and some of us did not.'[264] Ḥudhayfa said: 'I used to see things I had forgotten, and recognise them as a man recognises a man whom he sees after his absence.' The Prophet ﷺ also gave information about that which would come to pass after him until the Day of Resurrection.

Muslim narrates in his *Ṣaḥīḥ* collection that 'Amr b. Akhṭab al-Anṣārī ؓ said: 'The Messenger of Allah ﷺ lead us in the dawn prayer one day, and then ascended the pulpit, and spoke to us until the midday prayer arrived. He descended, and prayed, and then climbed the pulpit again, and spoke to us until the afternoon prayer. He came down, prayed, and climbed the pulpit again, and spoke to us until sunset. He informed us of everything that would come to pass until the Day of Resurrection; the best informed of us are those who remember best.'

He ﷺ did not leave a single matter that would come to pass until the Day of Resurrection except that he informed them of it. Abū Dāwūd narrated on the authority of Ḥudhayfa ؓ; who said: 'By Allah, I do not know if my companions were made to forget, or if they simply forgot. By Allah, the Messenger of Allah ﷺ did not omit a single bringer of strife until the end of the world, whose supporters numbered three hundred or more, except that he identified him by his name, his father's name, and the name of his tribe.'

---

[263] Literally: 'Those who remembered it remembered it; and those who forgot it forgot it.' [t]
[264] Literally: 'Those who know it know it; and those who are ignorant of it are ignorant of it.' [t]

He ﷺ also related information about the various stipulations of the Hour: the minor, the medial and the great; and about the condition of the hereafter and its partitions; and the state of the people of Paradise, and the people of Hell, and details of all that is concerned with them, all of which is clearly shown in the books of the Sunnah. This is evidence of the breadth of his learning, which Allah ﷻ bestowed upon him ﷺ.

Secondly: His ﷺ knowledge of the different worlds, as is attested to in the rigorously authenticated Ḥadīth of the Ascension, which tell how he ﷺ was taken up to the seven heavens, and entered them all one by one, and saw within them what he saw; and that he met with the Messengers, and was then taken up to the Lote-tree of the uttermost end, and saw its signs and wonders, and the revelations that bloomed upon it, and then to a level wherein he heard the scratching of the Pens, and all the other wonders of the higher worlds.

Allah ﷻ also revealed the world of the Throne[265] to him ﷺ, which is attested to by his ﷺ relating the Throne's magnitude, and that it is the vastest thing in all the worlds. Abū Dharr ﷺ related that he asked the Prophet ﷺ about the Footstool.[266] The Messenger of Allah ﷺ said: 'By He in whose hand is my soul, the seven heavens and the seven earths are naught in comparison to the Footstool except as a ring cast into the open desert; and the superiority of the Throne over the Footstool is like the superiority of the open desert over that ring.'[267]

He ﷺ also spoke about the Throne having lamps which constitute the worlds of the Throne, and having a shadow, and legs, and possessing treasure, as in the Ḥadīth related in the *Ṣaḥīḥ* collections of Bukhārī and Muslim, which includes: '...and Mūsā will hold onto one of the legs of the Throne.'

---

[265] The *'Arsh*. [t]
[266] The *Kursi*. [t]
[267] Narrated by Ibn Mardawayh; the like of it was narrated by Ibn Jarīr and others. (*Tafsīr Ibn Kathīr*)

He 🕌 also spoke of the bearers of the Throne, and their strength and might, as in narrated in the *Musnad*, that the Prophet 🕌 said: 'I am Muḥammad, the unlettered Prophet, and there is no Prophet after me!' which he repeated three times; 'I have been given the first and last of speech, and I have been taught the number of the keepers of Hell, and the bearers of the Throne...'

Abū Dāwūd narrated that the Prophet 🕌 said: 'I have been given permission to speak about one of Allah's angels, a bearer of the Throne. The distance between his earlobes and shoulders would take seven hundred years to traverse.' Ṭabarānī's narration has it: '...seven hundred years for a swift bird to traverse.'

Allah 🕌 also revealed to him 🕌 the world of Paradise and Hell, which were shown to him on numerous occasions, as in the Ḥadīth of the Ascension: '...Then, I was entered into Paradise, and in it were domes of pearl, and its dust was fragrant musk.'

Allah 🕌 also revealed to him 🕌 the world of the Isthmus, and its states and conditions; and the world of the Gathering, and the state of humanity therein; and the world of the Presentation,[268] of the Pool, and the collection of the Records, and the Reckoning, and the Scale, and the Bridge; and the condition of the denizens of Paradise, and the denizens of Hell; and he 🕌 spoke of all the worlds, and described them in detail.

Allah 🕌 also revealed to him 🕌 the higher worlds, and what takes place among the Highest Gathering, and their dispute over atonements and ranks; and all things were revealed to him, and he gained knowledge of them, as is related in the Ḥadīth narrated by Tirmidhī and Aḥmad, and others, that he 🕌 said: 'I woke one night and prayed that which was destined for me, and I fell asleep in my prayer, until my sleep became heavy. I found myself with my Lord 🕌, and He said to me: "O Muḥammad! Over what does the Highest Gathering dispute?" I said: "I do not know."'

This Ḥadīth shows that Allah 🕌 granted the Prophet 🕌 knowledge to the extent that he 🕌 said: 'And so all things were revealed to me, and I gained knowledge of them (in one narration: 'and so he taught me all things,' and in another:

---

[268] Of deeds.

'and so He did not ask me anything except that I knew it'). 'Then, He said to me: "O Muḥammad! Over what does the Highest Gathering dispute?" I said: "Over atonements, and ranks..."'[269]

Thirdly: All the communities were shown to him ﷺ: those who preceded his community, and those who came after. His ﷺ community was shown to him on several occasions.

The *Ṣaḥīḥ* collections of Bukhārī and Muslim narrate, on the authority of Ibn 'Abbās ﷺ, that the Prophet ﷺ said: 'The communities were shown to me, and I saw Prophets who had less than ten followers, and Prophets who had only one or two men with them, and Prophets who had no one with them at all. A huge multitude was then shown to me, and I thought it was my community; but it was said to me: "This is Mūsā and his people, but look to the horizon!" I looked, and saw a huge multitude. It was said to me "look to the other horizon!" I looked, and saw another huge multitude. It was said to me: "This is your community, and among them are seventy thousand who will enter Paradise with neither reckoning nor torment: they are those who do not use healing words, or seek them, or believe in ill omens (one narration adds 'and do not perform cauterisation'), and rely on their Lord."'[270]

Ṭabarānī and Ḍiyā' narrate on the authority of Ḥudhayfa b. Usayd that the Prophet ﷺ said: 'My community was shown to me yesterday in this very chamber, so that I know each man of them better than any of you know their companion: they were sculpted for me from clay.'

Fourthly: Allah ﷻ revealed this world for him ﷺ to see. Ṭabarānī narrated on the authority of Ibn 'Umar ﷺ that the Messenger of Allah ﷺ said: 'Allah revealed the world to me, and I saw it, and everything that would come to pass therein until the Day of Resurrection, as clearly as I see this, my own hand.'[271]

---

[269] See the full text of the Ḥadīth in my book *al-Ṣalāt fī al-Islām* ('Prayer in Islam').

[270] This is Muslim's narration in an abridged form.

[271] See *Sharḥ al-Mawāhib*.

This Ḥadīth is attested to by Muslim's narration in which the Prophet 🕮 said: 'Allah gathered before me the earth, and I saw the eastern and western extents of it...' as we have already mentioned. His 🕮 sight extended to all that there is, and he beheld it.

Fifthly: He 🕮 saw the results of unseen events before they took place. It is narrated in the *Ṣaḥīḥ* collections of Bukhārī and Muslim on the authority of Usāma b. Zayd 🕮, who said: 'The Prophet 🕮 climbed to the top of one of the tall buildings of Medina, and said: "Do you see what I see?" The people said "No." He 🕮 said: "I see the descent of civil strife [*fitna*] upon your houses like the descent of rain."'

Muslim narrates in his *Ṣaḥīḥ* collection that 'Umar b. al-Khaṭṭāb 🕮 said, speaking about the battle of Badr: 'The Messenger of Allah 🕮 showed us the places where the people of Badr would die, the day before, saying: "This is the place where so-and-so will die tomorrow, if Allah wills, and this is the place where so-and-so will die, if Allah wills." By He who sent him with the truth, not one of the places the Messenger of Allah 🕮 designated proved false.'

In Muslim's narration on the authority of Anas 🕮, the Messenger of Allah 🕮 said: 'This is the place where so-and-so will die,' placing his hand on the ground here and there. Anas 🕮 said: 'Not one of them erred from the place of the hand of the Messenger of Allah 🕮' i.e. they did not miss the place that the Messenger of Allah 🕮 specified and indicated.

Sixthly: Subtle, unseen matters were revealed to him 🕮 before they occurred, and he 🕮 related them. An example of this is the narration of Imam Aḥmad, and others, that the Prophet 🕮 was giving a sermon once, and something was shown to him therein. He 🕮 said: 'There will enter upon you presently from this door (or 'from this road') a man from amongst the most prosperous of people. Upon his face is the appearance of an angel.' Ṭabarānī's narration has it: 'There will appear to you the most prosperous of people; he has the appearance of an angel.' Jarīr b. 'Abdullāh 🕮 then came in.

Imam Aḥmad narrated that Anas ﷺ said: 'We were sitting with the Messenger of Allah ﷺ, when he said: "There will appear to you now a man from the people of Paradise." A man from the Anṣār then came in, drops of water from his ablutions falling from his beard.' Bayhaqī's narration has it: 'Saʻd b. Mālik then came and entered...'

Mazīda b. Mālik ﷺ said: 'The Messenger of Allah ﷺ was once speaking with his companions, when he said: "There will appear to you from this road presently a group of riders from the best of the people of the East." ʻUmar stood and made for that direction, and saw thirteen riders. He welcomed them, and bade them forth, and said: "Who are you?" They said: "A group from ʻAbd al-Qays..."'[272]

Seventhly: People's innermost thoughts were revealed to him ﷺ, and he would relate them. Ḥākim and Bayhaqī narrate on the authority of Ibn ʻAbbās ﷺ, and Ibn Saʻd narrates on the authority of Abū Isḥāq al-Sabīʻī ﷺ, that they both said:

'Abū Sufyān saw the Messenger of Allah ﷺ walking, and people walking behind him, and thought to himself: *What if I were to fight this man again, and gather a great horde against him?* The Prophet ﷺ came to him, and patted his chest, saying: "We would rout you!" Abū Sufyān said: "I repent to Allah, and seek Allah's forgiveness! I was not certain you were a Prophet until this moment. I was thinking it to myself!"'[273]

Another example of this is found in the narration of Aḥmad in his *Musnad*, on the authority of Abū Mūsā al-Ashʻarī ﷺ, who said: 'I once said to a man: "Let us devote this day to Allah ﷺ (i.e. to His worship)." By Allah, it was as though the Messenger of Allah ﷺ witnessed this day, for he gave a sermon, saying: "there are those who say *let us devote this day to Allah* ﷺ." He kept saying it until I wished the earth would swallow me.'

---

[272] The author of *Majmaʻ al-Zawāʼid* said: 'It was narrated by Ṭabarānī and Abū Yaʻlā, and the men of its chain are trustworthy; though some are differed upon.' Zurqānī said: 'Its chain of transmission is good, and this delegation is that of ʻAbd al-Qays that is mentioned in the collections of Bukhārī and Muslim.'

[273] See *Sharḥ al-Mawāhib*. This was the day of the conquest of Mecca.

Ṭabarānī narrated, with a chain of transmission consisting entirely of rigorously authenticated narrators [*rijāl al-ṣaḥīḥ*], as did the compilers of the Prophetic biographies, the story of ʿUmayr b. Wahb al-Jumaḥī, who was promised by Ṣafwān b. Umayya that all his debts would be settled, and his family supported, if he assassinated the Messenger of Allah 鑾. They kept the matter secret between them.

ʿUmayr then went to Medina, taking with him a poisoned sword, and sought audience with the Messenger of Allah 鑾, and was admitted. The Prophet 鑾 said to him: 'What has brought you [here]?' 'I have come for the prisoner of war in your custody,' said ʿUmayr. 'So what of the sword hung from your neck?' said the Prophet 鑾. 'Allah curse all swords!' said ʿUmayr, 'for have they availed us ought?' 'Tell me the truth,' said the Prophet 鑾, 'what have you come for?'

ʿUmayr said: 'I have only come for this.' 'Indeed, no,' said the Prophet 鑾, 'you sat with Ṣafwān b. Umayya in the chamber, and the two of you discussed the Quraysh of the pit,[274] and you said: "Were it not for my debts, and my family, I would ride out to Muḥammad and kill him!" Ṣafwān undertook to pay your debts and support your family if you killed me; yet Allah has come between me and that!' 'I testify that you are the Messenger of Allah,' said ʿUmayr, 'we used to deny that you brought news from the heavens, O Messenger of Allah, and we denied the revelation that was given to you; but there was no one present save Ṣafwān and I, and by Allah, I know that no one could have informed you of it but Allah. Praise be to Allah, who has guided me to Islam!'

Ibn Saʿd and others narrate that ʿAbdullāh b. Abū Bakr b. Ḥazm said: 'The Prophet 鑾 went out, and Abū Sufyān was sitting in the mosque. Abū Sufyān thought to himself: *I know not how Muḥammad has defeated us!* The Prophet 鑾 approached him, and patted him on the chest, saying: "With (the aid of) Allah we have defeated you!" Abū Sufyān said: "I testify that you are the Messenger of Allah."'

---

[274] Those who were killed at Badr, and whose corpses were buried in the pit.

Ibn Hishām and others narrate that Faḍāla b. ʿUmayr b. al-Mulawwaḥ intended to kill the Messenger of Allah ﷺ while he was circumambulating the Kaʿba in the year of the conquest of Mecca. When he approached him, the Prophet ﷺ said to him: 'O Faḍāla!' Faḍāla answered: 'Yes, O Messenger of Allah?' The Prophet ﷺ said: 'What were you thinking to yourself?' He replied: 'Nothing—I was making remembrance of Allah.'

The Messenger of Allah ﷺ smiled, and said to him: 'Seek Allah's forgiveness.'[275] The Messenger of Allah then placed his hand on Faḍāla's chest, and his heart became at ease, i.e. Islam became firm in his heart, as did the love of the best of humanity ﷺ. After this, Faḍāla would say: 'By Allah, he did not lift his hand from my chest until there was nothing in Allah's creation more beloved to me than him ﷺ.' Faḍāla said: 'I returned to my family, and passed by a woman with whom I used to enjoy conversation. She said to me: "Come and speak with me!"'

Faḍāla said:

> *She said 'Come and speak with me!' and I said, No,*
> *Allah and Islam do not allow it!*
> *If you had seen Muḥammad and his people*
> *In conquest, the day the idols were broken,*
> *You would have seen Allah's faith rise brightly,*
> *And the face of idolatry covered with shadow.*

Eighthly: The affairs of the heart were revealed to him ﷺ, and he answered questioners before they asked their questions (and this subject is vast).

An example of it is the narration of Imam Aḥmad, on the authority of Wābiṣa b. Maʿbad ﷺ, who said: 'I went to the Prophet ﷺ, intending not to leave any aspect of righteousness and iniquity without asking him concerning it. He said to me: "Approach, O Wābiṣa." I approached him, until my knees touched his. "O Wābiṣa,' he ﷺ said, "shall I tell you what you have come to ask me, or would you rather ask me yourself?" "O Messenger

---

[275] I.e. forgiveness from what he was thinking to himself, and then his saying 'nothing.'

of Allah," I said, "tell me." He 🕮 said: "You have come to ask me about righteousness and iniquity." I said: "Yes." He 🕮 put his three fingers together, and began to pat my chest with them. "O Wābiṣa," he 🕮 said, "Ask yourself: for righteousness is what your soul is at ease with, and you heart is at ease with; and iniquity is what confounds the heart and causes uncertainty in the breast, whatever counsel the people might give you.'"[276]

Ninthly: He 🕮 passed on glad tidings of the unknown. 'Abdullāh b. Busr 🕮 said: 'The Messenger of Allah 🕮 placed his hand on my head, and said: "this boy will live for a century."' He indeed went on to live for a hundred years. 'Abdullāh had a wart on his face, and the Prophet 🕮 said: 'He will not die before the wart disappears from his face.' And so it proved.[277]

A commentary of the aforementioned Qur'ānic verse, Allah's word: ⟪(He is) the Knower of the unseen, and He discloses His secret to none, save those Messengers whom He has chosen, and then He sends a guard to go before them, and another to go behind.⟫[278]

Allah 🕮 made it clear to His servants that it is He who has absolute knowledge of the unseen, inherently and without restriction, as He 🕮 said: ⟪Say: 'None in the heavens or the earth knows the unseen save Allah.'⟫[279] And He 🕮 said: ⟪To Allah belongs the unseen of the heavens and the earth.⟫[280]

And He 🕮 said: ⟪With Him are the keys to the unseen; none but He knows them.⟫[281] In this verse, Allah informed us that he discloses His knowledge of the unseen to those Messengers whom He chooses, and reveals to them what He wills of the unseen, according to His divine wisdom.

---

[276] Literally, 'even if the people counsel you and counsel you.'

[277] The author of *Majmaʿ al-Zawāʾid* said: 'it was narrated by Ṭabarānī and Bazzār, and the men of one of Bazzār's chains of transmission are all rigorously authenticated narrators, except for Ḥasan b. Ayyūb al-Ḥaḍramī; and he is trustworthy.'

[278] Qur'ān 72:26-27

[279] Qur'ān 27:65

[280] Qur'ān 16:77

[281] Qur'ān 6:59

He revealed some of the unseen to our Master 'Īsā ﷺ, in order that it be a sign of the veracity of his Prophethood, and a proof for his people. Allah said: ❴I inform you of that which you eat, and that which you store up in your houses. Herein is a portent for you, if you are believers.❵[282]

Allah ﷻ revealed to His Messengers whatever He willed of unseen matters, according to His wisdom, in order that this be a proof of the veracity of their Prophethood; for this could not be achieved by any ordinary means or devices, or derived by conventional indications; rather, it could only be the result of divine revelation of the unseen. From this, it is clear that the sciences of astronomy and meteorology, and the like of them, by the means of which certain unseen information might be derived, are all dependent on scientific principles, and based on conventional laws and forces, from which these derivations are obtained.

It should not be said that they are inherent forms of unseen knowledge, because the knowledge of the unseen must be arrived at without the use of materials, or created means and conventional methods, and the indications of local knowledge, as the rightly-guided scholars have pointed out.

A doctor who is able to establish the strength or weakness of the heart by the use of a stethoscope, and who diagnoses a patient's condition by examining them, is not described as having knowledge of the unseen. In the same way, a meteorologist, who ascertains the existence of changes in the earth's temperature by the use of meteorological instruments, is not described as having knowledge of the unseen.

Now the words of the Most High ❴(He is) the Knower of the unseen, and He discloses His secret to none, save those Messengers whom He has chosen, and then He sends a guard to go before them, and another to go behind❵ do not contradict His words ❴'And I do not say to you "I possess the treasures of Allah," nor do I know the unseen'❵[283] because that which is denied in this verse is the absolute knowledge of the unseen which encompasses everything—fully as well as partially, and this

---

[282] Qur'ān 3:49
[283] Qur'ān 11:31

[knowledge] belongs to Allah the Most High alone. And that is what He informed our Prophet 🕌 of about Nūḥ: ❨'And I do not say to you "I possess the treasures of Allah," nor do I know the unseen❩.

Or the meaning of this verse may be: 'I do not know the unseen except for that which Allah has taught me, and He discloses to me whatever of the unseen He wishes.'

Allah's words ❨(He is) the Knower of the unseen, and He discloses His secret to none, save those Messengers whom He has chosen...❩ do not negate the possibility that the Awliyā' of Allah could be allowed knowledge of some of the unseen. This is because the meaning of the word 'Messenger' [rasūl] in the verse means a human messenger[284] according to the majority of scholars; and so the disclosure of some unseen information to the Awliyā' only occurs because they have followed their Messenger, and by his means are they honoured. This means that the matter is considered a karāma,[285] and every karāma granted to a saint is considered a miracle for the Prophet they follow, for they were vouchsafed it by means of their following him. May Allah's benedictions and salutations be upon our Prophet, and upon all the Prophets!

If by 'Messenger' a message-bearing angel is intended, as some say, then these angels descend upon the Prophets with divine revelation, and they descend upon the saints with true inspiration,[286] casting it into their hearts.

How is it possible to deny that the Awliyā' are given knowledge of some of the unseen, when it has been confirmed in numerous sound Ḥadīth?

An example of this is the narration mentioned in the Ṣaḥīḥ collections of Bukhārī and Muslim, and elsewhere (and the wording here is that of Bukhārī), on the authority of Abū Hurayra 🕌, that the Prophet 🕌 said: 'There were, in the days before you, people who were inspired;[287] if there is such a one in my community, it is 'Umar.'

---

[284] I.e. not an angel. [t]

[285] A miracle Allah vouchsafes to a saint, as distinct from a miracle vouchsafed to a prophet. [t]

[286] Ar. Ilhām

[287] Literally 'those who are spoken to.'

Bukhārī also narrated on the authority of Abū Hurayra ؓ that the Prophet ﷺ said: 'There is, amongst those who came before you of the Children of Israel, people who were inspired without being prophets. If anyone from my community is one of them, it is 'Umar.'

The author of *Fath al-Bārī* said:

> 'The one who is spoken to' means someone who has something cast into his heart from the Highest Assembly,[288] as though someone is speaking to him. It is said that 'one who is spoken to' means one to whom the angels speak by means of other than Prophethood, and this is related in the Hadīth of Abū Saʿīd: 'It was said: "O Messenger of Allah, how are they spoken to?" He said: "The angels speak on their tongue."'
>
> His ﷺ statement: 'if there is such a one in my community, it is 'Umar' does not imply hesitation, or doubt; rather, it implies certainty, as when a man says: 'If I have a friend, it is so-and-so,' intending by this to specify the excellence of this friendship, not to deny that he has any friends. This is corroborated by Tirmidhī's narration on the authority of Ibn 'Umar, that the Prophet ﷺ said: 'Allah ﷻ has placed truth on 'Umar's tongue, and in his heart.'

These Hadīth are unambiguous in their confirmation of inspiration, and disclosure of the unseen. In Tirmidhī's *Sunan*, and elsewhere, it is narrated on the authority of Abū Saʿīd ؓ that the Messenger of Allah ﷺ said: 'Beware the believer's intuition, for he sees with Allah's light.' He ﷺ then recited: ﴿In this is surely a sign for those who see.﴾[289]

Ibn Jarīr narrated on the authority of Thawbān, quoting the Prophet ﷺ: 'Beware of the believer's intuition, for he sees with Allah's light, and Allah's mediation.' Bazzār narrated on the authority of Anas ؓ that the Prophet ﷺ said: 'Allah has servants who know people by means of insight.'

---

[288] The angels.
[289] Qurʾān 15:77

Another example of this is the story of 'Uthmān b. 'Affān 鑾 who, when a man who had looked at a woman who was not of his family came to him, said: 'One of you has come to us, with the mark of fornication in his eyes!' The man said: 'Is this revelation, after the Messenger of Allah, O Commander of the Faithful?' 'No,' said 'Uthmān, 'it is the true intuition of a believer.'

THE FOURTH PROOF:
HIS KNOWLEDGE 鑾 OF ALLAH'S CREATURES
AND THEIR VARIOUS TYPES

Another evidence of the breadth of his 鑾 learning is his 鑾 knowledge of the various species of creatures and types of living things, and the rulings regarding them, and their circumstances, and all the details concerning them.

Ṭabarānī narrated, with a chain of transmission consisting entirely of rigorously authenticated narrators, that Abū al-Dardā' 鑾 said: 'The Messenger of Allah 鑾 parted from us whilst there was not a single bird flying in the sky except that he had taught us some knowledge pertaining to it.'[290]

Imam Aḥmad narrated that Abū Dharr 鑾 said: 'The Messenger of Allah parted from us whilst there was not a single bird moving its wings in the sky except that had taught us some knowledge pertaining to it.' Ṭabarānī's narration added that the Prophet 鑾 said: 'There is nothing that draws one close to Paradise, and distances one from Hell, except that I have made it clear to you all.'

He 鑾 imparted to the Ṣaḥāba great knowledge concerning the world of the birds, which is evidence that his 鑾 knowledge of the species of the entire world was vast. It is also evidence that he 鑾 clarified every important matter of creation that pertained to the benefit of the world, and the happiness of humanity, in every aspect and expression. It was he 鑾 who took it upon himself to impart knowledge of the world of the birds; how could it be imagined that he neglected to clarify any detail concerning the betterment of humanity, and failed to mention it, yet concerned

---

[290] See *Majmaʿ al-Zawāʾid* (vol. 8), and several sections of *Tafsīr Ibn Kathīr*.

himself with mentioning the world of the birds, and its rulings? It cannot be imagined; rather, the Prophet ﷺ surely clarified every aspect of betterment, and the way to happiness for humanity, in its most complete form.

Abū Ya'lā narrated with his chain of transmission from Muḥammad b. al-Munkadir, that Jābir b. 'Abdullāh said: 'Locusts were scarce during one of the years of 'Umar's rule, and so he asked about them. He was not told anything, and so became distressed. He sent a rider to a certain place, and another to the Levant, and another to Iraq, each asking if any locusts had been seen or not. The rider from Yemen came to him with a handful of locusts, and cast them before him. When he saw them, he magnified Allah three times, and said: "I heard the Messenger of Allah ﷺ say: 'Allah created one thousand communities: six hundred in the sea, and four hundred on land. The first of these communities to be destroyed will be the locusts; when they are destroyed, the rest will follow like a pearl necklace when its string is cut.'"'[291]

These Ḥadīth explain Allah's words: ❨There is not a beast on land, nor a bird flying on two wings, but they are communities like unto you. We have left nothing out of the Book. Then, unto their Lord they will be gathered.❩[292]

The Prophet ﷺ also clarified that which is connected with the gathering mentioned in this verse, and what events will occur on the Day of Resurrection: Muslim and Tirmidhī narrate, on the authority of Abū Hurayra ﷺ, that the Messenger of Allah ﷺ said: 'All rights will be given to their possessors on the Day of Resurrection: even the hornless ram will be avenged of the horned.'

The narration of Aḥmad has it that the Messenger of Allah ﷺ said: 'All of creation will be avenged against one another: even the hornless against the horned, and the speck of dust against the speck of dust.'[293]

---

[291] The Ḥadīth can be found in *Tafsīr Ibn Kathīr*, and elsewhere.
[292] Qur'ān 6:38
[293] Ḥāfiẓ al-Mundhirī said: 'Its narrators are rigorously authentic.'

The birds, then, are a community, as are the ants, as in narrated in the *Ṣaḥīḥ*: 'An ant stung one of the Prophets, so he ordered its nest to be burned. Allah then revealed to him: "Because an ant stung you, you destroyed a community who praise (Me)!"' The bees are a community, as Allah informed us: ❨And your Lord inspired the bee, saying: 'Choose your habitations in the mountains, and the trees, and in that which they thatch...'❩²⁹⁴ The meaning of 'community' here is one of the created species, which has a system of living and reproduction, and an organised society, which contains leaders and followers, and so on.

Allah said: ❨An ant said: 'O ants! Enter your homes, lest Sulaymān and his armies crush you, without their knowing.❩²⁹⁵ When Sulaymān 🙋 wanted to pass by with his armies, the leader of the ants called them, and ordered them to enter their homes, fearing that the feet of the army would stamp on them. He made it clear to them that if they did not enter their homes, the feet would stamp on them, and the army would be excused this, for they would not be aware that the ants were beneath their feet.

After all this, the oceans of his 🙋 knowledge cannot be encompassed save by Allah 🙋, who showered them upon him. Bukhārī and Muslim narrated, (and the wording here is Bukhārī's) on the authority of Anas 🙋, that the Prophet 🙋 came out one day when the sun passed its zenith, and prayed the midday prayer. When the prayer ended, he ascended the pulpit, and mentioned the Hour, and said that before its arrival would come grave matters, and then said: 'Whoever wishes to ask about anything, let him ask now, for by Allah, there is nothing you might ask me except that I will inform you of it, as long as I stand here.'

Anas 🙋 said: 'The Anṣār began to weep, and the Messenger of Allah began to repeat: "Ask me!" A man stood up, and said: "Where will I go when I die,²⁹⁶ O Messenger of Allah?" He said: "Hell." ʿAbdullāh b. Ḥadhāqa stood, and said: "Who is my father, O Messenger of Allah?" He 🙋 said: "Your father is Ḥadhāqa."

---

²⁹⁴ Qur'ān 16:68
²⁹⁵ Qur'ān 27:18
²⁹⁶ Literally: 'where is my place of entrance?'

Then, he ﷺ repeated many times: "Ask me! Ask me!" 'Umar sank to his knees, and said: "We are pleased with Allah as our Lord, and with Islam as our religion, and with Muḥammad as our Messenger!" The Messenger of Allah ﷺ fell silent at 'Umar's words, and then said: "By the One in whose hand is my soul, Paradise and Hell were shown to me, in the place of this wall, as I was praying presently. I have not seen the like of today of good and evil.'"

The Prophet ﷺ allowed the Ṣaḥāba to ask about anything that occurred to them, as long as he stood in that place. This is the greatest evidence of the breadth of his learning, which Allah ﷻ taught him. Allah ﷻ said: ❨...and (He) taught you that which you knew not. The grace of Allah upon you has been great.❩[297]

HIS BLESSED HEART ﷺ

The heart of our Master Muḥammad ﷺ was the best and purest of hearts, and the broadest and strongest, and the most pious, and the most virtuous, and the softest and most gentle; a heedful, attentive heart, illuminated by the light of faith, and the Qur'ān.

His ﷺ heart is the finest of hearts. It is narrated in the *Musnad* of Imam Aḥmad, and elsewhere, on the authority of Ibn Mas'ūd ﷺ, who said: 'Allah looked at the hearts of humanity, and found the heart of Muḥammad ﷺ to be the finest of their hearts. He chose him for Himself, and sent him with His message. He then looked to the hearts of humanity, and found the hearts of his companions to be the finest of their hearts, and so He made them emissaries for His Prophet ﷺ, striving for His religion. What the Muslims see as good, Allah holds it to be good; and what the Muslims see as bad, Allah holds it to be bad.'[298]

His ﷺ noble heart was the purest and most wholesome of hearts. When he was young, his noble breast was opened, and Satan's allotment was removed from his heart, as is narrated by Muslim and others on the authority of Anas ﷺ, who said: 'Jibrīl ﷺ came to the Messenger of Allah ﷺ when he was playing with

---

[297] Qur'ān 4:113

[298] Narrated by Aḥmad, Bazzār and Ṭabarānī in *al-Kabīr*. The men of its chain of transmission are all trustworthy. (*Majma' al-Zawā'id*, vol. 1 & 8)

some boys (when he was still a young boy). He laid him on his back, opened his chest, and removed his heart. He took a morsel of flesh from the heart, and said: this is Satan's allotment over you.[299] He then washed the heart in a golden vessel with the water of Zamzam.

He then replaced it, and closed his chest. The boys went running to his (foster) mother, saying: "Muḥammad has been killed!" They then turned to him, and found that his colour had altered.'

Anas 🕌 said: 'I used to be able to see the mark left by the stitch in his 🕌 chest.' The opening of his 🕌 noble breast happened to him for the first time when he was a young boy, in the care of Ḥalīma 🕌. It is differed as to his 🕌 exact age at the time, and there are many different opinions.

Ḥāfiẓ al-Zurqānī said:

> The strongest opinion is that he 🕌 returned to his mother when he was four years old, and that the opening of his breast occurred when he was in his fourth year, as Ḥāfiẓ al-'Irāqī stated in *Naẓm al-Sīra*, as did his student, Ḥāfiẓ Ibn Ḥajar in his *Sīra*.

The second time his noble breast was opened, was when he 🕌 was ten years old, as was narrated by 'Abdullāh b. Aḥmad in *Zawā'id al-Musnad*, with a chain of transmission the men of which are trustworthy, and by Ibn Ḥibbān, Ḥākim, Ibn 'Asākir, and Ḍiyā' al-Maqdisī in *al-Mukhtāra*, on the authority of Ubayy b. Ka'b, that Abū Hurayra 🕌 said: 'O Messenger of Allah! How did you Prophethood first begin?' He 🕌 said: 'I was in the desert, ten years of age, when two men (angels in the form of men) appeared above my head, one of them saying to the other: "Is this him?" The other said: "Yes," and so they took me. I had never seen faces the like of theirs (because of their beauty), nor had I encountered the like of their souls, nor had I seen the like of their clothes

---

[299] I.e. the share of influence he would have over you if it remained.

(because of their beauty and resplendence). They walked up to me, each of them taking hold of one of my limbs. I could not feel their grasp. One of them said to the other: "Lie him down."'

Another narration has it: 'One of them said to the other: "Open his breast." They opened it, and I saw no blood, nor did I feel pain. One of them poured water into a golden vessel, and the other cleaned my chest, and then said: "Open his heart." He opened my heart, and removed from it all rancour, and envy. He took out something like a morsel of flesh, and discarded it...'[300]

The great scholar Muḥammad b. Yūsuf al-Shāmī said, in *al-Sīrat al-Shāmiyya*:

> The wisdom of this is that ten is close to the age of responsibility: his 🌸 heart was opened and sanctified, so that he would never be drawn into any of the things that tarnish men.

The third time his 🌸 noble breast was opened when Jibrīl 🌸 came to him with divine inspiration, when he was made a Prophet. Abū Dāwūd al-Ṭayālisī and Ḥārith Abū Muḥammad al-Tamīmī in their *Musnad* collections, and Bayhaqī and Abū Nu'aym in their *Dalā'il* collections, all narrated on the authority of 'Ā'isha 🌸 that the Messenger of Allah 🌸 spent a month in spiritual retreat with Khadīja in the cave of Ḥirā'; the month corresponding with Ramaḍān. The Messenger of Allah 🌸 came out, and heard: 'Peace be upon you!' Khadīja 🌸 said: 'I thought it was the sudden assailment of the Jinn.' He 🌸 said: 'Rejoice, for peace is surely good.'

Another day, he saw Jibrīl 🌸 covering the sun: one wing was in the East, the other in the West. The Prophet 🌸 said: 'I was startled by him.' He left to go to his family. He 🌸 described what happened when he was half-way to the door thus: 'He spoke to me, until I was felt at ease with him. He then set a meeting with me. I came to the meeting, but Jibrīl was late.'

---

[300] The whole text of the Ḥadīth can be found in *Sharḥ al-Zurqānī* 1:153.

When the Prophet 🕌 wanted to leave, Jibrīl 🕊 appeared, along with Mīkā'īl 🕊. Jibrīl came to earth, and Mīkā'īl remained between the heavens and the earth. The Prophet 🕌 said: 'Jibrīl took me, and turned me onto my back, and opened my stomach.'[301] Another narration has it: 'He turned me onto my back, opened my heart, and removed from it what Allah willed. He then washed it in a golden vessel, and replaced it. He then turned me as a jug is turned, and placed a seal on my back, until I felt the touch of the stamp.'

The wisdom of this opening, as the rightly-guided scholars have said, is that it was a source of increase in his 🕌 honour, and his succour, and his strengthening and preparation, so that he would receive what would be revealed to him with a firm heart, in the best of sacred and praiseworthy states.

The fourth time his 🕌 noble breast was opened on the night of the Ascent, as is narrated by Bukhārī and Muslim, on the authority of Anas 🕊, who heard from Mālik b. Ṣaʿṣaʿa 🕊 that the Messenger of Allah 🕌 told him about the night he was taken up. He 🕌 said: 'As I was reclining in the *Ḥaṭīm* (or perhaps he said 'in the *Ḥijr*'),[302] someone came to me, and made an incision between this, and this (his throat and the hair beneath his navel), and took out my heart. I was then brought a vessel of gold, full of faith (in Bukhārī's narration: 'full of wisdom, and faith'), and my heart was washed, then filled (i.e. with faith and wisdom), and then replaced.' Bukhārī's narration has it: 'I was then brought a vessel of gold, full of wisdom, and faith, which he emptied into my breast, and then closed it. I was then brought a steed, smaller than a mule and larger than a donkey, pure white...'

The wisdom of this opening, as those of sagacity have said, was to increase his 🕌 honour and magnificence, and to increase his support and preparation, to equip him for the moment when he would stand before Allah 🕌 and partake of intimate discourse with Him, and witness resplendent lights, and privileged secrets, and the theophanies of beauty, and majesty.

---

[301] This wording is the narration of the *Musnad* of Abū Dāwūd al-Ṭayālisī on page 215 of the first edition, published in Hyderabad. The other narrations can be found in *Sharḥ al-Zurqānī ʿalā al-Mawāhib* 1:225.
[302] Two chambers in the Sacred Mosque in Mecca.

The author of the *Mawāhib* and its commentary said:

> It is related that his ﷺ breast was opened a fifth time, when he was twenty years old, as it is said; but it is not confirmed, and so should not be mentioned without attention being drawn to the fact that it is uncorroborated.[303]

Ḥāfiẓ al-Qasṭalānī said:

> Everything that has been reported about the opening of the breast and the removal of the heart, and all other extraordinary events, must be accepted, without any attempt to remove it from its literal reality, because Allah's omnipotent power is well able to perform all this; none of it is impossible.

Zurqānī said, commenting on this:

> This is because Allah's omnipotence only relates to the possible, not the impossible, as Qurṭubī said in *al-Mufhim*, as did Ṭayyibī, Tūrbishī, Ḥāfiẓ [ʿAsqalānī] in *al-Fatḥ*, Suyūṭī, and others. This is further supported by the rigorously authenticated Ḥadīth in which it is stated that they could see the mark left by the stitch in his ﷺ chest.

He then quoted Suyūṭī:

> That which has emerged from some of the ignorant people of our times, of denying this, and explaining it away as a metaphor, and asserting that the 'heart' here is an allegory for spiritual realities, is clear ignorance, and hideous error, a result of Allah's ﷺ forsaking them, and their obsession with philosophy, and their detachment from the subtleties of the Sunnah, may Allah protect us from such calamities![304]

---

[303] *Sharḥ al-Zurqānī* 1:135
[304] Ibid., 6:25

How pure is the heart of our Master Muḥammad ﷺ, and how virtuous! How noble and magnificent it is! It is truly the mightiest and finest of hearts.

The breadth and strength of his ﷺ blessed heart: Allah ﷻ says: ⟨The faithful Spirit has brought it down to your heart, that you might be one of those who warn.⟩[305] This verse indicates the distinction of the Prophet's ﷺ noble heart, upon which the Qur'ān descended, above all other hearts. This is due to the perfection of its breadth, which Allah ﷻ bestowed upon him, and the immense strength it required to bear the mighty Qur'ān, which, had it been sent down upon towering, lofty mountains, would have cleaved and rent them asunder, by their fear of Allah ﷻ, as He says: ⟨Had we sent this Qur'ān down upon a mountain, you would have seen it humbled, and rent asunder from the fear of Allah.⟩[306]

A heart upon which the noble Qur'ān was revealed, with its illuminations and secrets, and its modes and meanings, and its spirit, and its realities, must surely be the broadest and strongest of hearts! Allah ﷻ says: ⟨Thus, We have revealed to you a spirit of Our command. You knew not what the scripture was, nor faith. But we made it a light, by which We guide whom We will of Our servants; and you indeed do guide to a straight path.⟩[307]

The ocean of the secrets of his ﷺ noble heart spread to the hearts of his followers, and the rays of his resplendent lights shone in the mirrors of their hearts. Whoever reflects on Allah's words: ⟨But we made it a light, by which We guide whom We will of Our servants; and you indeed do guide to a straight path⟩ will understand the meaning of this.

His ﷺ blessed heart was the most pious of hearts: Muslim narrated in his *Ṣaḥīḥ*, on the authority of Abū Dharr ﷺ, the Sacred Ḥadīth[308] in which Allah ﷻ said: 'O My servants! If the first

---

[305] Qur'ān 26:193-194

[306] Qur'ān 59:21

[307] Qur'ān 42:52

[308] A Ḥadīth in which the Prophet ﷺ reports a statement of Allah in his own words (as opposed to the Qur'ān, which is the uncreated word of Allah). [t]

of you, and the last of you, the humans and the jinn, were all equal to the heart of the most pious man amongst you, it would not increase my dominion ought...'

This heart, the most pious of hearts indicated by the Ḥadīth, is the heart of our Master Muḥammad 🕌, who said: 'By Allah, of all of you, I fear Allah the most, and I am the most pious.'[309]

His 🕌 blessed heart was the purest and soundest of hearts: It is narrated in the *Sunan* of Abū Dāwūd, on the authority of Ibn Masʿūd 🕌, that the Prophet 🕌 said: 'Let none of you tell me anything about any of my companions, for I love to come out to you with a sound heart.'

Ibn Mājah narrated, with a rigorously authentic chain of transmission that Ibn ʿUmar 🕌 said: 'It was said: "O Messenger of Allah, what person is best?" He 🕌 said: "Everyone with a clean heart,[310] and an honest tongue." The people said: "We know an honest tongue; but what is a clean heart?" He said: "This is the one who is pious, and pure; free of sin, transgression, rancour, and jealousy."'

His 🕌 noble heart was the softest and gentlest of hearts: Allah 🕌 said: ❨By the mercy of Allah, you dealt with them gently. Had you been stern, and fierce of heart with them, they would have dispersed from around you.❩[311] The Messenger of Allah 🕌 was not fierce-hearted; rather, he was gentle.

Ṭabarānī narrated on the authority of Abū ʿInaba al-Khawlānī that the Prophet 🕌 said: 'Allah has vessels among the people of the earth: the vessels of your Lord are the hearts of His virtuous servants. The most beloved of them to Him are the gentlest, and softest.'[312]

---

[309] Narrated by Bukhārī and Muslim.

[310] Literally 'a heart that has been swept out.'

[311] Qur'ān 3:159

[312] Ḥāfiẓ al-Haythamī said: 'Its chain of transmission is good.' His teacher ʿIrāqī said: 'Its chain contains Baqiyya b. al-Walīd, who was prone to relating without supplying a chain [*mudallis*]; but he explicitly stated that he was reporting it as a Ḥadīth.' (Munāwī, *Fayḍ al-Qadīr*)

The vigilance of his 🕌 blessed heart: Allah 🕌 gave His Messenger 🕌 vigilance of heart, and he was constantly focused on Allah, and aware of Him. He 🕌 was never overcome by heedlessness, and his heart was never taken by slumber. The visions he saw when asleep were all forms of divine inspiration. His sleep did not nullify his ablutions, and this is confirmed by numerous authentic Ḥadīth:

Bukhārī narrated in his *Ṣaḥīḥ*, as did others, that 'Ā'isha 🕌 said, in relation to the night prayer of the Prophet 🕌: 'I said: "O Messenger of Allah, do you sleep before you offer the *witr* prayer?" He said: "O 'Ā'isha, my eyes sleep, but my heart does not."'

Muslim narrated in his *Ṣaḥīḥ*, on the authority of 'Iyāḍ b. Ḥimār 🕌, that the Prophet 🕌 said: 'Allah 🕌 looked at the people of the earth, and despised them, the Arabs and the non-Arabs, save what remained of the People of the Scripture.[313] He said: "I have only sent you that I might test you, and test by means of you; I have sent down to you a book which cannot be washed by water,[314] which you recite both asleep and awake...'

Bukhārī narrated that Jābir 🕌 said: 'The angels came to the Prophet 🕌 while he slept. (The narration of Tirmidhī has: 'The Messenger of Allah 🕌 came out to us and said: "I saw in my sleep as though Jibrīl were at my head, and Mīkā'īl at my feet.) One of them said: "He is asleep." Another said: "The eye sleeps, yet the heart is awake." They said: "There is a similitude for your companion here." He said: "So draw the similitude!" They said:

---

[313] It is said that 'the Scripture' here means all previous divine revelation, which would mean that the Ḥadīth applies to the people before the Prophet 🕌 was sent, for ignorance has spread among them, and blinded them, and so Allah 🕌 despised them, except for those few who remained true to the Scripture, i.e. the divine revelation. (Munāwī, *Fayd al-Qadīr*)

[314] I.e. water cannot wash it from the face of the earth, for if it is washed from the page, it remains preserved in the hearts. This is because Allah 🕌 assured its preservation when He said: ❨We have revealed the Reminder, and We are its Guardian.❩ (Qur'ān 15:9) He preserved it on tablets that cannot be washed by water: the hearts of the scholars and the reciters. Allah 🕌 said: ❨Rather, it is clear signs in the breasts of those who have been given knowledge...❩ (Qur'ān 29:49)

"His likeness is that of a man who builds a house, and holds a great feast[315] therein. He sends a messenger to invite the people. Those who answer the messenger enter the house, and partake of the feast; those who do not answer the messenger do not enter the house, nor do they partake of the feast." They said: "Explain it to him so he understands." One of them said: "He is asleep." Another said: "The eye sleeps, yet the heart is awake." They said: "The house is Paradise, and the Messenger is Muḥammad 鄉: whoever obeys Muḥammad 鄉 has obeyed Allah, and whoever disobeys Muḥammad 鄉 has disobeyed Allah...'"

Dārimī narrated in his *Sunan* that someone came to the Prophet 鄉 and said: 'Let your eye sleep, and your ear hear, and your heart perceive!' The Prophet 鄉 said: 'And so, my eyes slept, and my ears heard, and my heart perceived. It was said to me: "A lord built a house, and held a great feast, and sent a messenger to invite the people. Those who answered the messenger entered the house, and partook of the feast, and the lord was pleased with them. Those who did not answer the messenger did not enter the house, nor did they partake of the feast, and the lord was angry with them." He said: "Allah is the lord, and Muḥammad is the Messenger, and the house is Islam, and the feast is Paradise.'"

The great scholars of times old and recent have compiled the various forms of divine revelation; they include the Prophet's 鄉 sleeping visions, as is borne out by the Ḥadīth of 'Ā'isha 鄉: 'The first revelation to visit the Messenger of Allah came in the form of visions in his sleep. He would not see a vision except that it came with the clarity of the sunrise...'

Suhaylī and others have adduced that it is a form of divine revelation from the words of Ibrāhīm, the Friend of Allah 鄉 to his son, as Allah informed us: ❨O my son! I have seen in a dream that I must sacrifice you.❩[316] He then set about implementing the vision.

---

[315] Ar. *ma'daba*: a feast that is prepared for a wedding, and what is meant here is Paradise.
[316] Qur'ān 37:102

It is confirmed by rigorously authenticated Ḥadīth that between the shoulders of the Prophet ﷺ was the Seal of Prophethood, which the scholars of the Ḥadīth identify as a piece of raised flesh on his noble back, near his left shoulder blade, with some hairs on it like a birthmark or mole. It shone with light, and bespoke dignity, and exuded a sweet fragrance.

Tirmidhī and others narrated that ʿAlī, the Commander of the Faithful ﷺ, when describing the Messenger of Allah ﷺ, would include in his description (as was mentioned in full previously): 'Between his shoulders was the Seal of Prophethood; and he was the Seal of the Prophets...'

Tirmidhī narrated on the authority of Rumaytha ﷺ who said: 'I heard the Messenger of Allah ﷺ—and had he willed, I would have kissed the seal that was between his shoulders, out of love for him—say about Saʿd b. Muʿādh, the day he died: "The throne of the Most Merciful trembles for him."'

The attributes of the Seal of Prophethood: The Seal of Prophethood was described with many attributes, none of which were contradictory, as we will make clear, if Allah ﷺ wills it:

Bukhārī and Muslim narrate (and the wording here is Bukhārī's) that Sāʾib b. Yazīd ﷺ said: 'My aunt took me to the Messenger of Allah ﷺ, saying: "O Messenger of Allah! My nephew is in pain."[317] The Messenger of Allah ﷺ rubbed my head, and prayed for my blessed increase. He then made ablutions, and I drank of the water he used. I then stood up behind him, and saw the Seal of Prophethood between his shoulders, like the tassel of a curtain.'[318]

---

[317] One narration has it 'he has had an accident.' He was complaining of pains in his leg.

[318] Imam al-Nawawī said, commenting on this Ḥadīth: "Tassel' here means the knots of the kind used to secure a tent. 'Curtain' here refers to the small, dome-shaped canopy that is hung over a bed, which has large tassels and knots. This is the correct meaning, according to the majority.'

Tirmidhī also narrated, on the authority of 'Āṣim al-Aḥwal, that 'Abdullāh b. Sarjis 🌼 said: 'I went to the Prophet 🌼 whilst he was with some of his companions, and went around so I was behind him. He knew what I intended, and so he took the cloak from his 🌼 back, and I saw the Seal of Prophethood on his shoulder, like a closed fist[319] around which was a nevus,[320] as though it were a mole. I returned until I was facing him, and said: "May Allah forgive you, O Messenger of Allah!" He 🌼 replied: "And you." The people said: "Did he ask forgiveness for you, the Messenger of Allah?" He 🌼 said: "Yes, and for you all." Then, he 🌼 recited the verse: ❨And seek forgiveness for your sin, and for the believers, men and women.❩' Muslim also narrated it, with the wording: '...Then, I went around his back and saw the Seal of Prophethood, between his shoulders, on the blade[321] of his left shoulder, like a clenched fist, a nevus upon it like some types of mole.'

Muslim narrated that Jābir b. Samura 🌼 said: 'I saw the Seal of Prophethood on the back of the Messenger of Allah 🌼; it was like a pigeon's egg.'

Imam Aḥmad and Tirmidhī (and the wording is his) narrated that Abū Naḍra al-'Awaqī said: 'I asked Abū Sa'īd al-Khudrī about the Seal of the Messenger of Allah 🌼. He said: "There was a piece of raised flesh on his back."'

Tirmidhī and others narrated, on the authority of 'Ulbā', that 'Amr b. Akhṭab al-Anṣārī 🌼 said: 'The Messenger of Allah 🌼 said: "O Abū Zayd, come to me and rub my back." I rubbed his back, and my fingers touched the seal.' 'Ulbā' said: 'What is the Seal?' 'Amr replied: 'A collection of hairs.'

The scholars say that the different statements of the narrators who described the Seal of Prophethood are not contradictory; rather, it is considered that each one of them drew a likeness according to whatever occurred to them. This is because the

---

[319] I.e. the shape of a hand when the fingers have been clenched, as though something is being clutched, as Nawawī and Zurqānī have explained.

[320] I.e. a mole or birthmark on the skin (and Allah knows best).

[321] Imam al-Nawawī said that the majority say this means the top of the shoulder; it is also said to mean the thin bone at the side of it, or that part of it that shows during movement.

Prophet 🕌 used to cover it, being as it was on his noble back, and so those who described it either saw it unintentionally, or were shown it by the Prophet 🕌; of course, anyone in this position would observe the proper respect, reverence and manners with the Prophet 🕌.

The great scholar Qurṭubī said, in his commentary on *Ṣaḥīḥ Muslim*:

> The sound Ḥadīth indicate that the Seal of Prophethood was prominent, and red, near his left shoulder. The smallest description of it is that it was the size of a (pigeon's) egg; the largest description of it is that it was the size of a clenched fist.[322]

The wisdom of its being placed between his 🕌 noble shoulders: The scholars have mentioned, in this regard, many aspects of wisdom. Ḥāfiẓ Ibn Kathīr said:

> One of the finest things mentioned by Ibn Duḥiyya 🕌, and by other scholars before him, concerning the wisdom of the seal being between the shoulders of the Messenger of Allah 🕌, is that it was a sign that there would be no prophet after him, coming from behind him.[323]

The author of *Fatḥ al-Bārī* said: 'The scholars say that the secret of this is that the heart is in that area.' The great scholar Suhaylī said, in *al-Rawḍ al-Unuf*:

> The wisdom of its being placed on the blade of the (left) shoulder is that he was immune to the whisperings of Satan, for this is the place through which Satan enters.

So, it was protection for him against Satan. Ibn 'Abd al-Barr narrated, with a strong chain of transmission leading back to Maymūn b. Mihrān, that 'Umar b. 'Abd al-'Azīz 🕌 said that a man asked his Lord to show him Satan's place (of entry) on the son of

---

[322] See all of this in *Sharḥ al-Zurqānī* and *Fatḥ al-Bārī*.
[323] See *al-Bidāya wal-Nihāya*, 6:28.

Adam. He was shown a transparent body, the innards of which could be seen from outside; and he was shown Satan in the form of a frog on its shoulder, opposite the heart, with a proboscis like that of a fly, which it had inserted through the left flank into the heart, and was whispering to it. When the servant mentions Allah 🕌, it creeps away.

The author of *Fatḥ al-Bārī* said:

> This [narration] does not go back to the Prophet 🕌;[324] but it is attested to by the Ḥadīth of Anas, narrated by Abū Yaʻlā and Ibn ʻAdī, which is as follows: 'Satan places his snout on the heart of the son of Adam...'
> Ibn Abī Dāwūd also narrated, in *Kitāb al-Sharīʻah*, by the relation of ʻUrwa b. Ruwaym, that ʻĪsā 🕊 asked his Lord to show him Satan's place (of entry) on the son of Adam.
> Suddenly, there appeared by his head something like a snake, placing its head onto the covering of the heart. When the servant mentions his Lord, it creeps away; when he is heedless, it whispers.[325]

When was the Prophet 🕌 sealed with the Seal of Prophethood? The scholars differ as to whether the Prophet 🕌 was born with the Seal of Prophethood, or whether it was placed upon him after his birth. It is said that he was born with it, as was reported by Ibn Sayyid al-Nās. This was repeated in *Fatḥ al-Bārī*, and followed by the following:

> Those of the second opinion (i.e. that it was placed on him after his birth) differed on the matter. It was said by some that when he 🕌 was born, the Seal of Prophethood was placed upon him. They adduced this with a Ḥadīth, the chain of which has some uncertainty. It is also said that it was placed upon him 🕌 when his breast was opened, when he was in Banī Saʻd, because of the Ḥadīth of ʻUtba b. ʻAbd, narrated by Imam Aḥmad and al-Ṭabarānī.

---

[324] I.e. it is *maqṭūʻ*.
[325] See *Fatḥ al-Bārī*, 7:374.

Ḥāfiẓ al-Zurqānī said: 'Qāḍī 'Iyāḍ pronounced this to be a fact, and Ḥāfiẓ Ibn Ḥajar said: "It is the strongest opinion."'

It is also said that it was placed upon him 🕌 when he was given his mission because of the previously mentioned Ḥadīth of 'Ā'isha 🕌 which included: '...and he placed a seal on my back, until I felt the touch of the stamp on my heart, and then he said: read! ...'

It is also said that it occurred on the night of the Ascent, because of the Ḥadīth of Abū Hurayra 🕌, narrated by Abū Ya'lā, Ibn Ḥarīr, and Ḥākim.[326]

Ḥāfiẓ al-Zurqānī said:

> The way to make sense of all these reports is that the sealing was repeated three times:
> In Banī Sa'd (when he 🕌 was young), then when his mission began, then on the night of the Ascent, as the (sound) Ḥadīth indicate. This combination is acceptable because it is in accordance with all of the Ḥadīth, without needing to discount some of them, and use some of them, for they are all authentic. Shāmī indicated this (in his *Sīra*), saying: 'With respect to the narration about after the birth: it is weak. As for his being born with it: it is also weak, and the one who claims it is required to present his evidence.'

The reason for its being named 'the Seal of Prophethood.' The great scholar Qurṭubī, and others, said that it was given this name because it is one of the clear signs that the people of divine scripture would know him 🕌 by. This is due to what was related concerning his attributes 🕌, and the signs of his veracity, in the previous divine revelations, stating that between his 🕌 shoulders would be the seal of Prophethood.

This is why a monk informed Salmān al-Fārisī 🕌 [327] that a Prophet would emerge in Ḥijāz, and described him to him. Among the signs of his veracity, the monk informed him, were

---

[326] See *Fatḥ al-Bārī* and *Sharḥ al-Mawāhib*.
[327] The Persian.

that he would not accept charity, but he would accept gifts, and that between his shoulders there would be the Seal of Prophethood. Salmān came to the Messenger of Allah 🕌 searching for these signs; when he saw the Seal, he believed in the Prophet 🕌.

Tirmidhī, Aḥmad and others narrate, on the authority of Burayda 🕌, that Salmān al-Fārisī 🕌 came to the Messenger of Allah 🕌 when he arrived in Medina, with a tray of dates. He placed the tray before the Messenger of Allah 🕌, who said: 'O Salmān, what is this? Salmān said: 'It is charity for you and you companions.' He 🕌 said: 'Take it, for we do not partake of charity,' so he lifted it up. The next day, Salmān came bearing the like of it, and placed it before the Messenger of Allah 🕌, who said: 'O Salmān, what is this?' He said: 'It is a gift for you,' so the Messenger of Allah 🕌 invited his companions to spread out and partake of the gift. Then, Salmān looked at the Seal of the Messenger of Allah's 🕌 back, and believed in him.

Salmān was a captive of the Jews.[328] The Messenger of Allah 🕌 purchased him,[329] for a sum of dirhams, with condition that he plant some palms for them, which Salmān would work with until they bore fruit.

---

[328] The reason for this was that he was in Persia, with the Zoroastrians, and he fled from them and joined a group of monks in Jerusalem. One of them told him of the emergence of the Prophet 🕌 in the land of the Arabs, so he left for Ḥijāz with a group of Bedouins, who sold him to the Jews. (*Shurūḥ Shamā'il al-Tirmidhī*)

[329] The great scholar Bayjūrī said: 'This means that he influenced the Jews to commission Salmān with this, in order to secure his freedom... Some narrations state that it was forty pieces of silver, or gold. This price remained on his head until the Messenger of Allah 🕌 was brought a piece of gold the size of a hen's egg. He 🕌 said: "What has the Persian seeking his freedom done?" Salmān was called forth, and the Prophet 🕌 said to him: "Take this, and use it to pay what you must." Salmān said: "How far will this go towards what I have to pay?" He 🕌 replied: "Take it, for Allah will secure you by it." Salmān said: "I took it, weighed out for them from it forty measures, and gave them their price." And so Salmān 🕌 was freed.'

The Messenger of Allah 🕌 planted them all, save one, which 'Umar planted; the trees all bore fruit within the year, except for that one. The Messenger of Allah 🕌 said: 'What of this palm?' 'O Messenger of Allah,' said 'Umar, 'It was I that planted it.' The Messenger of Allah 🕌 dug it up, and replanted it. It bore fruit within the year.

Another story is related of Buḥayrāʾ (or Baḥīrāʾ) the monk, and his recognition of the Prophet 🕌 because of the Seal of Prophethood, foretold in the divine scripture: Tirmidhī narrated that Abū Mūsā said: 'Abū Ṭālib travelled to the Levant, and the Prophet 🕌 accompanied him, along with some dignitaries of Quraysh.[330] When they came upon the monk (Baḥīrā), they stopped, and dismounted, and the monk came out to meet them. In the past, they had always rode past him; and he had never come out to them. They dismounted, and the monk began to search among them, until he took the hand of the Messenger of Allah 🕌, and said: "This is the Master of the worlds; this is the Messenger of the Lord of the worlds, whom Allah has sent as a mercy to the worlds!" The dignitaries of Quraysh said to him: "How do you know this?" The monk replied: "When you approached from the road, not a tree, nor a stone remained except that it fell prostrate. They do not prostrate except to a Prophet. I know him too by the Seal of Prophethood, below the cartilage of his shoulder, like an apple."

'He then returned, and prepared food for them. When he brought it to them, the Prophet 🕌 was herding the camels. The monk said: "Send for him." He came forward, and above him was a cloud, giving him shade. When he approached the people, he found that they had beaten him to the shade of the tree; yet when he sat 🕌, the tree's shadow inclined to him. "See how the shade of the tree inclines to him!" said the monk, "By Allah, I implore you, which of you is his guardian?" "Abū Ṭālib," they said. He did not cease to implore Abū Ṭālib until he took the Prophet 🕌 back to Mecca, out of fear that the Byzantines would kill him. Abū Bakr sent Bilāl with him, and gave the monk cake, and oil.' Tirmidhī said: 'It is a sound, singularly-narrated Ḥadīth [*ḥasan gharīb*].'

---

[330] When the Messenger of Allah 🕌 was still in his youth. [t]

Jazarī said:

> Its chain of transmission is rigorously authentic, and its men are those of the *Ṣaḥīḥ* collections,[331] or (at least) one of them. The mention of Abū Bakr and Bilāl is not preserved, and the scholars has considered it to be doubtful; and indeed it is so, for the age of the Prophet ﷺ at the time was twelve years, and Abū Bakr was two years younger than him, and Bilāl was likely not even born at the time.[332]

Ḥāfiẓ Ibn Ḥajar said in *al-Iṣāba*:

> The Ḥadīth is narrated by trustworthy men, and it has no other wording (i.e. with mention of Abū Bakr and Bilāl). It is possible that it has been taken from another Ḥadīth and mixed with this one accidentally by one of the narrators.

HIS EXALTED CHARACTER ﷺ

Allah ﷻ said: ﴿In the name of Allah, Most Gracious, Most Merciful. Nūn. By the pen, and by that which they write: by the grace of your Lord, you are not mad; and for you will be endless reward; and you are on an exalted character.﴾[333] Allah ﷻ swore by *nūn*, which means the showering of divine succour, from which sustenance comes to the limitless pen, which was the first of Allah's creations, as it related in the Ḥadīth narrated by Tirmidhī and Imam Aḥmad, on the authority of ʿUbāda b. al-Ṣāmit ؓ, who said: 'I heard the Messenger of Allah ﷺ say: "The first thing that Allah created was the pen. He said to it: 'Write!' it said: 'O Lord, what should I write?' He said: 'Write what will be until the Day of Resurrection...'"'

Then, Allah ﷻ swore by everything that the angels and the recorders write:

---

[331] I.e. of Bukhārī and Muslim.
[332] *Al-Mirqāt*
[333] Qur'ān 68:1-2

You, O Muḥammad, by the bounty of the grace of your Lord upon you of Prophethood, are not mad; because the implications of your message, and your wise call, and your upright law, are the peak of knowledge and wisdom.

How could this be imagined to be in accordance with what they say about you, that you are mad? Rather, the mad one is the one who accuses he who possesses such knowledge, wisdom and sagacity of being mad.

❨And for you❩, *O Messenger of Allah, because of your forbearance and patience in the face of their physical and verbal abuse,* ❨will be endless reward;❩ ❨And you❩, *O Messenger of Allah, because of the lofty qualities that you have Mastered, and reached the peak of, are truly* ❨on an exalted character.❩

He 🕮 is exalted in every aspect of perfect character: he 🕮 is exalted in his forbearance and tolerance; exalted in his generosity and munificence; exalted in his courage; exalted in his modesty; exalted in his noble companionship; exalted in his shyness; exalted in his manners; exalted in his compassion and his tenderness; exalted in all of his 🕮 characteristics! How should he not be in possession of such exalted character, when he took his character from the noble Qur'ān? It is related from ʿĀʾisha 🕮 that she was asked about the character of the Messenger of Allah 🕮. She replied: 'His character was the Qur'ān: he became angry for its sake, and was pleased for its sake.'[334]

Ibn Abī Shayba narrated, on the authority of ʿĀʾisha 🕮 that she was asked about the character of the Messenger of Allah 🕮. She said: 'He was the best of all people in character; his character was the Qur'ān: he was pleased for its sake, and angry for its sake. He was neither immoderate, nor slanderous; nor was he boisterous in the marketplace. He never repaid an ill deed with another; but would excuse, and forgive.' She then said: 'Recite: ❨The believers are successful...❩[335] until the tenth verse.' The questioner recited it. She said: 'This was his character.'

---

[334] Narrated by Muslim and Abū Dāwūd.
[335] Qur'ān 23:1

'Ā'isha ﷺ is related to have said: 'Nobody was ever of finer character than the Messenger of Allah ﷺ. No one from amongst his companions or household ever called him, except that he answered: 'At your service!' for this reason, Allah revealed: ❨And you are on an exalted character.❩'[336]

'Umar b. al-Khaṭṭāb ﷺ related that a man called the Prophet ﷺ three times; each time, he replied: 'At your service, at your service!'[337]

Our Master Muḥammad ﷺ
IS THE EXEMPLAR OF PHYSICAL AND MORAL PERFECTION

Bukhārī narrated that Anas ﷺ said: 'The Messenger of Allah ﷺ had the handsomest face and the most excellent character of all people.' He ﷺ was the most beautiful of Allah's creation, and his character was the most excellent; more than this, he was the fount of nobility and perfection in the world.

It is narrated in the *Musnad* of Aḥmad, and elsewhere, on the authority of Abū Hurayra ﷺ, that the Messenger of Allah ﷺ said: 'I was sent to perfect righteous character.'

Imam Mālik narrated in his *Muwaṭṭa'* that the Prophet ﷺ said: 'I was sent to perfect noble character.'

Imam Abū al-Qāsim al-Junayd ﷺ said: 'His character was only exalted because he ﷺ had no aspiration except Allah.'

The Messenger of Allah ﷺ embodied all the noble characteristics that the Prophets before him had brought, and he added to them perfection on top of perfection, and beauty on top of beauty.

---

[336] Narrated by Ibn Mardawayh and Abū Nuʿaym with a weak chain of transmission. (*Sharḥ al-Zurqānī*, 4:245)

[337] Narrated by Abū Yaʿlā in *al-Kabīr* on the authority of his Shaykh Jubāra b. al-Mughallis, whom Ibn Numayr considered trustworthy, though the majority considered him a weak narrator. The rest of the men of its chain of transmission are trustworthy, and rigorously authentic. (*Majmaʿ al-Zawāʾid*, 9:20)

Allah praised His beloved, our Master Muḥammad 𐎓, because of his exalted character, and his perfect conduct and his kindness, in the Torah and the Gospel, and all the other divine scriptures, just as He praised and lauded him because of them in the noble Qur'ān.

Bukhārī narrated that 'Aṭā' b. Yassār said: 'I met 'Abdullāh b. 'Amr b. al-'Āṣ, and said to him: "Tell me about the description of the Messenger of Allah 𐎓 in the Torah." He said: "Indeed, he 𐎓 is described in the Torah with some of the attributes mentioned concerning him in the Qur'ān:

O Prophet, We have sent you as a bearer of witness, and a bringer of tidings, and a warner,[338] *and a protector of the unlettered.*

You are My servant, and My Messenger. I have named you 'the one who relies on Me:' neither cruel nor fierce, nor boisterous in the marketplace.

He repays not an ill deed with another; but excuses, and forgives.

Allah will not take him until He has, by means of him, made a crooked way straight, so that they will say 'There is no god but Allah,' and has opened, by means of him, eyes that were blind, and ears that were deaf, and hearts that were enveloped.'"[339]

Wahb b. Munabbih related that Allah 𐎓 inspired a Prophet of the Israelites, whose name was Sha'yā': *Stand amongst the Children of Israel, for I will inspire your tongue.* He stood, and said: 'O sky, listen well! O earth, take heed! Allah wishes to decree a matter, and establish an affair, and here it is: He wishes to send an unlettered man, neither cruel nor fierce, nor boisterous in the marketplace. If he were to pass over a flame, he would not extinguish it, because of his tranquillity; if he walked upon kindling and dry earth, no sound would be heard beneath his feet:

---

[338] Qur'ān 33:45

[339] I.e. he will open hearts that were covered and hidden in darkness, by the light of faith that he 𐎓 brought.

I send him as a bearer of glad tidings; and a warner. His speech is not crude. By means of him, I will open eyes that were blind, and ears that were deaf, and hearts that were enveloped. I will fortify him with every thing of beauty; I will grant him every noble character.

I will make his serenity his raiment, and righteousness his badge, and piety his conscience, and wisdom his speech, and honesty and faithfulness his nature, and forgiveness and goodness his character, and the truth his law, and justice his conduct, and guidance his leader, and Islam his religion, and Aḥmad his name.

I will make him known, after obscurity; I will make his lot plenty, after it was sparse; I will enrich him, after poverty;

I will unite him, after he was divided. By means of him, I will unite communities that were alienated, and hearts that were at odds, and passions that were divided. By means of him, I will save a great throng of people from destruction.

I will make his community the finest ever to have emerged from humanity: they will enjoin good, and forbid evil: monotheists, and believers; sincere, and faithful in what the Messengers brought.'[340]

---

[340] Related by Ḥāfiẓ Ibn Kathīr in his *Tafsīr*, ascribed it to Ibn Abī Ḥātim; also related by al-Qasṭalānī in *al-Mawāhib*, ascribed it to Ibn Isḥāq.

PART IV
THE SUBLIME CHARACTER OF
OUR MASTER MUḤAMMAD ﷺ

HIS PERFECT KINDNESS
AND TENDER DISPOSITION ﷺ

ALLAH ﷻ said: ⟨It was by the mercy of Allah that you were gentle with them; had you been cruel, and fierce of heart, they would have dispersed from you about it.⟩[341]

The Prophet ﷺ was tender, and lenient in character. He treated his family, his companions, and all people with kindness, displaying to those who kept his company great magnanimity, benevolence, and friendliness.

Tirmidhī narrated on the authority of ʿAlī ؓ that, when he described the Messenger of Allah ﷺ, he would say: 'His heart was the soundest of hearts. His speech was the most truthful of speech. He was the gentlest of people, and the kindest of them in companionship...'

Bukhārī narrated that Ibn ʿUmar ؓ said: 'The Prophet ﷺ was neither immoderate, nor slanderous. He used to say: "The best of you are those with the finest characters."'

Out of his kindness, he would never confront a person with something they disliked. It is narrated that Anas b. Mālik ؓ said: 'The Prophet ﷺ was not an accuser, nor was he immoderate, nor did he curse. He used to say to us, when he rebuked them: 'What is wrong with him, may his forehead be covered in dust!'

---

[341] Qurʾān 3:159

More than this, he was the kindest of people: Abū Nuʻaym narrated in *al-Dalāʾil* that Anas ﷺ said: 'The Messenger of Allah ﷺ was the kindest of people. By Allah, he would never refuse any servant, male or female, who came to him bearing water on a cold morning, and he ﷺ would wash his face and forearms with the water. No one every asked him a question except that he listened to him; and he ﷺ would not leave until the questioner left him. No one ever reached for his hand except that he gave it to them; and he ﷺ would not remove his hand until the other man was the one who let go.'

HIS FRIENDLINESS ﷺ WITH FAMILY AND LOVED ONES

Muslim narrates in his *Ṣaḥīḥ* that Saʻd b. Abī Waqqāṣ ﷺ said: 'Once, ʻUmar asked permission to enter upon the Messenger of Allah ﷺ whilst he had with him some women[342] of Quraysh who were speaking with him, and asking many questions with raised voices.[343] When ʻUmar sought permission to enter, they began to rush to cover themselves.[344] The Messenger of Allah ﷺ gave him permission to enter, so he came in. the Messenger of Allah ﷺ was smiling, and so ʻUmar said: "May Allah ever cause your teeth to smile, O Messenger of Allah!"[345]

---

[342] Ḥāfiẓ Ibn Ḥajar said: 'This means women from among his wives; and possibly others were with them of his unmarriageable kin.'

[343] Qāḍī ʻIyāḍ said: 'This may have been before the prohibition of raising one's voice above his ﷺ; or it may be that the loudness of their voices was due to their being in a group, not because every individual from among them had a voice louder than his ﷺ.'
(Nawawī, *Sharḥ Ṣaḥīḥ Muslim*)

[344] Because ʻUmar ﷺ was not family to them, so it was obligatory for them to cover in his presence. Evidence may be adduced from this for the obligation of a woman covering in front of a man from outside her immediate family, even her face, which is also obligatory to cover.

[345] I.e. 'May Allah make constant the happiness that has caused your teeth to be revealed, and your light to emerge; but there must be some reason for it, some pleasing occurrence, so tell me of it, and honour me with an explanation of it!' (*Al-Mirqāt*)

'He ﷺ said: "I was amused by the ladies who were with me: when they heard your voice, they rushed to cover themselves." 'Umar said: "It is more fitting that they should fear you, O Messenger of Allah!" Then, he said: "O enemies of yourselves: do you fear me and not the Messenger of Allah ﷺ?" "Indeed yes," they said, "for you are fiercer, and crueller!"[346] He ﷺ said: "By the One in whose hand is my soul, Satan never came upon you following a path except that he followed a different one."'

His Kind Companionship and Amiability ﷺ
with His Wives and the rest of His Family

The Messenger of Allah ﷺ was amiable with his wives and the rest of his family, treating them with benevolence, and playing with them, and showing them love and affection.

Tirmidhī narrated on the authority of 'Ā'isha ﷺ that the Messenger of Allah ﷺ said: 'The best of you are the best of you to their families; and I am the best of you to my family.' Ibn 'Asākir's narration adds: 'No one honours women except an honourable man; no one disrespects them except a villain.' 'Ā'isha ﷺ also reported that the Messenger of Allah ﷺ said: 'The believers with the most complete faith are the best of them in character, and the kindest of them to their families.'[347]

Ḥākim narrated with a rigorously authentic chain of transmission, on the authority of Ibn 'Abbās ﷺ, that the Prophet ﷺ said: 'The best of you are the best of you to women.' Abū Hurayra ﷺ reported that the Messenger of Allah ﷺ said: 'The believers with the most complete faith are the best of them in character; and the best of you are the best of you to their women.'[348]

---

[346] I.e. 'You, O 'Umar, are very fierce, and cruel, in contrast to him ﷺ: for he is gentle, and kind.' Imam al-Nawawī said: 'The use of the comparative form here (i.e. 'fiercer,' 'crueller') does not suggest any comparison; rather, it means 'fierce' and 'cruel.''
[347] Narrated by Tirmidhī.
[348] Narrated by Tirmidhī, who said: 'It is sound, and rigorously authentic.'

Ibn Saʻd narrated that ʻĀʾisha ﷺ was asked how the Messenger of Allah ﷺ was when he was alone, amongst his household. She replied: 'He was the gentlest of people, smiling, and laughing. He was never seen stretching out his legs in front of his ﷺ companions.'

This was because of his exalted manners and his complete dignity. ʻĀʾisha ﷺ also is reported to have said: 'I went out with the Messenger of Allah ﷺ on one of his journeys, when I was young, having no flesh upon me, nor having yet become corpulent. He told the people to go on ahead, and so they did. Then, he said to me: "Come, I will race you!" So I raced him ﷺ, and beat him. He let me be until I had some flesh on me, and I became corpulent, and plump. I went out with him ﷺ on one of his journeys, and he ﷺ told them to go on ahead, and so they did. Then he said: "Come, I will race you!" He beat me, and began to laugh, saying: "This one for that one!"'[349]

He ﷺ would assist his family with the housework: Bukhārī narrated that Aswad said: 'I asked ʻĀʾisha ﷺ what the Prophet ﷺ used to do around the house. She replied: "He was at the service of his family; and when the time for the prayer came, he would go to pray."'

This is a direction for the Islamic community that they should act in accordance to this perfect example, and not be tyrannical men, especially where wives and families are concerned.

The Messenger of Allah ﷺ urged the importance of being good to women on numerous occasions, in both closed and open society. It is narrated in the *Ṣaḥīḥ* collections of Bukhārī and Muslim, on the authority of Abū Hurayra ﷺ, that the Prophet ﷺ said: 'Be sure to take care of women.' It is also narrated in the *Sunan* collections of Tirmidhī and Ibn Mājah that the Prophet ﷺ said, in his sermon at the farewell pilgrimage: 'Be sure to take good care of women.'

---

[349] I.e. 'I beat you this second time, after you had beat me the first time.' He intended by this that she should not be sad for losing. The Ḥadīth was narrated by Abū Dāwūd and Aḥmad.

Bukhārī, Muslim and Tirmidhī narrate (and the wording here is that of Tirmidhī), on the authority of 'Ā'isha ☙ that eleven women sat down together and made a pact that they would not conceal anything about their husbands.[350]

The first one said: 'My husband is the meat of an emaciated camel, on the peak of an insurmountable mountain: neither easy to climb to, nor meaty enough to move itself.'[351]

The second one said: 'I do not reveal ought about my husband, for I fear I will not leave him. If I mention him, I mention his flaws, both the open and the hidden.'[352]

The third one said: 'My husband is boorish:[353] if I speak, I am divorced; if I am silent, he will repudiate me.'[354]

The fourth one said: 'My husband is like a night in Tihāma:[355] Neither hot, nor cold; neither worrisome, nor dull.'

---

[350] I.e. they would not hide anything about them, praiseworthy or blameworthy, but would tell all.

[351] The meaning is that her husband is arrogant, and bad-tempered, and cannot be reached except with difficulty; and he does not benefit his wife with companionship, or anything else.

[352] 'For I fear I will not leave him' means either that she feared he would divorce her if she mentioned him, and this would lead to hardship for her, and the loss of her children; or, it means that if she started speaking about him, she feared that she would never stop!

[353] Or 'my husband is tall,' meaning there is nothing to say for him except that he is tall, for he has no other redeeming qualities. (Nawawī, *Sharḥ Ṣaḥīḥ Muslim*) [t]

[354] I.e. 'he will pronounce a conditional divorce, leaving me neither single nor married.' (Ibid.) [t]

[355] Tihāma is [the city of] Mecca and its surrounding locales. The meaning of this comparison is that her husband is completely just in his dealings, and amiable in his character (*Hāshiyat Bayjūrī*)

The fifth one said: 'My husband is like a lynx in the house, and a lion on the battlefield;[356] and he asks not about what he knows.'[357]

The sixth one said: 'When my husband eats, he eats the lot, and when he drinks, he empties the jug! When he lies down, he curls up, and he does not extend his hand to uncover any sorrow.'[358]

The seventh one said: 'My husband is hopeless—or she said 'iniquitous'—and fatuous. There is not an illness except he has it. He will either hurt your head, or break your bones, or both.'[359]

The eighth one said: 'My husband has the touch of a rabbit, and the fragrance of perfume.'[360]

The ninth one said: 'My husband is noble and refined of standing; and tall of stature.[361] His generosity is great,[362] and his house is near to the gathering-place.'[363]

---

[356] Literally: 'when he comes in, he is like a lynx; when he goes out (to fight), he is like a lion.' [t]

[357] I.e. he is like a lion in times of war, because of his strength and courage. 'He asks not about what he knows,' meaning about that which is stored in his house of food and drink, and so on, because of his great generosity.

[358] I.e. when he eats or drinks, he does not leave anything for his family; and he does not examine them when they are ill, or have any complaint—and other explanations have been given, as in Bayjūrī's *Hāshiya*.

[359] I.e. if he beats you, he will either injure you, or break your bones, or both.

[360] She praised him for the softness and gentleness of his touch, and the sweetness of his fragrance, like a sweet-smelling plant.

[361] Literally 'the scabbard of his sword is long,' an expression used by the Arabs to denote tallness.

[362] Literally 'he accumulates much ash,' because he has many guests, for whom he lights fires to cook meat, and bread, leaving much ash afterwards.

[363] This is a symbol of his generosity, because no one places their house near to the meeting-place of the tribe except those who are generous. (Nawawī, *Sharḥ Ṣaḥīḥ Muslim*)

The tenth one said: 'My husband owns much; and what does he own? Better than what you imagine! He has camels that are always kneeling, and rarely roaming. When they hear the sound of the lute, they know their days are numbered!'[364]

The eleventh one said: 'My husband was Abū Zarʿ: and who is Abū Zarʿ? He has made the jewellery on my ears swing to and fro,[365] and has filled my arms with flesh,[366] and has praised me until I praised myself.[367] He found me in a modest family of sheep-rearers, in hardship, and brought me to a family in which were heard the neighs of horses and the cries of camels, and threshing, and cleaning.[368] When I speak, he does not reject me; and I sleep through the morning, and I drink until I am satiated.

And the mother of Abū Zarʿ: who is the mother of Abū Zarʿ? Her containers of provisions are immense, and her house is spacious.

And the son of Abū Zarʿ: who is the son of Abū Zarʿ? His bed is like a thin palm leaf, and a single calf of a young she-goat is enough to satisfy his hunger.[369]

And the daughter of Abū Zarʿ: who is the daughter of Abū Zarʿ? Obedient to her father; and obedient to her mother. She is full-fleshed; a source of jealous rage to her husband's second wife.

---

[364] I.e. he has many camels, always kneeling in his courtyard. He does not let them roam except when it is necessary, so that when guests come to him, the camels are there, ready, so that he can offer them their milk, and their meat, and play music for them. When the camels hear the sound of the lute playing, they know that guests have come, and that they will be slaughtered. (Ibid.)

[365] I.e. 'He has given me such earrings that they sway to and fro on my ears because they are so many.' (Ibid.)

[366] I.e. she has become fat by his providing for her.

[367] I.e. 'he has made my happy, and exalted me until I exalted myself.'

[368] I.e. he found her in a family rearing a few sheep, in harsh living conditions, and took her to a family of horses, camels and cows, threshing crops with his feet to separate the grain from the ear, and cleaning the grain of hay after the threshing. This word could also mean the sound of the clucking of a chicken. (*Hāshiyat Bayjūrī ʿalā al-Shamāʾil*)

[369] This means that he eats little, which the Arabs deemed praiseworthy. (*Sharḥ al-Nawawī*)

And the servant-girl of Abū Zar': who is the servant-girl of Abū Zar'? She does not pass on our conversations;[370] nor does she interfere with our supplies;[371] nor does she let our house become a hovel.[372]

'One day, Abū Zar' went out, and the milkers were churning butter. He met a woman with two boys like lynxes, playing beneath her waist with pomegranates. He divorced me, and married her. After him, I married a noble man, with a robust steed,[373] adept with the spear, who showered me with many favours, and gave me a pair[374] of every kind of cattle, saying to me: "Take this, O Umm Zar', and with it provide for your family." If I had gathered everything that he gave me, it would not have amounted to the smallest vessel of what I received from Abū Zar'.'

'Ā'isha ﷻ said that, upon hearing this tale, the Messenger of Allah ﷺ said: 'I am for you what Abū Zar' was for Umm Zar'!' Haytham Ibn 'Adī's narration has it thus: 'I am for you what Abū Zar' was for Umm Zar': in companionship and loyalty; not in abandonment and departure.' Ṭabarānī's narration added: '...except that he divorced her, and I will not divorce you.' The narrations of Nasā'ī and Ṭabarānī add that 'Ā'isha ﷻ said: 'O Messenger of Allah ﷺ, you are indeed better even than Abū Zar'!' The narration of Nasā'ī has it that it was the Messenger of Allah ﷺ who began the story, saying to 'Ā'isha ﷻ: 'I am for you what Abū Zar' was for Umm Zar'!' 'Ā'isha ﷻ replied: 'My father and mother be sacrificed for you, O Messenger of Allah, who was Abū Zar'?' He ﷺ replied: 'Some women gathered together...'

Look, my brother, at the sweetness of his companionship ﷺ, and the kindness of his character with his family, as he listened to the story of 'Ā'isha ﷻ of an event that occurred in the pre-Islamic days of ignorance, when a group of women sat down together and made a pact that they would each tell the others about their relationships with their husbands, in respect to their characters, and their behaviour, and their companionship!

---

[370] I.e. she keeps our secrets.

[371] I.e. she does not damage them, or separate them, or steal them, for she is trustworthy.

[372] I.e. she takes good care of the house, and keeps it tidy.

[373] I.e. a horse that panted as it galloped, without needing breaks to rest.

[374] Or a large amount.

The scholars say that several things can be deduced from this Ḥadīth:

1 – The praiseworthiness of good companionship with one's family.

2 – The permissibility of conversing in the evening about good things, such as kindness to one's wife, and generosity to one's guests.

3 – The permissibility of mentioning a person who is unknown to both the speaker and listener with something that they would dislike; for it does not amount to backbiting. The most that 'Ā'isha ﷺ did is mention some unnamed women, some of whom mentioned the faults of their husbands, who were also unnamed, and whose identity is unknown. This does not constitute backbiting, as Imam al-Nawawī made clear in his commentary.

The author of *al-Tarātīb al-Idāriyya* said:

> The scholars have deduced from this Ḥadīth that it is permissible to speak about the past nations, and the previous generations, and to draw parables from their histories, because their chronicles contain much that inspires contemplation and insight, and much benefit can be deduced from them. This Ḥadīth contains particular benefit if it is related to women, for it reminds them of the importance of loyalty to their husbands.

Qāḍī 'Iyāḍ said:

> The understanding that can be drawn from [this Ḥadīth] includes the permissibility of telling stories, and novel tales, as a means of entertaining the soul,[375] and illuminating the heart. Abū 'Īsā al-Tirmidhī included this Ḥadīth in the section he named *What has been reported of the Messenger of Allah's ﷺ evening conversation.*

---

[375] As can be adduced by this Ḥadīth because of our lady 'Ā'isha's enjoyment of it.

It was narrated that the Commander of the Faithful, ʿAlī b. Abī Ṭālib 🕊 said: 'Amuse these souls of yours time and again, for they become rusty, just as iron does.' He also said: 'If the heart is coerced, it will become blind.' It is narrated that Ibn ʿAbbās 🕊 that he used to say: 'Entertain yourselves: if you become bored with jurisprudence, turn to poetry, and the chronicles of the Arabs.'

All of this is acceptable as long as it is not constant and uninterrupted. As for if it is a man's habit, for which he is known, and he habitually uses it to please the people, this is blameworthy, and not commendable from the position of the Sacred Law. Because of the many benefits which can be adduced from this Ḥadīth, many scholars authored entire works on it. [He then goes on to mention their names]

HIS KIND COMPANIONSHIP 🕊 WITH ALL PEOPLE

Bukhārī and Muslim narrate that Anas 🕊 said: 'I served the Prophet 🕊—Aḥmad's narration adds 'both home and abroad'—for ten years;[376] and not once did he say to me "*Uff*,"[377] nor did he ever say about anything I did: "Why did you do this?" nor about anything I did not do: "Why didn't you do it?"'

Abū Nuʿaym's narration has it that Anas 🕊 said: 'Not once did he 🕊 revile me, nor did he beat me, nor did he scold me, nor did he frown at me, nor did he ever reprimand me for being negligent with something that he had instructed me to do. If anyone from his family reprimanded me, he would say: "Leave him: if something is predestined, it will be."'

---

[376] Muslim's narration has 'nine years.'
[377] An Arabic expression of displeasure or disrespect. [t]

His Lofty Manners ﷺ
with Those Who Spoke to Him

The Messenger of Allah ﷺ would listen intently to those with whom he spoke, or those who asked him a question; and he would approach them with kindness: Abū Dāwūd narrated that Anas ﷺ said: 'I never saw the Prophet ﷺ speak to a man in confidence, and be the one to turn his head away, until it would be the other man who would turn his head away; and I never saw the Messenger of Allah ﷺ take hold of a man's hand and then let it go, until the man would be the one who let go of his hand.'

Muslim narrated in his *Ṣaḥīḥ*, on the authority of Abū Qatāda ﷺ, the Ḥadīth about their sleeping through the dawn prayer, in which it is mentioned that they were thirsty, and all rushed *en masse* to the water. The Messenger of Allah ﷺ said: 'Behave properly;[378] you will all drink.' They did as he said. The Messenger of Allah ﷺ began to pour the water.

Abū Qatāda ﷺ said: 'I gave them all to drink, until there was only myself and the Messenger of Allah ﷺ left. He said to me: "Drink." I replied: "I will not drink until you have drunk, O Messenger of Allah." He said: "The one who gives a group of people to drink should be the last of them to drink." So I drank, and then the Messenger of Allah ﷺ drank.'

The Warm Reception He ﷺ
Would Grant to His Guests

It is narrated that Abū Hurayra ﷺ said that if anyone ever took the hand of Messenger of Allah ﷺ, he would not withdraw his hand until the other man would be the one to do so; and his knees—or 'his knee'—would never be seen to be withdrawn from

---

[378] Ibn al-Athīr said: 'Most of the narrators of the Ḥadīth have it: 'Fill the jug properly' (The words are similar in Arabic [t]), but it is of no consequence.'

the knee of his guest;[379] and no one would greet him except that he would turn his face to them, and he would not leave them until they had finished speaking with him.[380]

'Umar b. al-'Āṣ ﷺ is reported to have said: 'The Messenger of Allah ﷺ would turn his face and converse with even the most wicked of people, in order to gain their affection. He used to turn to me and engage me in conversation until I thought I was the best of people, so I said: "O Messenger of Allah, am I better, or is Abū Bakr?" "Abū Bakr," he said. "O Messenger of Allah," I said: "Am I better, or is 'Umar?" He replied: "'Umar." "O Messenger of Allah," I said: "Am I better, or is 'Uthmān?" He replied: "'Uthmān." When I asked the Messenger of Allah ﷺ this, he turned away from me, and I wished that I had never asked him.'[381] And when he ﷺ sent an envoy, he used to say: 'Gain people's affection!'[382]

HIS SMILE ﷺ
AND HIS CHEERY DISPOSITION WITH PEOPLE

The Messenger of Allah ﷺ was the cheeriest of people in his countenance, and the most joyful. Bazzār narrated with a sound chain of transmission on the authority of Jābir ﷺ, who said: 'When the Messenger of Allah ﷺ was visited by revelation, or was counselling the people, you would say: "He is the warner of a people to whom punishment has come!" but when this state had passed, you would see him the cheeriest of people, and the quickest of them to smile, and the most joyful of them.'[383]

---

[379] I.e. he ﷺ would sit close to them so that their knees touched. [t]

[380] Narrated by Bazzār and Ṭabarānī with a sound chain of transmission (*Majma' al-Zawā'id* 9:15); and by Ibn Sa'd in *al-Ṭabaqāt*, and by Ibn Mājah. (*Ghidhā' al-Albāb*)

[381] Narrated by Tirmidhī in *al-Shamā'il*, and by Ṭabarānī. Its chain of transmission is sound, and some of it is recorded in the *Ṣaḥīḥ* in a different context. (*Majma' al-Zawā'id* 9:15)

[382] *Al-Iṣāba*, 3:152

[383] *Majma' al-Zawā'id* 9:17

We have already made mention of what 'Ā'isha 🌸 said when she was asked how the Messenger of Allah 🌸 was when he was alone, amongst his household. She replied: 'He 🌸 was the gentlest of people, smiling, and laughing. He was never seen stretching out his legs in front of his companions.'

THE WAY HE 🌸 RESPONDED TO GREETINGS

Salmān al-Fārisī 🌸 reported that a man came to the Prophet 🌸 and said: 'Peace be upon you, O Messenger of Allah!' 'And upon you, with Allah's mercy!' said the Prophet 🌸. Another man then came, saying: 'Peace be upon you, O Messenger of Allah, with Allah's mercy!' He 🌸 replied: 'And upon you, with Allah's mercy and blessings!'[384]

THE WARM WELCOME HE 🌸 EXTENDED
TO THOSE WHO APPROACHED HIM

It is narrated that 'Alī 🌸 said: 'Ammār asked permission to enter upon the Prophet 🌸, who recognised his voice, and said: 'Welcome to the good, sweet-smelling one!'[385]

It is also narrated that 'Ā'isha 🌸 said: 'Fāṭima came walking up to us, and it was as though her gait were the gait of the Prophet 🌸. He 🌸 said to her: 'Welcome to my daughter!' He 🌸 then bade her sit down next to him, on the right or the left.[386]

Bukhārī and Muslim narrated, on the authority of Ibn 'Abbās 🌸, that when a delegation came from 'Abd al-Qays to the Prophet 🌸, he said to them: 'Welcome to the delegation, neither infamous nor rueful!'

---

[384] Narrated by Aḥmad in *al-Zuhd*, and by Ibn Jarīr, Ibn al-Mundhir, Ibn Abī Ḥātim, Ṭabarānī, and Ibn Mardawayh, with a sound chain of transmission. (*Al-Durr al-Manthūr*)
[385] Narrated by Tirmidhī, Ibn Mājah and Ibn Mardawayh with a sound chain of transmission.
[386] Narrated by Bukhārī in *al-Adab al-Mufrad*.

He ﷺ also said to 'Ikrima b. Abū Jahl: 'Welcome to the emigrant horseman!'

Umm Hānī' ؓ said: 'I went to the Prophet ﷺ while he was bathing, and greeted him. He said: "Who is that?" I said: "Umm Hānī'." He said: "Welcome to Umm Hānī'!"'

HIS ENQUIRIES ﷺ INTO HIS COMPANION'S HEALTH

Imam Aḥmad narrated on the authority of Anas ؓ that the Prophet ﷺ would meet a person by asking them: 'How are you?' The person would respond: 'I am well, praise be to Allah!' The Prophet ﷺ would respond: 'May Allah make you well!'[387]

Abū Ya'lā narrated with a sound chain of transmission, on the authority of Ibn 'Abbās ؓ, that a man came to the Prophet ﷺ, who said to him: 'How are you?'[388] He replied: 'I am well, from a people who have neither visited any ill person, nor witnessed any funeral!'

Ṭabarānī also narrated with a sound chain of transmission, on the authority of Ibn 'Umar ؓ, that the Messenger of Allah ﷺ said to a man: 'How are you, O (so-and-so)?' He replied: 'I proclaim Allah's praises to you, O Messenger of Allah!' The Prophet ﷺ said: 'That is what I wanted from you.'

THE HONOUR THAT HE ﷺ EXTENDED TO NOBLES

The Messenger of Allah ﷺ used to honour nobles, saying: 'If a nobleman comes to you, honour him.'[389] Ṭabarānī narrated that Ibn Jarīr b. 'Abdullāh al-Bajalī ؓ said: 'When the Prophet ﷺ was

---

[387] The men of its chain of transmission are all rigorously authenticated, except for Mu'mal b. Ismā'īl, who was trustworthy, although he had some weakness. (*Majma' al-Zawā'id*)

[388] Literally 'how have you reached the morning?'

[389] Narrated by Ibn Mājah with a weak chain of transmission on the authority of Ibn 'Umar, and by Abū Dāwūd on the authority of Sha'bī with a rigorously authentic chain of transmission, without mention of the Companion who related it, as is mentioned in *Kashf al-Khafā'* and elsewhere. (*Al-Maqāṣid al-Ḥasana*)

sent, I went to him, and he said: "What has brought you [here]?" I replied: "I have come to accept Islam." He threw his robe around me, and said: "If a nobleman comes to you, honour him!'"

Bazzār's narration has it: 'I went to the Prophet 🌿, and he spread his cloak out for me, and said: "Sit down on this." I said: "May Allah honour you, as you have honoured me!'" The Ḥadīth then continued with the same wording.

Ḥākim narrated that the Prophet 🌿 entered one of his houses, and his companions came to him until the space was overcrowded and full. Jarīr al-Bajalī came in, but could not find a space, so sat at the door. The Messenger of Allah 🌿 took of his cloak, and offered it to him. Jarīr took it, and drew it to his face and began to kiss it, weeping. He tossed it back to the Prophet 🌿, and said: 'I would never sit on your clothes; may Allah honour you, as you have honoured me!' The Prophet 🌿 looked right and left, and said: 'If a nobleman comes to you, honour him!'[390]

'Adiyy b. Ḥātim related that he once went to the Prophet 🌿, who gave him a cushion. 'Adiyy said: 'I bear witness that you do not desire dominance in the land, nor corruption!' So 'Adiyy b. Ḥātim entered Islam, and then the Messenger of Allah 🌿 said: 'If a nobleman comes to you, honour him!'[391]

'Abd al-Raḥmān b. 'Abd said that he went to the Prophet 🌿 along with one hundred men from his people. The Prophet 🌿 honoured him, and bade him sit down, and dressed him in his cloak, and gave him his staff, and he embraced Islam.

A man from amongst those sitting with him said: 'O Messenger of Allah, what is this honour we see you extending to this man?' He 🌿 said: 'This is the chief of his people; if the chief of a people comes to you, honour them!'[392]

This is further supported by what Ibn 'Umar 🌿 and Abū Hurayra 🌿 both narrated: 'If a noblewoman is with you, honour her.'[393]

---

[390] The numerous chains of transmission strengthen this Ḥadīth, even though individually they may have some weakness. (Ibid.)

[391] Narrated by 'Askarī with a weak chain of transmission, as mentioned in *Kashf al-Khafā'* and *al-Maqāṣid al-Ḥasana*.

[392] *Al-Maqāṣid* ascribes it to Dūlābī.

[393] See *Kashf al-Khafā'*. These Ḥadīth present a warning to all husbands that they preserve the honour of their wives, especially the daughters of

An example of this is the Prophet's 🕌 honouring the commander of the delegation of 'Abd al-Qays, bidding him to sit on his right side, and enjoining the honouring of the delegation:

Shihāb b. 'Abbād related that he heard some of the delegation of 'Abd al-Qays saying: 'We went to the Messenger of Allah 🕌, and they were very pleased (i.e. the Ṣaḥāba). When we reached them, they made room for us, and we sat. The Prophet 🕌 welcomed us and prayed for us, and then looked to us and said: "Who is your Master, and leader?" We all pointed to Mundhir b. 'Ā'idh. "Do you mean Ashajj?"[394] asked the Prophet 🕌. "Yes, O Messenger of Allah," we said. He was lingering behind after the people, tying the camels and securing their provisions. He then took out his sack, and removed his travelling clothes and put on his best clothes. Then, he approached the Prophet 🕌, who was reclining with his legs spread out.

'When Ashajj approached, the people made room for him, and said: "Sit here, O Ashajj!" The Prophet 🕌 sat up and drew in his legs, and said: "Here, O Ashajj!" He sat on the right hand side of the Messenger of Allah 🕌, who welcomed him and treated him kindly, and asked him about their homeland, mentioning the names of each village: al-Ṣafā, and al-Mashqar, and other villages in Hajar. Ashajj said: "May my father and mother be sacrificed for you, O Messenger of Allah, you know more of the names of our land than we do!"

'The Prophet 🕌 said: "I visited your land, and was well accommodated there." Then, he 🕌 approached the Anṣār, and said: "O Anṣār, honour your brothers, for they are your equals in Islam, resembling you most in their hair and their skin; they embraced Islam willingly, neither through force nor affliction, while other people refuse to surrender until they are killed."

'The next morning, he 🕌 said: "How did you find the honour and hospitality of your brothers to you?" They replied: "The best of brothers: they made soft our beds, and delicious our food, and

---

noblemen amongst them. We have already mentioned the Ḥadīth narrated by Ibn 'Asākir in which the Prophet 🕌 said: 'No one honours women except an honourable man; no one disrespects them except a villain.'

[394] I.e. 'the split-headed one,' a nickname. [t]

they spent the night until morning teaching us the Book of our Lord ﷻ, and the Sunnah of our Prophet ﷺ." The Prophet ﷺ was pleased, and delighted.'"[395]

By this, the noble, generous nature of the Prophet ﷺ, and his friendliness, and his perfect character, and his thoughtfulness, is revealed to us. People who are by nature ignoble always love to pour scorn on the dignity of noble people, and diminish their stature; and we ask Allah's protection.

HIS FRIENDLINESS AND RELAXED MANNER ﷺ WITH HIS COMPANY

The Messenger of Allah ﷺ would always extend, to those he sat with, relaxed, wholesome companionship with both his state and his words, without stifling them, or repressing them. If they spoke about something, he would join them in conversation, as long as it was not of a sinful nature.

Khārija b. Zayd related that a group of people visited his father, Zayd b. Thābit ﷺ, and said: 'Tell us a story about the Prophet ﷺ.' He replied: 'What can I tell you? I was his neighbour, and when the revelation visited him, he would send for me, and I would go to him, and write it down. When we would speak about this worldly life, he would speak about it with us; and when we spoke about the hereafter, he would speak about it with us. And when we spoke about food, he would speak about it with us. All of this, I tell you about him ﷺ.'[396]

Imam Aḥmad narrated that Jābir b. Samura ﷺ said: 'The Messenger of Allah ﷺ would be silent for long periods, and would laugh little. The Ṣaḥāba would speak in his company about poetry, and their stories from the time of ignorance, and they would laugh; and occasionally he would smile with them.'[397]

---

[395] Ḥāfiẓ al-Mundhirī said: 'This Ḥadīth in its entirety was narrated by Aḥmad with a rigorously authentic chain of transmission.'

[396] Narrated by Tirmidhī in *al-Shamā'il* and by Bayhaqī. The author of *Majmaʿ al-Zawā'id* said: 'It was narrated by Ṭabarānī with a sound chain of transmission.'

[397] Tirmidhī narrated the like of it.

Abū Salama b. 'Abd al-Raḥmān said: 'The companions of the Messenger of Allah ﷺ were not repressed, nor were they listless.[398] They used to recite poetry in their gatherings, and speak about the time of ignorance. If any of them were prompted about anything in relation to Allah's ﷻ religion, their eyes would widen as though they were mad.'[399]

It is related in *al-Nihāya,* in explanation of the word 'listless:' 'A man is listless if he shows himself to be subdued, and slack in relation to worship, asceticism and fasting.' The meaning of this Ḥadīth is that they were not withdrawn and repressed; rather, they were relaxed, and sociable.

Muslim narrated that Simāk b. Ḥarb said: 'I said to Jābir b. Samura: "Did you use to sit with the Messenger of Allah ﷺ?" Jābir replied: "Yes, often. The Messenger of Allah ﷺ would not rise from the place he prayed the dawn prayer until the sun had risen. When it rose, he would stand. They would converse, and mention the affairs of the time of ignorance, and laugh; and he would smile."'

THE WAY HE ﷺ SPREAD JOY AMONGST HIS COMPANY BY JOKING WITH THEM

The Prophet ﷺ used to joke with his companions to spread joy amongst them, and to make them relax, so that they might follow his guidance and take on his characteristics. If he ﷺ had not been cheery and relaxed with his companions, and instead had been austere and stern, they would have charged themselves to be the same way, as would have those who followed them.

Thus he ﷺ joked so that they would joke, at the same time clarifying for them that he always spoke the truth when he joked, never indulging in falsehood, frivolity or silliness.

Bukhārī (in *al-Adab al-Mufrad*) and Bayhaqī narrated on the authority of Anas ﷺ that the Messenger of Allah ﷺ said: 'I have nothing to do with imbeciles, and they have nothing to do with

---

[398] I.e. they were of strong action, and resolution.
[399] I.e. out of intense anger for the sake of Allah's religion ﷻ. this Ḥadīth was narrated by Bukhārī in *al-Adab al-Mufrad,* and by Ibn Abī Shayba.

me.'[400] This means: 'I am not from the people of frivolity and silliness, and they are not from me.' Ṭabarānī and Bazzār also narrated it on the authority of Anas 鑾, with the addition: '...and I am not from falsehood, and falsehood is not from me.'[401]

Bukhārī and Muslim narrated that Anas 鑾 said: 'The Prophet 鑾 would joke with us, even saying to a brother of mine: "O Abū ʿUmayr, what did the bird do?"'[402]

Tirmidhī also narrated this Ḥadīth, saying:

> The *fiqh* (jurisprudential understanding) of this Ḥadīth is that the Prophet 鑾 was joking; and that he 鑾 gave a young child a nickname, calling him 'Abū ʿUmayr;' and that it is permissible to give a child a bird to play with, as long as he does not expose it to torment, hunger or thirst. The Prophet 鑾 said to him: 'O Abū ʿUmayr, what did the bird do?' because he had a pet bird that died, and he was sad, so the Prophet 鑾 cheered him up by saying to him 'O Abū ʿUmayr, what did the bird do?'[403]

Tirmidhī narrated on the authority of Anas 鑾 that a man from the countryside named Zāhir used to give the Prophet 鑾 gifts from the countryside. The Prophet 鑾 used to give him provisions when he wanted to return to the countryside. Once the Prophet 鑾 said: 'Zāhir is our countryside, and we are his townsfolk!' The Prophet 鑾 loved Zāhir, and he was a deformed man. One day, the Prophet 鑾 went to him whilst he was selling his wares, and embraced him from the back, so he could not see him. 'Who is that?' said Zāhir. 'Let me go.'

---

[400] This means that the Prophet 鑾 uttered nothing but serious matters, and true speech.

[401] *Sharḥ al-Mawāhib*

[402] In Arabic the words have a pleasant rhyme to them. [t]

[403] People have derived many rulings from this Ḥadīth. Abū al-ʿAbbās b. al-Qāṣ of the Shāfiʿī school adduced more than one hundred, and devoted a whole volume to them. It is reported that Ibn al-Ṣabbāgh deduced four hundred beneficial lessons from the Ḥadīth. (*Al-Tarātīb*, vol.2)

Then, he looked round and recognised the Prophet 畿, and so he began to cleave his back to the chest of the Prophet 畿 when he recognised him. The Prophet 畿 began to say: 'Who will purchase this servant?' 'O Messenger of Allah,' Zāhir said, 'by Allah, you will find no demand for me!' The Prophet 畿 said: 'But in Allah's sight, you are not worthless.' (Or, he said: 'in Allah's sight, you are valuable.')

Abū Dāwūd narrates in his *Sunan* that 'Awf b. Mālik al-Ashja'ī said 畿: 'I went to the Messenger of Allah 畿 during the battle of Tabūk. He was in a small, leather tent. I greeted him, and he returned my greeting, and said: "Come in." I said: "All of me, O Messenger of Allah?" He 畿 replied: "All of you!" So I entered.'

Here are some examples of his 畿 joking: Anas 畿 reported that a man came to the Prophet 畿, requesting a mount. The Prophet 畿 said to him: 'I will give you the child of a she-camel.' 'O Messenger of Allah,' he replied, 'what will I do with the child of a she-camel?'[404] The Prophet 畿 replied: 'Aren't all camels the children of she-camels?'

A woman came, saying: 'O Messenger of Allah, grant me a camel!' He replied: 'Give her the child of a camel.' 'What will I do with that?' she said, 'will it bear me?' The Prophet 畿 replied: 'Does a camel produce any offspring other than a camel's child?'[405]

Ibn Bikār narrated, on the authority of Zayd b. Aslam, that a woman named Umm Ayman al-Ḥabashiyya came to the Messenger of Allah 畿, saying: 'My husband invites you.'

'Who is your husband,' he 畿 asked, 'is he the one with the white in his eyes?' 'There is no whiteness in his eyes,' she said. 'Indeed, there certainly is whiteness in his eyes,' he 畿 replied. 'No, by Allah,' she said. The Prophet 畿 said: 'Everyone has whiteness in their eyes!'[406]

---

[404] The man erroneously believed that he 畿 would give him an infant camel.

[405] Narrated by Tirmidhī, Abū Dāwūd, Aḥmad, and others. The great scholar Zurqānī said: 'The two incidents (of the man and the woman) occurred separately.'

[406] I.e. the white of the eye that surrounds the iris.

Then there is the story of his 👑 joking with the old woman: Tirmidhī narrated, on the authority of Ḥasan al-Baṣrī[407] 👑 that an old woman came to the Prophet 👑 and said: 'O Messenger of Allah, pray for me that I will enter Paradise.' He replied: 'O mother of so-and-so, no old woman will enter Paradise.' The woman turned to go, weeping, but then the Prophet 👑 recited: ❨We have created them in a new creation, and made them virgins; faithful lovers, equal in age.❩[408]

These Ḥadīth show the way he 👑 would joke to be convivial with those to whom he spoke, and to cheer them up, and make them happy, because joking should be cheery, relaxed behaviour with someone, without hurting their feelings. For this reason, the Ṣaḥāba 👑 would often joke with one another, as is narrated in *al-Adab al-Mufrad*, on the authority of Bakr b. ʿAbdullāh, who said: 'The companions of the Prophet 👑 used to throw melon seeds at one another; and when matters became serious, they were true men.'

As for the Ḥadīth related that seem to prohibit joking, such as the narration of Tirmidhī in his *Sunan*, on the authority of Ibn ʿAbbās 👑, that the Prophet 👑 said: 'Do not argue with your brother, and do not joke with him, and do not make him a promise and then break it,' this prohibition is understood to mean excessive joking, because it distracts one from remembering Allah, or thinking about religious duties; and because too much laughter hardens the heart, and too much joking can lead to enmity, hurt and rancour, and to young people disrespecting the elderly. ʿUmar 👑 said: 'He whose laughter is excessive has little dignity; and he who jokes is looked down upon,' i.e. if his joking is excessive.

---

[407] Ḥāfiẓ al-Tirmidhī said: 'This narration is *mursal* (the companion who related it is not mentioned); but there is another narration through (the companion) Anas 👑.

[408] Qurʾān 56:35-37. 'Lovers' here means women whose love for their husbands is pure. Allah will make all women in Paradise equal of age, and this is the meaning of the Prophet's 👑 joke that no old woman will enter Paradise. [t]

The Prophet's 🙵 prohibition of joking could also mean the kind of joking that causes hurt or sadness to others. Abū Dāwūd and Tirmidhī narrate in their *Sunan* collections, on the authority of 'Abdullāh b. al-Sā'ib, who heard it from his father, who heard from his grandfather that he heard the Messenger of Allah 🙵 say: 'Let one of you not take his brother's possessions, whether in play or in earnest; whoever takes his brother's staff, let him return it.'

Abū Dāwūd also narrated that 'Abd al-Raḥmān b. Abī Laylā said: 'The companions of Muḥammad 🙵 told me that they were travelling once with the Prophet 🙵, and a man from amongst them fell asleep, so one of them took hold of a rope he was carrying and pulled it, and startled him. The Messenger of Allah 🙵 said: "It is not allowed for a Muslim to frighten a Muslim."'[409]

On the Day of the Battle of the Trench, Zayd b. Thābit 🙵 was shifting soil with the Muslims, and fell asleep. 'Umāra b. Ḥazm 🙵 came and took his weapon without his knowing, and the Messenger of Allah 🙵 forbade him from doing so.

It is narrated on the authority of 'Āmir b. Rabī'a 🙵 that a man took another man's shoe and hid it as a joke. This was mentioned to the Messenger of Allah 🙵, who said: 'Do not alarm a Muslim, for to alarm a Muslim is a grave transgression.'[410]

Therefore, joking is praiseworthy between brothers and friends, as long as it is not hurtful, defamatory, slanderous, dishonouring to reputation or religion, or disdainful.

As for a man's joking with his wife and being amiable with her, it is praiseworthy and laudable; and it is from the characteristics of the Prophets, and the traits of the believers. 'Umar 🙵 said: 'A man should be like a child with his family; and if anything of his is threatened, he should become a man.'

---

[401] Zayn al-'Irāqī ascribed the Ḥadīth to Aḥmad and Ṭabarānī, and declared it to be sound. (*Fayḍ al-Qadīr*)

[410] Ḥāfiẓ al-Mundhirī said: 'It was narrated by Ṭabarānī and Ibn Ḥibbān.'

His Smile 鑿 when He Met His Companions and Spoke with them

The Messenger of Allah 鑿 would smile much when he met his companions and when he spoke to them, because of his affection and fondness for them. Jarīr b. 'Abdullāh 鑿 said: 'The Messenger of Allah 鑿 never once refused (to see) me after I entered Islam,[411] nor did he ever see me and fail to smile.'[412]

Imam Aḥmad narrated on the authority of Umm al-Dardā' 鑿 who said: 'Abū al-Dardā' would always smile when he spoke, and so I said to him: "Stop, for people say you are a madman!"[413] Abū al-Dardā' said: "I never saw or heard the Messenger of Allah 鑿 speak except that he smiled."' So, Abū al-Dardā' would smile when he spoke, following the example of the Messenger of Allah 鑿.

His Laugh 鑿

The companions of the Prophet 鑿 used to examine the characteristics of the Prophet 鑿, and his states and mannerisms, in order that they could emulate him.

An example of this is their examining his manner of laughing, and the things that would make him laugh, in order to discover those things that a Muslim is permitted to laugh at, and those things that he is not. This is because the Sacred Law permits laughter in some instances, and forbids it in others, and this cannot be adduced except by referring back to the example of the Messenger of Allah 鑿.

For the most part, his 鑿 laughter took the form of smiling: Tirmidhī and others narrated the Ḥadīth on the authority of Hind b. Abī Hāla 鑿 in which he described the Prophet 鑿, which included: 'His laughter was mostly smiles, revealing something

---

[411] I.e. 'he never prevented me from entering upon him if he was in his house, and I asked permission to enter.' (*Fatḥ al-Bārī*)
[412] Narrated by Tirmidhī.
[413] I.e. because of his smiling.

like hailstones.' This means that he 🌸 would laugh pleasantly, revealing his teeth, which were as shining white and pure as hailstones.

Tirmidhī also narrated that 'Abdullāh b. Ḥārith 🌸 said: 'The laugh of the Messenger of Allah 🌸 was nothing but a smile.'

It is narrated in the *Sunan* collection of Abū Dāwūd that 'Ā'isha 🌸 said: 'I never once saw the Messenger of Allah 🌸 laugh so raucously that I could see his tonsils; he would merely smile.'

Occasionally, he 🌸 would laugh so that his incisors could be seen: 'Āmir b. Sa'd reported that Sa'd b. Abī Waqqāṣ 🌸 said: 'I saw the Prophet 🌸 laugh on the day of the Battle of the Trench until his incisors were revealed.' 'Āmir said: 'I said to Sa'd: "What was his laugh like?" Sa'd replied: "There was a man who had a shield, and Sa'd was firing arrows. The man was saying such-and-such, and covering his forehead with the shield. Sa'd drew an arrow and aimed it at the man. When he (the idolater) lifted his head, Sa'd fired, and his arrow did not miss its mark (his forehead). The man fell, and kicked out his leg. The Prophet 🌸 laughed until his incisors were revealed." I said: "What was he laughing at?" He said: "At what he did with the man,"' i.e. what Sa'd did with the idolater, firing at him and hitting his mark despite his hiding behind his shield.

Muslim narrated in his *Ṣaḥīḥ* collection, on the authority of Ibn Mas'ūd 🌸, that the Messenger of Allah 🌸 said: 'I know who will be the last of the denizens of Hell to leave it, and the last of the denizens of Paradise to enter it: A man will come crawling out of Hell, and Allah 🌸 will say to him: "Go, and enter Paradise." He will come to it, and it will seem to him that it is full, so he will return, saying: "O my Lord, I found it full!" Allah 🌸 will say to him: "Go, and enter Paradise." He will come to it, and it will seem to him that it is full, so he will return, saying: "O my Lord, I found it full!" Allah will say: "Go, and enter Paradise, for you possess therein the like of the entire world, and ten more besides it!"[414]

---

[414] Or, he 🌸 said: '... "For you possess therein ten times the like of this world!"'

So he will say: "Do you mock me,[415] and you are the King?"' Ibn Masʿūd 🌺 said: 'Then, I saw the Messenger of Allah 🌺 laugh, until his incisors were revealed, saying: "This is the lowest ranked of the denizens of Paradise."'

Abū Dharr 🌺 reported that the Messenger of Allah 🌺 said: 'I know who will be the last of the denizens of Paradise to enter Paradise, and the last of the denizens of Hell to leave Hell: A man will be brought forth on the Day of Resurrection, and it will be said: "Show him his venial sins, and keep from him his grave sins." His venial sins will be shown to him, and it will be said: "You did such-and-such on such a day," and he will say: "Yes," unable to deny it, all the while anxious that his grave sins will be shown to him. It will then be said to him: "In place of every sin, you are granted a good deed!" He will say: "My Lord, I did other things that I do not see here!"' Abū Dharr 🌺 said: 'Then, I saw the Messenger of Allah 🌺 laugh, until his incisors were revealed."[416]

Imam Aḥmad narrated, on the authority of Umm Salama 🌺 that Abū Bakr 🌺 travelled to Buṣrā with Nuʿaymān 🌺 and Suwaybiṭ b. Ḥarmala 🌺, both of whom fought at Badr. Suwaybiṭ was in charge of the provisions, and Nuʿaymān said to him: 'Feed me.' Suwaybiṭ replied: 'Not until Abū Bakr comes.' Nuʿaymān was a joker, and a wag, and so he approached some people who were trading camels, and said to them: 'Would you like to purchase a young Arab servant?' They said they would. Nuʿaymān said: 'He has quite a mouth on him, and he might well say: "I am free;" so if you would leave him for this, then let me go now, and do not cheat me.' 'No,' they said, 'we will buy him.'

They purchased him for ten young she-camels, and he began to lead them away, saying: 'Take him, he is there.' Suwaybiṭ said: 'He is lying, I am a free man!' They said: 'He told us you would say as much,' and they put a rope around his neck and took him away. Abū Bakr came, and was told what had happened. He went to them with his companions, and returned the camels and recovered Suwaybiṭ. Then, they told the Prophet 🌺 about it, and he and his companions laughed heartily.

---

[415] Or 'do you laugh at me...'
[416] Narrated by Muslim, and Tirmidhī in *Shamāʾil*, and the wording is his.

The third volume of *al-Iṣāba* contains the report of Zubayr b. Bakkār, who said that no rare product would enter Medina except that Nuʿaymān would buy some of it, and then take it to the Prophet ﷺ, and present it to him as a gift. When the owner would come asking Nuʿaymān for payment, he would take him to the Prophet ﷺ, and say: 'O Messenger of Allah, pay him for his wares!' The Prophet ﷺ would say: 'Didn't you give it to me as a gift?' Nuʿaymān would reply: 'By Allah, I didn't have enough to pay for it, but I wanted you to have it.' The Prophet ﷺ would laugh, and have one of his companions pay for it.

He ﷺ would also laugh upon hearing humorous stories: Imam Aḥmad narrated in his *Musnad*, on the authority of ʿĀʾisha ﷺ that Salmā, the wife of Abū Rāfiʿ, a slave that the Prophet ﷺ freed, saying that Abū Rāfiʿ had beaten her. The Prophet ﷺ said: 'What happened between you and her?'

'She insulted me, O Messenger of Allah,' he said. 'How did you insult him, Salmā?' asked the Prophet ﷺ. She replied: 'I did not insult him at all; rather, when he broke wind whilst praying, I said to him: "O Abū Rāfiʿ, the Messenger of Allah ﷺ has commanded the believers to make ablutions if they break wind," and so he stood up and struck me.'

The Messenger of Allah ﷺ began to laugh, and said: 'O Abū Rāfiʿ, she did not exhort you except to what is good!'[417]

Ibn ʿUmar ﷺ was once asked if the companions of the Prophet ﷺ used to laugh. He said: 'Yes, and the faith in their hearts was like the mountains,' or perhaps he said: '...and the faith in their hearts was mightier than the mountains.'

As for the laughter not permitted by the Sacred Law: it is that which results from mocking people, and finding fault with them; or that which entails disrespect to the religion or the Muslims; or that which is excessive, because excessive laughter kills the spiritual heart by means of the heedlessness that it leads to, which causes the heart to harden, and also kills the physical heart by weakening it through excessive palpitations.

---

[417] See *Sharḥ al-Mawāhib*, 2:302.

Imam al-Ghazālī 🌸 said that excessive laughter and worldly joy is a deadly poison, which runs in the veins, and instils fear and sadness in the heart.

Bukhārī[418] and Ibn Mājah narrated, on the authority of Abū Hurayra 🌸, that the Prophet 🌸 said: 'Do not laugh excessively, for excessive laughter kills the heart.' There are many other Ḥadīth that affirm the prohibition of excessive laughter.

HIS KINDNESS 🌸 TO CHILDREN

Imam Aḥmad narrated with a sound chain of transmission, on the authority of ʿAbdullāh b. Ḥārith, that the Messenger of Allah 🌸 would line up ʿAbdullāh, and ʿUbayd Allah, and many of the children of ʿAbbās, and then say: 'Whoever wins the race to me will win such-and-such.'

They would race to him, and pile onto his back, and chest 🌸, and he would kiss them and hug them.[419] Ibn Ḥibbān narrated in his *Zawāʾid* that Anas 🌸 said: 'The Messenger of Allah 🌸 used to visit the Anṣār, and greet their children, and pat their heads.

Bukhārī[420] and Ṭabarānī narrated that Abū Hurayra 🌸 said: 'These, my two ears, heard, and these, my two eyes, saw the Messenger of Allah taking hold of the hands of Ḥasan or Ḥusayn, his feet on the Messenger of Allah's feet 🌸, and say to him: "Climb!" The boy climbed until his feet reached the chest of Allah's Messenger 🌸, who then said to him: "Pucker up!" and then kissed him. He then said: "O Allah, love him, for I love him!"'

This is also recorded in *al-Iṣāba*, which adds that the Prophet 🌸 recited a sing-song poem for the boy as he played with him: *khuzuqqah khuzuqqah, taraqqa ʿayna baqqah.* ('Step by step, climb, little one!')

ʿAbdullāh b. Jaʿfar 🌸 is reported to have said: 'When the Messenger of Allah 🌸 returned from a journey, he would be welcomed by the children of his household. Once he returned from a journey, and I was the first to be taken to him. He picked

---

[418] In *al-Adab al-Mufrad.*
[419] *Majmaʿ al-Zawāʾid,* 9:17
[420] In *al-Adab al-Mufrad.*

me up, and then one of the sons of Fāṭima 🕊 was brought to him, either Ḥasan or Ḥusayn, and he sat him down behind him, and the three of us entered Medina on the same mount.' ʿAbdullāh b. Jaʿfar also said to Ibn al-Zubayr: 'Do you remember when you, Ibn ʿAbbās, and I met the Messenger of Allah 🕊?' He said yes. ʿAbdullāh said: 'He picked us up, and left you!'

HIS PERFECT KINDNESS AND CONCERN 🕊 FOR ANYONE, MAN OR WOMAN, WHO ASKED HIM ABOUT THE RELIGION

Imam Muslim narrated that Abū Rifāʿa 🕊 said: 'I went to the Prophet 🕊 whilst he was giving a sermon, and said: "O Messenger of Allah, a stranger has come asking about his religion, for he does not know what his religion is." The Messenger of Allah 🕊 came to me, and left his sermon. A chair with iron-coated legs was brought, and the Messenger of Allah 🕊 sat on it, and began to teach me that which Allah had taught him. Then, he returned to his sermon, and finished it.'[421]

Bukhārī narrated that Anas 🕊 said: 'Once, while we were sitting with the Prophet 🕊 in the mosque, a man entered, riding a camel, which he made to kneel down in the mosque, and then tied. He then said to the people: "Which one of you is Muhammad?" The Prophet 🕊 was reclining amongst them. We said: "He is this white man, reclining here." The man said to him 🕊: "Son of ʿAbd al-Muṭṭalib!" the Prophet 🕊 answered him.

'The man said: "I will ask you strong questions, so do not be angry with me!" The Messenger of Allah 🕊 patted him gently, and said: "Ask about whatever occurs to you." He said: "I ask you by your Lord, and the Lord of those before you: did Allah send you to all humanity?" The Prophet 🕊 replied: "By Allah, yes!"'

Muslim's narration continues: 'The man said: "So who created the heavens?" The Prophet 🕊 said: "Allah." He said: "So who created the earth?" He 🕊 said: "Allah." He said: "So who raised these mountains, and placed within them what they contain?"

---

[421] See the strength of his concern for those who asked him 🕊 about the religion, and how he even left his sermon to teach the one who asked him!

He ﷺ said: "Allah." The man then said: "By the One who created the heavens, and the earth, and raised the mountains, and placed within them what He placed: did Allah send you?" He ﷺ said: "By Allah, yes!"

'The man then said (as Bukhārī's narration also has it): "I ask you by Allah: did Allah command you to pray[422] five prayers every day and night?" He ﷺ said: "By Allah, yes!" He then said: "I ask you by Allah: did Allah command you to fast this month of the year?" He ﷺ said: "By Allah, yes!" He then said: "I ask you by Allah: did Allah command you to take charity from the rich and divide it amongst the poor?" He ﷺ said: "By Allah, yes!" (In Muslim's narration, the man asked also about the pilgrimage.) Then, the man said: "I believe in what you have brought, and I am a messenger to those in my charge from my people, and I am Ḍimām b. Thaʿlaba, brother of Banī Saʿd b. Bakr!"'

Ibn ʿAbd al-Barr narrated, in his *al-Istīʿāb*, the biography of Asmāʾ bint Yazīd b. al-Sakan ﵂ mentioning therein that she was a woman of intellect and religion, and that it is narrated that she went to the Prophet ﷺ, and said: 'I am a messenger to those Muslim women in my charge: all of them say as I say, and think as I do: Allah sent you to the men, and the women, and so we believed in you, and followed you. We women are restricted, and confined to our houses, and the men are honoured with attending Friday prayers, and funerals, and fighting Jihād. When they go out to fight, we keep their wealth safe for them, and raise their children. Do we have a share in their reward, O Messenger of Allah?' The Messenger of Allah ﷺ turned his face to his companions, and said:

'Have you ever heard any woman ask a finer question about her religion than this?' 'Never, O Messenger of Allah,' they said. The Messenger of Allah ﷺ then said: 'Go, O Asmāʾ, and tell the women in your charge that being a faithful wife to your husbands, and seeking his pleasure, and meeting his approval, is equal to all that you mentioned that men do.' Asmāʾ left, proclaiming Allah's unity and magnificence, delighted with what the Messenger of Allah ﷺ had told her.

---

[422] Or 'that we pray,' and so on, in the first person plural.

This Ḥadīth is strengthened by the report of Ibn 'Abbās ﷺ, who said: 'A woman came to the Prophet ﷺ and said: '"O Messenger of Allah! I am an envoy of the women, sent to you. This Jihād that Allah has ordained for the men: if they are injured, they are rewarded; if they are killed, they are alive with their Lord, and provided for. We women serve them, so what do we gain by this?" The Messenger of Allah ﷺ said: "Pass on to any women that you meet: obedience to the husband, and acknowledging his rights, is equal to this; yet so few of you do it!"'[423]

Ṭabarānī narrated a Ḥadīth containing at the end: '...then, a woman came to the Prophet ﷺ, saying: "I am the messenger of the women to you, and there is not a woman amongst them, whether she knew it or not, that did not want me to come to you. Allah is the Lord of men and women, and their God; and you are the Messenger of Allah, to men and to women. Allah has ordained Jihād for men: if they are injured, they are rewarded; if they are martyred, they are alive with their Lord, and provided for. What act of worship is equal to these works of theirs?" The Prophet ﷺ said: "Obedience to husbands, and acknowledging their rights; yet so few of you do it!"'[424]

HE ﷺ WOULD REPAY GENEROSITY
WITH GREATER GENEROSITY

Bayhaqī[425] and Ibn Isḥāq narrated, on the authority of Abū Qatāda, that the delegation of Najāshī[426] came to the Prophet ﷺ, who began to serve them. His companions said to him: 'We will suffice you,' i.e. we will accommodate them and serve them for you. The Prophet ﷺ said: 'They were generous to our companions, and I would like to repay them.'

---

[423] Ḥāfiẓ al-Mundhirī said: 'It was narrated by Bazzār in this abridged form.'
[424] See Mundhirī's *Targhīb wal-Tarhīb*.
[425] In *al-Dalā'il*.
[426] The Negus.

Our Master the Messenger of Allah ﷺ would never let a good turn go unrewarded if it was offered to him by anyone. If someone did him a good turn, or did something nice for him, he would remind them of it, and repay it with something even better and nicer. This is adduced to by many sound reports:

It is narrated that ʿAmr b. Akhṭab al-Anṣārī ﷺ said: 'The Messenger of Allah ﷺ asked for some water to drink, so I brought him a cup of water. There was a hair in the cup, so I took it out.' The Prophet ﷺ said, in response to ʿAmr's fine action: 'O Allah, make him beautiful!' The narrator said: 'I saw ʿAmr when he was ninety years old, and his beard did not contain a single white hair.'

Abū Ayyūb al-Anṣārī ﷺ reported that the Messenger of Allah ﷺ was walking between al-Ṣafā and al-Marwa, and a feather fell into his beard. Abū Ayyūb rushed to take it out, and so the Prophet ﷺ said to him:

'May Allah remove from you that which you dislike.' See how the Prophet ﷺ did not overlook the good deed of the one who removed a single feather from him!

Muslim narrated that Rabīʿa b. Kaʿb al-Aslamī ﷺ said: 'Once, when I was staying with the Messenger of Allah ﷺ, I brought him water for his ablutions, and the other things he needed.[427] He said to me: "Ask."[428] I replied: "I request your company in Paradise." The Prophet ﷺ said: "Or [would you ask for] other than this?" I said: "It is as I said." He ﷺ said: "In that case, assist me for your own sake by offering much prostration."'

Ṭabarānī also narrated it in *al-Kabīr*, with this wording: Rabīʿa b. Kaʿb said: 'I used to serve the Prophet ﷺ by day. When night fell, I would go to the Messenger of Allah's ﷺ door, and sleep there, and I would hear him saying "Glory be to Allah, Glory be to Allah," until I tired, or sleep overcame me. One day, he ﷺ said to me: "O Rabīʿa, ask me, and I will grant it to you!" I said: "Let me think on it." I reflected that this world will perish, and is limited,

---

[427] I.e. his tooth stick, etc.

[428] I.e. 'ask for what you need in return for the service you have rendered.'

and so I said: "O Messenger of Allah, I ask that you beseech Allah to save me from Hell, and enter me into Paradise." The Messenger of Allah was silent for a moment, and then he said: "Who told you to say this?" "No one told me," I said, "but I realised that this world is limited, and it will perish; and you occupy the status before Allah that you do, so I wanted you to pray to Allah for me." He ﷺ said: "In that case, assist me for your own sake by offering much prostration."'[429]

HE ﷺ WOULD MISS HIS COMPANIONS

Tirmidhī and others narrated the Ḥadīth on the authority of Hind b. Abī Hāla ﷺ in which he described the Prophet ﷺ, which included: 'He ﷺ would miss his companions, and ask people about others...' as in the Ḥadīth which will be mentioned in full later, if Allah ﷻ wills it. This means that he ﷺ would ask after them when they were absent from him.

Abū Yaʿlā narrated, with a chain of transmission containing some weakness, that Anas ﷺ said: 'If the Prophet ﷺ missed a man from amongst his brethren for three days, he would ask after him. If he was away, he would pray for him; and if he was in town, he would go to him; and if he was sick, he would visit him.'[430]

HIS PRESERVATION ﷺ OF THE BONDS OF LOVE

Allah ﷻ said: ﴾And forget not kindness amongst yourselves; Allah sees all that you do.﴿[431] Bukhārī narrated in his Ṣaḥīḥ collection, in the chapter on preserving covenants:[432] ʿĀ'isha ﷺ said: 'I never envied any woman like I envied Khadīja, though she died three years before the Messenger of Allah ﷺ married me, because of

---

[429] See Mundhirī's *Targhīb*, the section on the excellence of prostration.
[430] See *al-Jāmiʿ al-Ṣaghīr* and *Majmaʿ al-Zawāʾid*.
[431] Qur'ān 2:237
[432] 'Upholding covenants' here means the preservation of respect, and honour, without negligence or disregard.

the way I heard him praise her. His Lord commanded him to give her glad tidings of a house of silver and gold in Paradise, and he 卐 used to slaughter sheep and give the meat to her friends.'

He 卐 would present the sheep's meat to our lady Khadīja's female friends and companions, out of deference to her, and in preservation of the bond of love between them. Ḥākim and Bayhaqī[433] narrated that 'Ā'isha 卐 said: 'An old woman came to the Prophet 卐, and he said to her: "How are you? How do you do?" She replied: "I am fine, my father and mother be sacrificed for you, O Messenger of Allah!" When she left, I said: "O Messenger of Allah! Why did you greet this old woman so?" He 卐 said: "O 'Ā'isha, she used to come to us in Khadīja's time, and preserving covenants is part of faith."' So he 卐 would preserve covenants, and the bonds of love.

Bukhārī narrated in *al-Adab al-Mufrad* that al-Ṭufayl said: 'I saw the Prophet 卐 in al-Ji'rāna[434] dividing meat, when I was still a young boy, carrying camel meat. A woman came to him, and he 卐 spread out his cloak for her to sit on. "Who is that?" I said. It was said: "She is his mother by breastfeeding,"' i.e. our lady Ḥalīma al-Saʿdiyya 卐.

Abū Dāwūd narrated that the Prophet's 卐 father by breastfeeding[435] came to him 卐, so he laid down one of his cloaks for him to sit on. Then, his mother by breastfeeding came, so he 卐 laid down part of his cloak from the other side for her to sit on. Then, his brother by breastfeeding came, so the Messenger of Allah 卐 stood for him, and bade him sit down before him.

HE 卐 WOULD KEEP HIS PROMISES

The Messenger of Allah 卐 would always keep his promises, even if it caused him hardship. Abū Dāwūd narrated that 'Abdullāh b. Abī al-Ḥamsā' said: 'I made a contract of sale with the Prophet 卐 before he was sent on his mission, and part of it remained, so I promised him I would meet him at a certain place to give it to

---

[433] In *al-Shuʿab.*
[434] A place in Mecca. [t]
[435] I.e. the husband of the woman who nursed him. [t]

him, but then I forgot. After three days, I remembered, I went to the place, and there he ﷺ was. He said: "My son, you have inconvenienced me! I have been here for three days awaiting you!"'

HIS GENEROUS VISITS ﷺ TO HIS COMPANIONS

The Messenger of Allah ﷺ used to visit his companions in order to honour them, and make them happy, and to benefit them with his guidance and teachings. 'Abdullāh b. Qays ﷺ said: 'The Messenger of Allah ﷺ would often visit the Anṣār, both privately and publicly. If it was a private visit, he would go to the man's house; if it was public, he would go to the mosque.'[436] Tirmidhī and Nasā'ī narrated that Anas ﷺ said: 'The Messenger of Allah ﷺ used to visit the Anṣār, and greet their children and pat their heads.'[437]

Bukhārī narrated in *al-Adab al-Mufrad*, in the chapter on visiting people and eating with them, that Anas b. Mālik ﷺ said: 'The Messenger of Allah ﷺ visited a family of the Anṣār, and ate with them.

'When he wanted to leave, he asked for a space in the house to be covered with a rug, and he prayed upon it, and supplicated for them.' He ﷺ did so in order that they would be blessed by his prayer, and by the place where he prayed, so that they could appoint this place as the permanent place of prayer in their house. Jubayr b. Muṭ'im reported that the Messenger of Allah ﷺ said: 'Come with us to Banū Waqāf, to visit Baṣīr (a blind man there).'[438]

---

[436] Narrated by Aḥmad; the chain contains a narrator who is not named, and the rest of the narrators are rigorously authenticated. (*Majma' al-Zawā'id*, 8:173)

[437] The Ḥadīth is rigorously authenticated, as shown in *Fayḍ al-Qadīr*.

[438] Ḥāfiẓ al-Haythamī said: 'It was narrated by Bazzār (and the wording is his), and by Ṭabarānī. The narrators of Bazzār's chain are all rigorously authenticated, except Ibrāhīm b. al-Mustamirr al-'Arūqī, who is trustworthy.' (8:174)

Imam Aḥmad narrated in the *Musnad*, on the authority of Qays b. Saʿd, who said: 'The Messenger of Allah ﷺ visited us at our house, and said: "Peace be upon you, and the mercy of Allah!" Saʿd answered silently.' Abū Dāwūd's narration continues that Qays continued: 'I said: "Will you not give the Messenger of Allah ﷺ leave to enter?" Saʿd said: "Leave him, so he will greet us further!" The Prophet ﷺ again said: "Peace be upon you, and the mercy of Allah!" Saʿd again answered silently. The Prophet ﷺ then repeated a third time: "Peace be upon you, and the mercy of Allah!" and then turned to leave.

'Saʿd followed him, saying: "O Messenger of Allah! I heard your greetings, and answered you silently, so that you would give us extra greetings." The Messenger of Allah ﷺ returned with Saʿd to the house, and asked him for some water to wash with. It was brought forth, and the Messenger of Allah ﷺ washed. Then, Saʿd gave him[439] a blanket decorated with saffron and yellow dye. The Messenger of Allah ﷺ wrapped himself up in it, and then raised his hands, and said: "O Allah, send Your blessings and mercy upon the family of Saʿd b. ʿUbāda!"

'Then, we ate. When the Messenger of Allah ﷺ wanted to leave, Saʿd presented him with a donkey saddled with velvet, and the Messenger of Allah ﷺ mounted it. Saʿd said: "O Qays, accompany the Messenger of Allah!" The Messenger of Allah ﷺ said to me: "Get on!" I declined, and so he said: "You can either get on, or go (back home)," so I went.'

Ibn Mandah's narration has it:[440] 'Saʿd sent his son Qays with the Messenger of Allah ﷺ to return the donkey. The Messenger of Allah ﷺ said to Saʿd: "Put him (i.e. Qays) in front of me (on the donkey)." Saʿd said: "Glory be to Allah! Will I put him in front of you, O Messenger of Allah?" The Prophet ﷺ said: "Yes! He has more right to his own donkey." Saʿd replied: "It is yours, O Messenger of Allah!" He ﷺ said: "So put him behind me."' See his perfect kindness and amiability, and how he preserved the rights of others, and gave everyone their due rights, may Allah bless him, and give him peace!

---

[439] Or he said 'they gave him.'
[440] As mentioned in *Sharḥ al-Mawāhib*.

HIS VISITS 🕮 TO THE WEAK AMONGST THE MUSLIMS IN GENERAL, AND THE PEOPLE OF THE LEDGE IN PARTICULAR

The Messenger of Allah 🕮 used to visit those Muslims who were weak, and treat them with kindness and compassion, and sit with them, and visit those of them who were sick, and attend their funerals. This was for them a source of honour and blessing, and consolation and beneficence, so that they would feel proud, and noble, and joyful.

Sahl b. Ḥunayf 🕮 said: 'The Messenger of Allah 🕮 would go to the weak from amongst the Muslims, and visit their sick, and witness their funerals.'[441]

Abū Saʿīd 🕮 said: 'I was sitting in a group of the weak from amongst the Muhājirūn (Immigrants), some of whom had been reduced to using each other as shields against their own nakedness; and someone was reciting the Qurʾān to us. The Messenger of Allah 🕮 came and stood before us. As he 🕮 stood before us, the reciter became silent. The Messenger of Allah 🕮 greeted us, and then said: "What were you doing?" We said: "We were listening to the Book of Allah 🕮." He said: "Praise be to Allah, who has made, from my community, those with whom I am commanded to keep myself, patiently."[442]

'He 🕮 sat down so he was at the same level as us, and then indicated with his hand, like this, so they formed a circle, turning their faces to him, and he said: "Rejoice, O you destitute of the Muhājirūn, with glad tidings of perfect light on the Day of Resurrection: you will enter Paradise half a day before the rich; and that is equal to five hundred years."'

The ledge[443] of the Prophet's mosque was a school for the destitute. The poverty-stricken from amongst the Ṣaḥāba who

---

[441] In *al-Jāmiʿ al-Ṣaghīr*, the author ascribes the Ḥadīth to Ṭabarānī, Abū Yaʿlā and Ḥākim, and indicated its rigorous authenticity.

[442] An allusion to Qurʾān 18:28. [t]

[443] Ar. *ṣuffa*, translated by some as 'bench;' but the appropriate translation is 'ledge,' Allah willing, as it is mentioned in several reports that it alluded to the ledge in the Prophet's 🕮 mosque beneath which shade was sought. (See *Lisān al-ʿArab*) [t]

had no family would go there and study the Qur'ān, and the affairs and rulings of the religion, and then spread throughout the land, teaching it to the people.

He 🪑 Would Miss His Companions at night, and Listen Out for their Voices reciting Qur'ān

Bukhārī and Muslim narrated on the authority of Abū Mūsā 🪑 that the Messenger of Allah 🪑 said: 'I know the voices of the Ash'arī companions at night when they enter; and I know where they each camp by their voices when reciting the Qur'ān at night, even if I did not see them when they made camp by day.'

Abū Dāwūd and Tirmidhī narrated that Abū Qatāda 🪑 said: 'The Prophet 🪑 went out one night, and came across Abū Bakr 🪑 praying with a low voice. He then passed by 'Umar b. al-Khaṭṭāb, who was praying with a loud recitation. When the two of them met with the Prophet 🪑, he said: "O Abū Bakr, I passed by you as you were praying with a low voice." Abū Bakr replied: "I spoke loudly enough for the One I addressed to hear me, O Messenger of Allah." The Prophet 🪑 said: "Raise your voice a little."[444]

'Then, he said to 'Umar: "I passed by you as you were praying with a loud voice." 'Umar said: "O Messenger of Allah, I rouse those who are sleepy, and keep Satan at bay!" The Prophet 🪑 said: "Lower your voice a little."'

'Abū Dāwūd's narration adds: 'The Prophet 🪑 then said: "And I heard you, O Bilāl, reciting first from one chapter, and then from another." Bilāl replied: "Beautiful speech, which Allah links together!" The Prophet 🪑 said: "All of you were correct."'

Abū Sa'īd 🪑 said: 'The Messenger of Allah made a spiritual retreat in the mosque, and heard them reciting out loud. He drew back the veil, and said: "All of you are addressing your Lord, so let not one of you disturb the other: do not raise your voices above one another while reciting." (Or, he 🪑 said: '...while praying.')[445]

---

[444] According to one narration.
[445] Narrated by Abū Dāwūd, Tirmidhī, and others.

The Messenger of Allah ✲ would patiently bear the coarseness of Bedouin folk, and would be kind to them, and meet their harshness with kindness, in order to make their faith firm, or to prevent them from being drawn to dissent. He would show them mercy, gentleness and informality, in order that they would not be repelled, or be scared off.

It is narrated in the *Ṣaḥīḥ* collections of Bukhārī and Muslim that Anas ✲ said: 'I was walking with the Messenger of Allah ✲, who was wearing a thick-seamed Ethiopian robe. A Bedouin man came across him, and tugged sharply on the robe, until I saw that the seam of the robe had left a mark on the Messenger of Allah's ✲ neck because of the violence of the tug. The Bedouin then said: "O Muḥammad, give me some of the wealth of Allah that you possess!" The Prophet ✲ looked at him, and smiled, and then ordered that his request should be granted.'

Abū Hurayra ✲ also related that a Bedouin came to the Messenger of Allah ✲ asking for something. The Messenger of Allah ✲ gave him something, and said to him: 'Have I been good to you?' The Bedouin man said: 'No, and you have not acted decently!' Some of the Muslims became angry, and made as if to stand up to him. The Messenger of Allah ✲ indicated to them that they should stand down.

When the Messenger of Allah stood to go home, he called the Bedouin to the house, and said: 'You only came to us to ask us, and we gave you; then you said what you said.' The Messenger of Allah ✲ then gave the Bedouin more, and said: 'Have I been good to you?' The Bedouin replied: 'Yes, so may Allah reward you with goodness of family and kinsfolk!' The Prophet ✲ said: 'You only came to us to ask us, and we gave you; then you said what you said, and this has provoked something in the souls of my companions; so when you come, say before them what you just said before me, so it leaves their hearts.' He said: 'Yes.'

When the Bedouin came, the Messenger of Allah ✲ said: 'Your companion came to us, and asked us, and we gave him, and he said what he said. We called him, and gave him, and he claimed to be satisfied. Is that right, O Bedouin?' The Bedouin said: 'Yes, may Allah reward you with goodness of family and kinsfolk!' The Prophet ﷺ said: 'The example of myself and this Bedouin is like the example of a man who had a camel that ran away, and the people followed it, but did naught but make it run further. The owner of the camel said to them: 'Go from between me and my camel, for I am gentler than you with it, and I know it better.' He then went to it, and took for it some vegetation, and called it, until it answered him. Then, he secured to it its saddle. Had I given you [what you wanted] when he said what he said, he would have gone to Hell.'"[446]

HIS GREAT HUMILITY ﷺ WITH HIS COMPANIONS

Allah ﷻ said: ﴾And lower your wing (in kindness and humility) to the believers who follow you.﴿[447] The Messenger of Allah ﷺ was the exemplar of humility and modesty, despite his high station and noble status. His humility ﷺ was manifested in all of his states, both public and private, and in all of his affairs, both in society and in the household.

One aspect of his ﷺ humility is that he would serve himself: 'Ā'isha ﷺ said: 'The Messenger of Allah ﷺ used to sew his own clothes, and repair his own shoes, and would carry out the tasks that men perform in their houses.'[448]

---

[446] Ḥāfiẓ Ibn Kathīr mentioned this Ḥadīth in his *Tafsīr*, at the end of Sūrat al-Tawba, and then said: 'It was narrated by Bazzār, and we are not aware of any other version narrated by him but this. It is a weak narration because of Ibrāhīm b. al-Ḥakam b. Abān, and Allah knows best.' The author of *Majmaʿ al-Zawāʾid* also narrated it, and pointed out its weakness. ʿAllāmah al-Khafājī said, 'This Ḥadīth was narrated by Bazzār and Abū al-Shaykh with a weak chain of transmission on the authority of Abū Hurayra ﷺ, and by Ibn Ḥibbān in his *Ṣaḥīḥ*, and by Ibn al-Jawzī in *al-Wafāʾ*.' (*Sharḥ al-Shifā*, 2:17)

[447] Qurʾān 26:215

[448] I.e. he ﷺ would busy himself with serving both the family and himself.

Another narration has it: 'He would draw the pail from the well, and clean his clothes, and milk his ewes, and serve himself 鸞.'[449]

Another aspect of his 鸞 humility is that he would ride donkeys, and not insist on horses in the manner of a king: Tirmidhī and others narrated that Anas 鸞 said: 'The Messenger of Allah 鸞 would visit the sick, and attend funerals, and ride upon donkeys, and accept people's invitations. On the day of (the war of) Banū Qurayẓa, he rode a donkey with a halter of palm fibres, and a saddle of palm fibres.'

Another aspect of his 鸞 humility is that he would seat behind him, on his mount, women from his household: Bukhārī narrated that Anas 鸞 said: 'We came back from Khaybar with the Messenger of Allah 鸞. I was sitting behind Abū Ṭalḥa on his mount, and one of the women from the household of the Messenger of Allah 鸞 was behind him on his mount. The camel began to stumble, and so I said: "The woman!"[450] and dismounted. The Messenger of Allah 鸞 said: "She is your mother,"[451] so I went on, and the Messenger of Allah 鸞 mounted. When he approached[452] Medina, he said: "We return, repentant worshippers, praising our Lord."'

He would also seat his companions behind him, and their children, and would not disdain such a thing, as luminaries and princes are wont to do. Bukhārī narrated, on the authority of

---

[449] This does not contradict the fact that he 鸞 would allow some of his companions to serve him, such as Anas and others, in order that they could have the honour of serving him, and gain his 鸞 blessings; this was not a case of grandiosity, or affectation. The Ḥadīth was narrated by Aḥmad and Ibn Ḥibbān, and Ibn Sa'd declared it to be rigorously authentic.

[450] I.e. 'The woman has fallen! Help us!'

[451] He 鸞 reminded them of the necessity of honouring her and showing her respect. The woman was Ṣafiyya bint Ḥuyayy, the Mother of the Believers 鸞.

[452] Or 'when he saw...'

Ibn 'Abbās 🕌, that the Messenger of Allah 🕌 came to Mecca, carrying Qutham (Ibn 'Abbās) in his hands, with Faḍl (his brother) behind him 🕌.[453]

Bukhārī and Muslim narrated in their *Ṣaḥīḥ* collections that Mu'ādh b. Jabal 🕌 said: 'I was behind the Prophet 🕌, nothing between me and him but the cantle[454] of the saddle. He 🕌 said: "O Mu'ādh b. Jabal!" "At your service, O Messenger of Allah," I replied. He 🕌 went on for a moment in silence, and then said: "O Mu'ādh b. Jabal!" "At your service, O Messenger of Allah," I replied. He 🕌 went on for a moment in silence, and then said again: "O Mu'ādh b. Jabal!" I replied: "At your service, O Messenger of Allah!" "Do you know what Allah's right is over the servants?" he 🕌 asked. I said: "Allah and His Messenger know better." He 🕌 said: "Allah's right over the servants is that they worship Him, and do not associate anything with Him." He 🕌 went on for a moment in silence, and then said: "O Mu'ādh b. Jabal!" I replied: "At your service, O Messenger of Allah!" "Do you know what the servants' right is over Allah, if they do this?" I said: "Allah and His Messenger know better." He 🕌 said: "That He does not punish them."'

Another aspect of his 🕌 humility is that he would walk with widows, poor people, and servants: Bukhārī and Muslim narrate that Anas 🕌 said: 'A woman who was mentally unstable came to the Prophet 🕌, and said: "I have a need of you!" He 🕌 replied: "Sit in any street in the city you wish, and I will sit with you until I fulfil your need."' Bukhārī also narrated that Anas 🕌 said: 'If a servant-girl ever took the hand of the Messenger of Allah 🕌, she would lead him wherever she wished.' Aḥmad's narration has it: '...she would lead him to her need,' i.e. so that he would fulfil her requirement himself 🕌. Nasā'ī narrated that Ibn Abī Awfā 🕌 said: 'The Messenger of Allah 🕌 used to remember Allah often and chat seldom, and lengthen the prayer and shorten the sermon. He did not disdain to walk with widow and poor people, and fulfil for them their needs.'

---

[453] Or perhaps it was the other way round (the narrator was unsure).

[454] The raised part of the back of the saddle, as opposed to the pommel, which is at the front.

Another example of his 🕊 humility was his honouring of Allah's Muslim servants: Imam Aḥmad and others narrated, on the authority of Ibn ʿAbbās 🕊, that the Prophet 🕊 went to the well and asked for water. They said: 'The people have dipped (their hands) into this water; we will bring you water from the house.' He 🕊 replied: 'I have no use for it; give me to drink from that which the people drink.'

See this great humility, from the possessor of such exalted character! He did not accept to be given water specially reserved for him 🕊, and insisted on drinking from the same water the people drank from, though their hands had plunged into it. Ibn ʿUmar 🕊 reported that the Prophet 🕊 would send for water from public pools and fountains,[455] and drink it, seeking the blessing of Muslims hands.[456]

Another example of his 🕊 humility: Tirmidhī and Abū Dāwūd narrated in their *Sunan* collections, as did others, that ʿUmar b. al-Khaṭṭāb 🕊 asked leave of the Messenger of Allah 🕊 to perform ʿUmra. He 🕊 gave him permission, and said: 'O brother, O ʿUmar, include me in your prayers!' (In one narration, he 🕊 said: '...do not forget me in your prayers!')

His Enjoining 🕊 of Humility

Imam Muslim narrated in part of a long Ḥadīth on the authority of ʿIyāḍ b. Ḥimār that the Messenger of Allah 🕊 said: 'And Allah Almighty revealed to me that you must all be humble, so that no one thinks themselves better than any other, and no one oppresses another.'

---

[455] Munāwī said: 'That is, the pool, ponds and fountains provided for people to use for ablutions.'

[456] Narrated by Ṭabarānī, and by Abū Nuʿaym in his *Ḥilya*, as is mentioned in *al-Jāmiʿ al-Ṣaghīr*. Ḥāfiẓ al-Haythamī said: 'The men of its chain are trustworthy, and they include ʿAbd al-ʿAzīz b. Abī Rawād, who is trustworthy, although said to be upon *irjāʾ* [i.e., of the Murjiʾā sect].

One of the clearest evidences of the Prophet's ﷺ humility is that when Allah ﷻ gave him the choice whether to be a Prophet-Servant or a Prophet-King, he chose servanthood, out of humility before Allah ﷻ.

Ṭabarānī narrated, with a sound chain of transmission, that Ibn ʿAbbās ﷺ said: 'One day, the Messenger of Allah ﷺ was with Jibrīl ﷺ on al-Ṣafā, when he ﷺ said: "O Jibrīl, by the One who sent you with the Truth, the family of Muḥammad has not left in its possession a single grain of flour, nor a handful of barley." As soon as he had spoken, he heard a tremendous crash in the heavens, which startled him, and so he ﷺ said: "Has Allah commanded the Resurrection to begin?" Jibrīl said: "No, but He commanded Isrāfīl to come to you when He heard your words." Isrāfīl came to him, and said: "Allah heard what you said, and He sent me to you with the keys of the earth's treasures, and commanded me to propose to you that I send with you the like of the mountains of Tihāma in emeralds, sapphires, gold and silver. If you wish it, you will be a Prophet-King; and if you wish it, you will be a Prophet-Servant." Jibrīl gestured to him to humble himself, so he said: "Rather, I will be a Prophet-Servant," repeating it three times.'

Mundhirī narrated it thus in *al-Targhīb*, commenting that Bayhaqī also narrated it in *al-Zuhd*, as did others, and that Ibn Ḥibbān narrated a shorter version of the Ḥadīth in his *Ṣaḥīḥ* collection, on the authority of Abū Hurayra ﷺ, as follows: 'Jibrīl sat with the Prophet ﷺ. He looked to the sky, and saw an angel there descending. Jibrīl said to him: "This angel has not descended, before this moment, since it was created."

'When the angel had descended, he said: "O Muḥammad, your Lord sent me to you: should I make you a king, or a servant and a messenger?" Jibrīl said to him: "Humble yourself before your Lord, O Muḥammad!" The Messenger of Allah ﷺ said to him: "No, rather a servant and a messenger."'[457]

---

[457] This is the narration in *al-Targhīb*, and the Ḥadīth with this wording is also narrated in the *Musnad* of Aḥmad, also on the authority of Abū

There is no doubt that there is a difference between kinghood and servanthood; for kinghood requires the maintenance of an army, and chamberlains and horses, and servants and palaces, and the seeking of revenge against any who expose the king's person to harm. As for servanthood, it required him to serve himself, and help his family, out of his ﷺ humility; and it required that he forgive and pardon those who harmed him ﷺ personally. If the sacraments of Allah were violated, however, he would seek recompense for the cause of Allah ﷻ.

For this reason, he ﷺ would say: 'I eat as a servant eats.'[458] He ﷺ resembled a servant in the way he sat, and in the manner he ate, and in his satisfaction with whatever there was to eat, out of humility before Allah ﷻ, and good etiquette with Him. He did not eat in a reclined position, like the people who seek comfort and repose in this world and its delights. He ﷺ would also say: 'I sit as a servant sits.' He did not sit as tyrant kings sit, for to adorn oneself with the characteristics of servanthood is the finest of human attributes.

'Ā'isha ﷺ reported that the Messenger of Allah ﷺ said: "'O 'Ā'isha, had I willed it, mountains of gold would have followed me! An angel came to me in the chamber of the Ka'ba, saying: 'Your Lord sends you greetings, and says to you that if you will, you will be a Prophet-King; and if you will, you will be a Prophet-Servant.' Jibrīl indicated that I should humble myself, and so I said: 'A Prophet-Servant.' After this, he would never eat whilst reclining, and would say: 'I eat as a servant eats, and I sit as a servant sits.'[459] Bayhaqī's narration adds: '...for I am nothing but a servant.'[460]

Hurayra. Ḥāfiẓ al-Haythamī said: 'It was narrated by Aḥmad, Bazzār, and Abū Ya'lā, and the men of the early part of its chain are rigorously authenticated.'

[458] 'Allāmah Munāwī said: 'The meaning of 'servant' here is a person who is meek and humble before his Lord ﷻ.'

[459] Narrated by Abū Ya'lā, Ibn Ḥibbān and Ibn Sa'd.

[460] Narrated on the authority of Yaḥyā b. Abī Kathīr without mention of the Ṣaḥābī who related it. (*Fayḍ al-Qadīr*)

Hannād's narration adds: 'For by the One in whose hand is my soul, if this world were equal to the weight of a single gnat's wing to Allah, He would not grant the disbeliever to drink a single glass.'[461]

Abū Dāwūd and Ibn Mājah narrate in their *Sunan* collections that 'Abdullāh b. Busr 🕮 said: 'The Prophet 🕮 had a large serving-dish called a *gharrā'*, which needed four men to carry it. When midmorning came,[462] and they prayed the midmorning prayer, this dish was brought out, filled with *tharīd*.[463] They gathered around it, and because there were so many, the Messenger of Allah 🕮 sat in a kneeling position. A Bedouin man said: "Why do you sit like this?" The Messenger of Allah 🕮 replied: "Allah made me a noble servant, and did not make me a headstrong tyrant." Then he 🕮 said: "Eat from the sides, and leave the top; you will find blessed increase thereby."'

Because our Master Muḥammad 🕮 was the greatest of all those who realised the station of servanthood and devotion to Allah 🕮, and the noblest of those for whom the lofty ranks of it were perfected, Allah 🕮 described him with the highest attributes of servanthood, saying: ❲And when the servant of Allah stood and beseeched Him, they fell upon him, almost cleaving together.❳[464]

He 🕮 also said, concerning the revelation of the scripture to him 🕮: ❲Praise be to Allah, who has revealed the Scripture unto his servant.❳[465] And He 🕮 said, concerning the discrimination between right and wrong, and victory, and clear proofs: ❲...if you believe in Allah, and in what We revealed unto Our servant on the Day of Discrimination, the day when the two forces met...❳[466]

Again He 🕮 said, concerning the challenge of the Qur'ān: ❲And if you are in doubt concerning what We have revealed to Our servant, produce a single chapter of the like thereof.❳[467]

---

[461] See (*Fayḍ al-Qadīr*, 1:55). The author said: 'Because of the Ḥadīth's numerous chains of transmission, Suyūṭī indicated that it is sound.'

[462] I.e. after the sun had risen completely.

[463] A dish of sopped bread, meat and broth.

[464] Qur'ān 72:19

[465] Qur'ān 18:1

[466] Qur'ān 8:41

[467] Qur'ān 2:23

Again He ﷺ said, concerning the Night Ascent: ❪Glory be to He who raised up His servant by night...❫[468]

For this reason he ﷺ was granted the position of *al-Wasīla*,[469] the highest station in Paradise, as he ﷺ said: '...and ask Allah to grant me *al-Wasīla*, for it is a (unique) place in Paradise, unsuitable for anyone but a servant; and I hope that I will be the one, so whomever asks Allah to grant me *al-Wasīla* will have my intercession of the Day of Resurrection.'[470]

---

[468] Qur'ān 17:1
[469] Literally 'the intermediary.'
[470] Narrated by Muslim in his *Ṣaḥīḥ*.

PART V
Our Master Muḥammad ﷺ
The Messenger of Mercy

His Great Forbearance and Mercy ﷺ

ALLAH ﷻ said: ❨But pardon them, and forgive. Allah loves those who are kind.❩[471] And He ﷻ said: ❨Pardon them, and ask forgiveness for them, and seek their advice in the conduct of affairs.❩[472] The Prophet ﷺ was a man of great forbearance, who would not return one ill-deed with another, but rather would pardon and forgive. He never once sought revenge for his own sake, unless Allah's sacraments were violated, in which case he would seek recompense for the sake of Allah's ﷻ cause.

Bukhārī, Muslim and Abū Dāwūd narrate that ʿĀʾisha ﷺ said: 'The Messenger of Allah ﷺ was never given the choice between two matters except that he chose the easier one, as long as it entailed no sin; if it entailed sin, he was the furthest person from it. The Messenger of Allah ﷺ never sought vengeance for his own sake, unless Allah's sacraments were violated, in which case he would avenge Allah's cause.'

His ﷺ forbearance extended to all of Allah's ﷻ creatures, even those who had shown him enmity, and hurt him ﷺ. At the battle of Uḥud, when his ﷺ tooth was broken, and his lower lip cut, and his noble forehead cleaved until blood ran from it, he mopped up the blood before it could touch the ground, saying: 'Were any of it to touch the ground, chastisement would be cast upon them

---

[471] Qurʾān 5:13
[472] Qurʾān 3:159

from the heavens.' This weighed heavily upon the Ṣaḥāba, and they said: 'If only you were to pray against them!' He ﷺ replied: 'I was not sent as a curser, rather was I sent as a preacher, and a mercy. O Allah! Forgive my people (one narration has it 'guide my people'), for they know not!'

An example of his ﷺ great forbearance and mercy is found in the story of Zayd b. Saʿna, one of the rabbis who embraced Islam when they recognised the amazing signs and clear indication of the Prophethood of our Master Muḥammad ﷺ. It is narrated that Zayd b. Saʿna said: 'There was not a single sign of Prophethood that I did not see it in Muḥammad's ﷺ face when I saw him, except two that I had not yet tested: *his forbearance will overcome his being mistreated*, and *severe mistreatment will only increase his forbearance*. I began to treat him kindly, so that I might keep his company, and thereby come to know his forbearance, and his manner when being mistreated. I bought some dates from him, deferring their delivery but paying in advance.

(Abū Nuʿaym's narration mentions that Zayd gave the Prophet ﷺ eighty miskals[473] of gold in return for a number of dates to be delivered at a specific time.) Two or three days before the day delivery was due, I went to Muḥammad ﷺ, and took hold of his shirt and the cloak around his neck, and looked at him angrily, and said: "Will you not give me my right, O Muḥammad? By Allah, you sons of ʿAbd al-Muṭṭalib are procrastinators!"

"Umar said: "What enemy of Allah speaks to the Messenger of Allah ﷺ in such a way as this?[474] By Allah, were I not wary of what would be lost,[475] I would strike your head with my sword!" The Messenger of Allah ﷺ looked at ʿUmar calmly, and smiled, then said: "He and I needed other than this from you, O ʿUmar: that you encourage me to repay properly, and that you encourage him to ask properly." Then, he ﷺ said: "Go, ʿUmar, and give him his due, and then add twenty Ṣāʿ[476] for alarming him."

---

[473] *Mithqāl*, an Arabic measurement, the metric equivalent of which is 4.235 grams. (Keller, *Reliance of the Traveller*, w15:1) [t]

[474] Abū Nuʿaym's narration has it that ʿUmar looked at Zayd, his eyes revolving in his head like the orbit of a celestial body.

[475] I.e. the truce between the Muslims and the Jews at the time.

[476] A measurement equivalent to 2.03 litres. (*Reliance of the Traveller*, w15:1) [t]

"Umar did as he was bid. I said: "O ʿUmar, I recognised all the signs of Prophethood in the face of the Messenger of Allah 🕮 when I looked at him, except two that I had not yet tested: *his forbearance will overcome his being mistreated,* and *severe mistreatment will only increase his forbearance.* I have tested him with them now, so bear witness, O ʿUmar, that I accept Allah as my Lord, and Islam as my religion, and Muḥammad 🕮 as my Prophet.'"

Another narration has it that Zayd said: 'Nothing drove me to do what you saw me do, O ʿUmar, except that I saw upon him all the attributes that are mentioned in the Torah except forbearance; so today I tested his forbearance, and found it to be in accordance with the Torah's description. I call you to bear witness that all of these dates, and half my wealth, are hereby given to the destitute Muslims.' Zayd accepted Islam, along with all the members of his household, except one old man who was conquered by misery.[477]

His 🕮 mercy and forbearance were manifested many times, when he bore the torment of those who hurt him, and the boorishness of those who were coarse with him, meeting all this with tolerance and forgiveness.

Abū Dāwūd narrated Abū Hurayra 🕮 said: 'The Messenger of Allah 🕮 spoke with us one day, and then stood, and told us to stand. We saw a Bedouin man approach him, and pull hard on his cloak, leaving a red mark on his neck; and it was a rough cloak. The Prophet 🕮 looked at the Bedouin, who said to him: "Load my two camels with food from the wealth of Allah that is in your possession, for you will not give me from your own wealth, or the wealth of your father!" The Prophet 🕮 said to him: "No, and I ask Allah's forgiveness."'[478]

The narration of Bayhaqī has it: 'The Prophet 🕮 was silent, and then said: "The wealth is Allah's wealth, and I am His servant. No, and I ask Allah's forgiveness, I will not give to you until you

---

[477] Narrated by Ṭabarānī, Ibn Mājah, Ḥākim, Bayhaqī, Abū al-Shaykh, and others, with a chain of transmission the men of whom are trustworthy, reported by ʿAbdullāh b. Salām on the authority of Zayd b. Saʿna. (*Sharḥ al-Mawāhib*)

[478] I.e. 'No, I will not give you from my own wealth, or the wealth of my father.'

give me my requital for pulling me as you did."[479] The Bedouin said: "By Allah, I will give you no requital." The Prophet ﷺ replied: "Why not?" He said: "Because you do not repay one ill-deed with another." The Prophet ﷺ smiled, and then called a man (one narration states it was 'Umar ﴾), and said to him: "Load his two camels with food: one camel with dates, the other with oats.'"[480]

So when he ﷺ was injured personally, he would forgive, and pardon; but when the sanctity of any part of Allah's religion was violated, he would avenge Allah's ﷻ cause. When his noble face was cleaved on the day of Uḥud, he forgave, saying: 'O Allah, guide my people, for they know not!' Yet, when they kept him from praying on the day of the Ditch, he did not pardon; rather, he ﷺ said: 'May Allah fill their houses, and their graves, with fire; for they have kept us from the middle prayer, until the sun has set...'[481]

HIS ANGER ﷺ FOR THE SAKE OF ALLAH ﷻ
AND HIS DEEP CONCERN FOR ALLAH'S COMMAND

The Prophet ﷺ would be angry for the sake of Allah ﷻ and pleased with what pleased Allah. No affair of this worldly life would ever make him angry, nor would he become angry for his own sake; rather, he would only become angry for the sake of his Lord ﷻ. The Ḥadīth of Hind b. Abī Hāla, narrated by Tirmidhī and others, includes this description of the Prophet ﷺ: 'The affairs of this worldly life would not make him angry; but if the truth was threatened, no one would recognise him, and nothing would quiet his anger until he had achieved justice. He would never become angry for his own sake, nor would he seek to avenge himself.'

---

[479] I.e. 'Allow me to do to you what you did to me, pulling my cloak violently.'

[480] Narrated by Abū Dāwūd and Bayhaqī, and the origin of the Ḥadīth is in Bukhārī's Ṣaḥīḥ.

[481] Narrated by Bukhārī and Muslim in their Ṣaḥīḥ collections.

If one looks into the things that caused the Prophet 🕋 to become angry, one will find that every single one of them was for the sake of Allah 🕋, and for the sake of His command, and the ascendancy of His religion, and in the cause of the truth He established.

One example of this is his 🕋 anger upon seeing a curtain decorated with illustrations of animate objects: Bukhārī and Muslim narrate that ʿĀʾisha 🕋 said: 'The Prophet 🕋 came to see me, and there was a curtain in the house decorated with pictures. His face filled with colour, and he took down the curtain and tore it up. The Prophet 🕋 said: "Some of the most severely punished on the Day of Resurrection will be those who fashion such pictures as these."'

Another example of this is his 🕋 anger upon hearing of any action that might frighten off a believer: Bukhārī, Muslim, and others narrate that Abū Masʿūd 🕋 said: 'A man came to the Prophet 🕋 and said: "O Messenger of Allah, I delay joining the dawn prayer because of so-and-so, as he makes the prayer too long for us." I never saw the Messenger of Allah 🕋 more angry in admonition than he was that day. He 🕋 said: "O people! Some of you are a cause of alienation! Whichever of you leads the people in prayer, let him be light; for amongst them are the sick, and the elderly, and those who have needs."'

Another example of this is his 🕋 anger when he saw people spitting towards the front of the mosque, as Bukhārī and Muslim narrated in their *Ṣaḥīḥ* collections. A Muslim must be vigilant in preserving the cleanliness and sanctity of mosques; and it is not permissible to throw rubbish in them, or spit in them, as was mentioned in the section on the Prophet's enjoining the upkeep of the cleanliness of the mosque.

Another example of this is his 🕋 anger at people overburdening and harassing others. Bukhārī in his *Ṣaḥīḥ* and others narrated that Zayd b. Thābit 🕋 said: 'The Messenger of Allah made a small chamber for himself out of palm reeds or mats. He came out to pray there (a non-obligatory prayer), and some men followed him, and prayed with him. Another night, they returned, and the Messenger of Allah 🕋 was late for them, and did not come out to them.[482] They raised their voices, and threw pebbles at the door. The Messenger of Allah ﷺ came out to them in an angered state, and said: "You kept up your action until I thought it would be written against you! Pray in your houses, for the best of a person's prayer is that which is in his house, except for the obligatory prayers."'

Ḥāfiẓ al-'Asqalānī says in *Fatḥ al-Bārī*:

> The apparent meaning is that his ﷺ anger was caused by their gathering without his instruction. They were not sufficed by the hint he gave them by not coming out to them; rather, they went too far by throwing pebbles at his door and following him. Or, his anger was caused because he delayed coming out because of his concern for them, so that the prayer would not seem to be obligatory upon them, but they thought otherwise.

THE SEVERITY OF HIS ANGER ﷺ NEVER DIVERTED HIM FROM THE TRUTH, AND UPRIGHT SPEECH AND CONDUCT

Anger causes turmoil in the soul, and alters the temperament. An angry person might be diverted from upright speech and conduct in such a situation. To this end, the Messenger of Allah ﷺ said: 'Teach, and make things easy; teach, and make things easy; teach, and make things easy. And if you become angry, be silent; and if you become angry, be silent; and if you become angry, be silent.'[483]

Allah ﷻ, however, protected His Prophet, our Master Muḥammad ﷺ from all of this, and so his anger did not divert him ﷺ from the truth, nor from absolute impartiality in all of his words and deeds. Abū Dāwūd narrated that 'Abdullāh b. 'Amr ﷺ said: 'I used to write down everything I heard from the Messenger of Allah ﷺ in order to commit to memory. Quraysh

---

[482] I.e. he ﷺ prayed in his house instead.
[483] Narrated by Aḥmad in his *Musnad* , and by Bukhārī in *al-Adab al-Mufrad*, on the authority of Ibn 'Abbās ﷺ.

prohibited me from doing so, saying: Would you write down everything you hear, when the Messenger of Allah 🌸 is a human being, who speaks both when angry and when content?" I stopped writing, and mentioned the matter to the Prophet 🌸. He 🌸 pointed to his mouth, and said: "Write, for by the One in whose hand is my soul, nothing comes from it but the truth.'" [484]

HIS GREAT GENEROSITY 🌸

Anas 🌸 said: 'The Messenger of Allah 🌸 was the best of people, and the most generous of people, and the bravest of people.' [485] These three attributes are of the essence of sublime character. He 🌸 was the finest of people in appearance and in character, and in beauty and perfection. His was the bravest of hearts; and he was the most generous of people, and the most beneficial of them to others. The generosity that characterised him was for naught but the sake of Allah 🌸, and out of a desire to please Him. For this reason, his 🌸 generosity was directed to certain matters, which included:

- Spending money on Jihād in the cause of Allah 🌸.
- Spending money on poor and needy people.
- Striving to unite the hearts of the believers.

Muslim narrated that Anas 🌸 said: 'The Messenger of Allah was never asked for anything except that he gave it. A man (Ṣafwān b. Umayya) came, and he 🌸 gave him all the sheep between two mountains. The man returned to his people, and said: "O my people, embrace Islam, for Muḥammad gives like one who does not fear poverty!'"

On the day of Ḥunayn, in order to open their hearts to Islam, the Prophet 🌸 gave each of the freed captives one thousand camels. One of those who were freed was Mālik b. 'Awf, who composed a poem of praise in his 🌸 honour.

---

[484] Dārimī's narration has it: 'He 🌸 said: "Write, for by the One in whose hand is my soul, nothing came from it but the truth."'
[485] Narrated by Bukhārī and Muslim.

Tirmidhī narrated, on the authority of Saʿīd b. al-Musīb, that Ṣafwān b. Umayya ﷺ said: 'The Messenger of Allah ﷺ gave me what he gave me, and he was the most hateful of people to me. He did not cease giving to me until he was the most beloved of people to me.'

Wāqidī narrated in his *Maghāzī* that Ṣafwān went around with the Prophet ﷺ examining the battle-spoils on the day of Ḥunayn, when they came upon a ravine filled with camels and sheep. Ṣafwān was impressed by it, and began to stare at it. The Prophet ﷺ said to him: 'Does this ravine please you, O Abū Wahb?' He replied: 'Yes.' The Prophet ﷺ said: 'It is yours, along with all that it contains.' Ṣafwān said: 'I testify that you are the Messenger of Allah, for none but a Prophet could be willing to do such a thing!'

An aspect of his generosity was that no one would ask him for anything he ﷺ had except that he would give it to them, until he had nothing left. Tirmidhī narrated that the Prophet ﷺ was brought seventy thousand dirhams, which were laid out on a mat. He ﷺ then began to divide it, and did not refuse anyone who asked for it until he had gone through it all.

It is narrated that Abū Saʿīd ﷺ said: 'Some people from the Anṣār asked something of the Messenger of Allah ﷺ, and he gave them what they asked. Then, they asked him again, so he ﷺ gave them what they asked. Then, they asked him again, so he ﷺ gave them what they asked, until all he had was spent, whereupon he ﷺ said: 'Whatever good I possess, I would not keep it from you. Whosoever seeks modesty will be granted modesty by Allah, and whosoever is satisfied with his lot will be sufficed by Allah, and whosoever acts patiently will be granted patience by Allah; and no one was ever given any gift finer and more abundant for him than patience.'[486]

The Prophet ﷺ was generous in spirit, and would give to beggars himself, not too proud to go to a beggar and give them charity. He would not entrust the delivery of his charity to someone else; rather, he would be the one to put the charity in the beggar's hand.

---

[486] Narrated in all of the six major collections.

Ibn Mājah narrated that ʿĀʾisha ﵞ said: 'I never saw the Messenger of Allah ﷺ entrust the delivery of his charity to another person, so that he would be the one to put it in the beggar's hand.'

Ibn Saʿd narrated that Ziyād, the freed servant of ʿAyyāsh b. Abī Rabīʿa said: 'There were two things that the Messenger of Allah ﷺ would never appoint anyone else to see to: his water for ablutions when he rose at night; and the beggar, to whom he ﷺ would give in person.'[487]

Another aspect of his generosity ﷺ was that if he did not have enough to meet the need of a person, he would tell him to go and borrow it in his ﷺ name. Bayhaqī and Abū Dāwūd narrate in their *Sunan* collections that ʿAbdullāh al-Hawzanī said: 'I met Bilāl, and said to him: "O Bilāl, tell me how the Messenger of Allah ﷺ used to spend." He replied: "He had nothing, and I was the one who would arrange his financial affairs, from the time Allah ﷺ sent him until he passed away. If there ever came to him ﷺ a Muslim person whom he ﷺ saw to be without clothing, he would have me go and borrow some money to clothe and feed them."'

Tirmidhī narrated on the authority of ʿUmar b. al-Khaṭṭāb ﵞ that a man came to the Prophet ﷺ and asked him to give him something. The Prophet ﷺ said: 'I have nothing, but buy something in my name, and when I get something, I will pay for it.' 'O Messenger of Allah,' said ʿUmar, 'you gave to him! Allah did not make you responsible for what you have not the means to do!' The Prophet ﷺ did not like what ʿUmar said, and so a man of the Anṣār said: 'O Messenger of Allah, spend, and do not fear any decrease from the Possessor of the Throne!' The Messenger of Allah ﷺ smiled, and his face showed delight in what the Anṣārī had said. Then, he ﷺ replied: 'This is what I was commanded with.'

What is more, his ﷺ great generosity entailed that he never once said no to any request. Tirmidhī narrated that Jābir ﵞ said: 'The Messenger of Allah was never asked for anything to which he said no.'

---

[487] See *al-Tarātīb*, 1:31.

Bukhārī and Muslim narrate in their *Ṣaḥīḥ* collections that Ibn 'Abbās 🌿 said: 'The Messenger of Allah 🌿 was the most generous of people, and he would be at his most generous during Ramaḍān, when he met with Jibrīl, who would come to him every night of Ramaḍān to study the Qur'ān with him. Indeed, the Messenger of Allah 🌿 was more generous in bestowing goodness than the very wind.'

From all of this and more, it is clear to every person of sagacity that the Prophet 🌿 was the most generous of Allah's 🌿 creation, and his generosity was not surpassed, nor equalled, nor even approached. His munificence was such that he 🌿 would sometimes spend money on the poor and needy, and sometimes in Allah's cause and on Jihād, and sometimes would soften hearts by giving such gifts that would outdo kings. He 🌿 would give all of this, until there was not left for him even the sustenance of a single night, so that both he 🌿 and his wives would go hungry; and they chose this when he gave them the choice, and they were happy with it. Because of the severity of his hunger, he 🌿 would sometimes have to fasten stones to his stomach, as is confirmed by the Ḥadīth narrated by Tirmidhī and others, as will be mentioned later, if Allah 🌿 wills it. Due to all this, he 🌿 was truly the most generous of people, as Ibn 'Abbās 🌿 described him, saying: 'The Messenger of Allah 🌿 was the most generous of people.'

HIS GREAT COURAGE 🌿

Our Master 'Alī 🌿 said, describing the Prophet 🌿: 'The Messenger of Allah 🌿 had the soundest of hearts, and the boldest. His speech was the most truthful of speech. He was the gentlest of people, and the kindest of them in companionship.'

If the Ṣaḥāba were ever exposed to danger, he 🌿 would rush to their aid, and protect them. Anas 🌿 said: 'The Messenger of Allah 🌿 was the best of people, and the most generous, and the bravest. The people of Medina were frightened one night (by a loud noise that they heard). Some people went out towards the source of the sound, and met the Messenger of Allah 🌿 on his way back, for he had gone before them to see what was going on. He 鑿 was riding bareback on one of Abū Ṭalḥa's horses, his sword round his neck, saying: "Do not worry."'[488]

Another narration has it that the horse was moving slowly, and when the Prophet 鑿 mounted it, it began to gallop, and he said: 'We found it to be swift!' Ibn 'Umar 鑿 is reported to have said: 'I never saw anyone braver, nor bolder, nor finer, nor pleasanter than the Messenger of Allah 鑿.'[489]

When the companions of the Prophet 鑿 were met with misfortune and surrounded by danger, they would take refuge by his noble side, and seek the shelter of his 鑿 impenetrable protection. Our Master 'Alī 鑿 said: 'When times became hard, and eyes became red, we would seek the protection of the Messenger of Allah 鑿, and no one would be closer to the enemy than he. On the day of Badr, we sought the Prophet's 鑿 shelter, and he was the closest of us to the enemy, and on that day he was amongst the bravest of people in the face of the enemy.' Muslim narrates in his *Ṣaḥīḥ* collection that Barā' b. 'Āzib used to say: 'The brave man is the one who would be willing to stay close to the Prophet 鑿 when he approached the enemy.'[490]

He stood firm on the day of Ḥunayn 鑿, and strengthened the hearts of the Ṣaḥāba, and approached the ranks of the enemy on his mule, neither concerned nor hesitant, and said, with complete boldness and certainty: *I am the Prophet, no lie! I am the scion of 'Abd al-Muṭṭalib!* [491] That is, 'I am not a liar, who will be put to flight; I am the truthful Prophet, aided by Allah's 鑿 aid and succour, completely sure of His 鑿 might, and His power and succour!'

Bayhaqī narrated in *al-Dalā'il* on the authority of 'Urwa b. al-Zubayr[492] that on the day of Uḥud, the idolater Ubayy b. Khalaf

---

[488] Narrated by Bukhārī and Muslim.

[489] Narrated by Aḥmad and others.

[490] I.e. the bravest of Muslims in battle were the ones who stayed close to the Prophet 鑿 in the midst of battle, because he would be so close to the enemy.

[491] Mundhirī ascribed it in *al-Targhīb* to Imam Muslim, Abū Dāwūd, and Tirmidhī.

[492] 'Allāmah al-Khafājī said: 'This Ḥadīth is rigorously authentic; it was narrated by Bayhaqī on the authority of 'Urwa and Sa'īd b. al-Musīb as a

said: 'Where is Muḥammad? Let me survive not if he survives!' Ubayy had said to the Prophet 🕊 when he ransomed (his son) on the day of Badr: 'I have a horse that I feed every day on many measures of corn, upon which I will slay you.' The Prophet 🕊 replied: 'It is I who will slay you, if Allah wills.'

When Ubayy saw the Prophet 🕊 on the day of Uḥud, he spurred his horse towards him 🕊, and some men from amongst the Muslims opposed him. The Messenger of Allah 🕊 said: 'Stand aside, and do not come between me and Ubayy b. Khalaf!' The Prophet 🕊 then took a spear from the companion Ḥārith b. al-Ṣimma, and leapt forward with it. Ubayy and the idolaters around him scattered like flies from a camel's back, and the Prophet 🕊 faced Ubayy b. Khalaf, the spear in his hand, and thrust him in the neck with a thrust that made him sway atop his horse several times; and it is said that he broke one of his ribs. Ubayy returned to Quraysh, saying: 'Muḥammad 🕊 has killed me!' They said to him: 'You are fine.' Ubayy replied: 'If what afflicts me now were to afflict all people, it would surely kill them! Did he not say: 'It is I who will slay you'? By Allah, had Muḥammad but spat upon me, he would have slain me!' Sure enough, Ubayy died upon their return to Mecca.

His Patience 🕊
in the Face of the Idolaters' Persecution;
and His Willingness to Bear All Manner of
Hardships for the Sake of Allah's Cause 🕊

Allah 🕊 said: ❴Be then, patient, as the strong-willed among the Messengers were patient; and hasten not for their sake.❵[493]

The patience of the Messenger of Allah 🕊 for the sake of Allah's 🕊 cause was beyond that of the most patient of people; and the forbearance he 🕊 showed in the face of the persecution of his detractors was above the forbearance of all sentient beings.

---

mursal narration, and by ʿAbd al-Razzāq in his *Muṣnaf*, and by Wāqidī in his *Maghāzī*, and by Ibn Saʿd in his *Ṭabaqāt*.(*Sharḥ al-Shifā*)
[493] Qurʾān 46:35

How severe was the harsh, shameless treatment he ﷺ received from the impudent villains of Quraysh! There is no doubt that vile and obscene language deeply impacts those of high moral rectitude, and affects them more than it does others; and acts of persecution work upon their souls much more than they do upon those who have no morals or manners. If this is so, then what about the disposition of our Master, the Messenger of Allah ﷺ, which is the embodiment of all perfections and virtues, and the source of them; and what about the effect their offensive language and acts of persecution would have on him ﷺ?

Imam Aḥmad and Tirmidhī narrate on the authority of Anas ﷺ that the Messenger of Allah ﷺ said: 'I have been frightened in Allah's cause as no other has been frightened; and I have been hurt in Allah's cause as no other has been hurt; and I have been visited by thirty people in a single night and day, and neither I nor Bilāl had any food for a needy person to eat, save something concealed under Bilāl's armpit.'[494]

The idolaters would confront him ﷺ with enmity, and all forms of persecution, in their hordes, and their groups, and individually, involving even their women and children.

Ṭabarānī narrated that Ḥārith b. Ḥārith said: 'I said to my father: "What is this horde?" He replied: "It is a tribe who have gathered against one of their own." We went down, and there we found the Messenger of Allah ﷺ, calling the people to the Oneness of Allah ﷺ, and to faith; and they were rejecting him, and persecuting him, until midday arrived and they dispersed from around him. A woman approached, her breast exposed, carrying a vessel of water and a cloth. He ﷺ took them from her, and drank and made ablutions, and then raised his head, and said: "Daughter, cover your breast, and worry not about your father." I said: "Who is this?" They replied: "It is Zaynab, his daughter."'[495]

---

[494] Mundhirī said: 'It was narrated by Tirmidhī and Ibn Ḥibbān in his *Ṣaḥīḥ*, and Tirmidhī declared it to be rigorously authentic.' (*Al-Targhīb wal-Tarhīb*)
[495] Ḥāfiẓ al-Haythamī said: 'The men of its chain of transmission are trustworthy.'

It is reported that ʿUrwa b. al-Zubayr said to ʿAbdullāh b. ʿUmar ﷺ: 'What is the worst thing you saw Quraysh afflict the Messenger of Allah ﷺ with, of all the enmity they showed him?' He replied: 'I was amongst them when their nobles had gathered in the precinct, and said: "We have never seen the like of what we have borne from this man: he has ridiculed our aspirations, and insulted our forefathers, and criticised our religion, and divided our faction, and slighted our gods! We have borne from him a grave matter indeed!" Whilst they were in the midst of this, the Messenger of Allah ﷺ appeared to them, and approached on foot until he reached the pillar, and then passed by them, circumambulating the Sacred House.

'As he passed by them, they secretly disparaged him with some of his own words, and I recognised in his face that he had heard, and then he moved on. Then, when he passed by a second time, they disparaged him again, and I recognised it in his face that he had heard, and then he moved on. Then, when he passed by a third time, they disparaged him again. He ﷺ said: "Do you hear, O hordes of Quraysh? By He in whose hands is Muḥammad's soul, I bring you slaughter!"[496]

'The people were so shocked by his words that there was not a man amongst them upon whose head a bird did not land; until he of them who had been the most severe in abusing him ﷺ before began to appease him ﷺ,[497] with the best words he could muster, saying: "Go, O Abū Qāsim, go with honour; for by Allah, you are no fool!" The Messenger of Allah ﷺ went, and the next day they gathered in the precinct again, and I was among them. One of them said to another: "You mentioned what he had done to you, and what you had heard about him; and then, when he confronted you with what you disliked, you left him be?"

'Whilst they were in the midst of this, the Messenger of Allah ﷺ appeared to them, and they fell upon him in unison, and surrounded him, saying: "Are you the one who says such-and-such?" mentioning what they had heard, of his ﷺ criticising their gods, and their religion. The Messenger of Allah ﷺ said:

---

[496] Literally 'I have brought upon you slaughter.'
[497] I.e. he began to act kindly towards the Messenger of Allah ﷺ, out of fear for what he had said to them.

"Yes, I am the one who says this." I saw one of them take hold of his 🕮 cloak. Abū Bakr stood between them, saying: "Will you kill a man for saying *My Lord is Allah*?" Then, they left him be. That was the worst thing I saw Quraysh afflict the Messenger of Allah 🕮 with.'[498]

Ibn Masʿūd 🕮 is reported to have said: 'Once, the Messenger of Allah 🕮 was praying in the Sacred House, and Abū Jahl and his companions were sitting there. Abū Jahl had slaughtered a camel the day before, and he said to his companions: "Which of you will take the intestines of the camel of the tribe of so-and-so, and throw them onto Muḥammad's back as he prostrates?" The worst man of the lot, ʿUqba b. Abī Muʿayṭ, went and took it, and when the Prophet 🕮 prostrated, he threw them. They began to laugh, leaning upon one another. I was standing there watching; if only I had the strength,[499] I would have taken it off his 🕮 back.

'The Prophet 🕮 remained in prostration, not rising, until someone went and told Fāṭima, who came, and she was still a young girl at this time, and removed it from him 🕮, and then confronted them, and scolded them. When the Prophet 🕮 finished his prayer, he raised his voice and prayed against them. When he 🕮 prayed, he used to repeat his prayer three times. He 🕮 said: "O Allah, have at Abū Jahl b. Hishām, and ʿUtba b. Rabīʿa, and Shayba b. Rabīʿa, and Walīd b. ʿUtba, and Umayya b. Khalaf, and ʿUqba b. Abī Muʿayṭ!" And he 🕮 mentioned a seventh whose name I have forgotten. By He who sent Muḥammad 🕮 with the truth, I saw every one of those he mentioned cut down on the day of Badr, and dragged to the well!'[500]

When the Prophet's 🕮 uncle Abū Ṭālib died, the idolaters intensified their persecution, and set upon him with all their severity. The Prophet 🕮 decided to go to Ṭāʾif, in the hope that the tribe of Thaqīf would be a source of support and succour for him against his own people in Mecca.

---

[498] Ḥāfiẓ al-Haythamī said: 'Parts of this Ḥadīth are found in the *Ṣaḥīḥ* collections; it was narrated by Aḥmad, and Ibn Isḥāq made it clear that he had heard it, and the rest of the men of its chain of transmission are rigorously authenticated.' (*Majmaʿ al-Zawāʾid*, vol. 6)
[499] Meaning either physical strength, or strength of numbers.
[500] Narrated by Bukhārī and Muslim.

When he got there, however, they extended to him the worse possible welcome, and responded with the worst possible response. He only sought their aid, as Maqrīzī has said, because they were his relatives, and there was no enmity between them.

Bukhārī and Muslim narrate that ʿĀʾisha 🌸 said: 'I said: "O Messenger of Allah, was any day worse for you than the day of Uḥud?" He 🌸 replied: "I encountered from your people what I encountered; and the worst that I ever encountered from them was on the day of al-ʿAqaba, when I opened myself to Ibn ʿAbd Yālayl b. ʿAbd Kulāl, and he did not respond to me as I had hoped. I left, my head hanging in sorrow, and I did not recover until I had reached the Fox-horn,[501] whereupon I raised my head, and saw above me a cloud that was giving me shade.

'"I looked, and saw that within it was Jibrīl, who called me, saying: 'Allah Almighty has heard the words of your people to you, and how they have rejected you; and He has sent to you the angel of the mountain, whom you may command to do with them as you like.' He called the angel of the mountain, who greeted me, and said: 'O Muḥammad, Allah Almighty has heard the words of your people to you, and I am the angel of the mountain, whom He has sent to you, that you command me (Ṭabarānī's narration adds 'as you like'). If you desire it, I will cause the Akhshabayn[502] to tumble down upon them!'" He 🌸 said: "Rather, I have hope that from their progeny will come forth those who worship Allah, and associate nothing with Him."'

Abū Nuʿaym narrated in *al-Dalāʾil* that ʿUrwa b. al-Zubayr 🌸 said: 'Abū Ṭālib died, and the severity of the persecution of the Messenger of Allah increased, so he set out to Thaqīf, hoping they would give him shelter, and support him. He would meet three men from the leaders of Thaqīf, the brothers ʿAbd Yālayl b. ʿAmr, Khubayb b. ʿAmr, and Masʿūd b. ʿAmr. The Prophet 🌸 opened himself to them, and told them of his troubles, and of what his people had done to him. One of them said: "If Allah sent you with anything, I will steal the hangings from the Kaʿba!"

---

[501] A small mountain, used as the rendezvous point of the people of Najd, one day-and-night's journey from Mecca.
[502] The two mountains of Mecca, Abū Qubays and Qaʿīqaʿān.

'Another said: "By Allah, I will never speak another word to you again after this meeting! For, if you are a Messenger from Allah, you are far too noble that the likes of me should speak to you!"[503] The third one said: "Could Allah find none to send but you?"

'They made what he had said to them known throughout Thaqīf, and they gathered to ridicule the Messenger of Allah 🪶, and sat before him in two rows either side of the path he walked, picking up stones. Every time he lifted his foot, or put it down, they pelted it with stones, ridiculing and disparaging him. When he had left the two rows behind, his feet streaming with blood, the Prophet 🪶 made for a vineyard of theirs, and sought the shade of one of the vines. He sat at its root, sorrowful and in pain, his feet bleeding.'

The narrations of Ibn Isḥāq and Ṭabarānī mention that 'Abdullāh b. Jaʿfar 🪶 said: 'When Abū Ṭālib died, the Prophet 🪶 went on foot to Ṭā'if, and called them to Islam; but they did not answer his call, so he sought the shade of a vine, and prayed two cycles of prayer [raqʿatayn], then said: "O Allah, unto You I complain of my weakness, and my helplessness, and my lowliness before the people. O Most Merciful of the merciful! You are the Most Merciful of the merciful, and You are the Lord of the Oppressed. To whom do you entrust me? To a distant enemy, who despises me? Or to a near one, whom you have empowered against me? If You are not angry with me, I care not; but Your protection would be for me the broader way!

'"'I seek refuge in the light of Your noble countenance, by which the heavens and the earth are lit, and the darkness is illuminated, and the concerns of this world and the next are made right, lest Your wrath descend upon me, or Your anger beset me! Yet, Your pleasure will be sought until You are pleased, and there is no power and no might except through You.'"[504]

---

[503] Ibn Isḥāq added that he continued: "...and if you are lying against Allah, it does not befit me that I should speak to you."

[504] See details of all this in Zurqānī's Sharḥ al-Mawāhib.

The Messenger of Allah ﷺ was the most equitable of Allah's creatures with regard to the rights of Allah ﷻ, and the rights of Allah's servants. He maintained justice and supported the truth wherever it lay; whether with the weak or the strong, or the rich or the poor, or the old or the young, or the man or the woman, or the freeman or the slave.

Bukhārī and Muslim narrated (and the wording here is Bukhārī's) on the authority of 'Urwa that a woman stole something during the time of the Messenger of Allah ﷺ, at the conquest of Mecca, so her family went to Usāma b. Zayd to plead for his intercession. When Usāma spoke to him about her, the face of the Messenger of Allah ﷺ coloured (in anger), and he ﷺ said: 'Do you speak to me concerning one of the ordinances of Allah Almighty?' Usāma replied: 'Seek forgiveness for me, O Messenger of Allah!' That evening, the Messenger of Allah ﷺ stood and delivered a sermon. He praised Allah as He should be praised, and then said: 'The people[505] only came to ruin because if a nobleman from amongst them stole, they left him; but if a lowly person stole, they carried out his punishment. By He in whose hand is my soul, if Fāṭima, the daughter of Muḥammad, stole, I would amputate her hand!' Then, the Messenger of Allah ﷺ instructed that the woman's hand be amputated, and she made good her repentance afterwards, and went on to marry. 'Ā'isha ﷺ said: 'After that, she used to come to me, and I would mention her needs to the Messenger of Allah ﷺ.'[506]

Behold, O you of sagacity, his ﷺ great equity, and upright judgement! More than this, his ﷺ equity even extended to his enemies, to whom he would give their lawful rights without mitigation. Imam Aḥmad narrated that 'Abdullāh b. Abī Ḥadrad al-Aslamī owed four dirhams to a Jew, who appealed to the Messenger of Allah ﷺ to secure its repayment.

---

[505] I.e. the previous nations.

[506] Ḥāfiẓ al-Mundhirī also narrated it in *al-Targhīb* in an abridged form, ascribing it to Bukhārī, Muslim, and the authors of the four *Sunan* collections. (*Al-Targhīb wal-Tarhīb*, 3:247)

He ﷺ said to him: 'Pay him his due.' Ibn Abī Ḥadrad replied: 'I don't have it.' The Prophet ﷺ repeated three times: 'Pay him his due.' If the Messenger of Allah ﷺ said something three times, he would not change his mind.

Ibn Abī Ḥadrad went to the marketplace, removed his turban to use as a loincloth, and removed the cloak he had been wearing, selling it for four dirhams, which he used to pay back the Jew. An old woman passed by Ibn Abī Ḥadrad, and asked after him. He told her about what had happened, and so she gave him a cloak she had with her.[507]

Abū Hurayra ﷺ reported that the Messenger of Allah ﷺ owed a camel to a man,[508] who came to him to ask him to settle the debt. He spoke to him harshly, until some of the Ṣaḥāba present were on the brink of challenging him. The Prophet ﷺ said: 'Leave him, for the one who is owed has a right to speak.' Then, he ﷺ said: 'Give him (his due).' They called for a camel to be brought, but the only one they could find was of a better condition than the one owed. The Prophet ﷺ said: 'Give it to him.' The man said: 'You have reimbursed me in full; may Allah Almighty repay you in kind!' The Prophet ﷺ replied: 'The best of you is the one who repays in the best way.'[509]

The Prophet ﷺ would be sought out to give judgement even before his mission, because all recognised his equity and trustworthiness. Ibn Masʿūd ﷺ said: 'The Messenger of Allah ﷺ would be sought out to give judgement in the pre-Islamic time of ignorance.' Ibn Abī Shayba narrated, on the authority of Abū Rāfiʿ, that the Prophet ﷺ said: 'By Allah, I am reliable in the heavens, and reliable on earth.'[510]

---

[507] See *al-Iṣāba* (vol. 2) for the biography of ʿAbdullāh b. Abī Ḥadrad.

[508] Ibn Mājah reported that he was a Bedouin.

[509] Narrated by the authors of the five collections, except Abū Dāwūd. (*Jāmiʿ al-Uṣūl*)

[510] Or 'I am reliable in what I say about the heavens, and reliable in what I say about the earth.' See *al-Shifā* and its commentaries.

Allah ﷻ said: ⟨And we have not sent you except as a mercy to the worlds.⟩[511] He ﷺ is the Messenger of mercy, whom Allah ﷻ sent as a mercy to all created beings: a mercy to the believers, and a mercy to the disbelievers, and a mercy to the hypocrites; a mercy to all humanity, men women and children, and a mercy to the birds, and the animals. He is an all-embracing mercy to all of Allah's creation.

As for his mercy to the believers: it lay in his guiding them to happiness in this world and the next, and by the effort he extended on their behalf to improve the affairs of both their religious and worldly lives, and to warn them against that which would corrupt them, out of compassion and mercy for them, as Allah ﷻ said: ⟨With the believers he is compassionate, and merciful.⟩[512] Compassion entails that he ward off all evil, corruption, and harm; mercy entails that he brings all manner of goodness, virtue, and wellbeing.

Allah ﷻ placed him, by his compassion and mercy to the believers, in the position of being closer to them than their own selves. He ﷻ said: ⟨The Prophet is closer to the believers than their own selves.⟩[513] This means that he ﷺ is more compassionate and kinder to them, and more beneficial for them, than their own selves; and his command is better for them to follow than the commands of their own selves, so they must give them up for his ﷺ sake. For this reason, he ﷺ would teach this principle in his sermons and meetings, as was mentioned in the examination of his ﷺ speech and sermons.

Bukhārī narrated on the authority of Abū Hurayra ﷺ that the Prophet ﷺ said: 'There is not a single believer to whom I am not the closest of people in this world and the next. Read, if you will: ⟨The Prophet is closer to the believers than their own selves.⟩

---

[511] Qur'ān 21:107
[512] Qur'ān 9:128
[513] Qur'ān 33:6

So, if any believer leaves behind wealth, let whichever of his family remain inherit it; and if he leaves behind a debt, or a loss, or dependents, I am his patron.'

Aḥmad's narration on the authority of Jābir 靈 has it that the Prophet 靈 said: 'I am closer to every believer than his own self, so if any man dies leaving behind debt, it is for me; and whoever leaves behind wealth, it is for his heirs.'

As for his mercy to the hypocrites: it lay in their security from being fought, and captured, out of deference to the appearance of their adherence to Islam.

As for his mercy to the disbelievers: it lay in their being saved from annihilation in this world; for the previous communities, when Allah 靈 sent to them Messengers in whom they disbelieved, were visited by punishment that encompassed them all. Allah 靈 informed us about the people of Nūḥ, ʿĀd, Thamūd, Lūṭ, and others, and how punishment enveloped them, and how that which they had scorned before overwhelmed them.

As for the disbelievers of this Muḥammadan community, Allah spared them the encompassing punishment that would have annihilated them, just as the disbelievers of the previous communities were totally annihilated. This was a tribute to this noble Messenger 靈, whom Allah 靈 sent as a mercy to the worlds.

Ibn ʿAbbās 靈 said, commenting on Allah's word ❨And we have not sent you except as a mercy to the worlds❩: 'Whoever believes has gained mercy in this world and the next; and whoever does not believe has been spared that which afflicted the previous communities, of instantaneous punishment; of mutation, disgrace, and ignominy.'[514]

As for *some* of the disbelievers of this community being punished, it occurs, without doubt.

This understanding—that Allah 靈 will not punish the disbelievers of this Muḥammadan community with total annihilation, as was the case for the disbelievers before them—is

---

[514] Narrated by Ṭabarānī, Bayhaqī in *al-Dalāʾil*, Ibn Mardawayh, and others, as mentioned in *Tafsīr Ibn Kathīr* and elsewhere.

the understanding that the diligent scholars have taken from Allah's word: ❨And Allah would not punish them whilst you are amongst them; and Allah would not punish them whilst they yet seek forgiveness❩,[515] i.e. 'Allah would not punish them whilst you are sent as a Messenger to them.' The punishment that is negated here is absolute, all-encompassing punishment.

As for punishment specific to certain individuals or groups from amongst them, it occurs, as is borne out by Allah's word in the very next verse: ❨And why should Allah not punish them, when they bar off passage to the Sacred Mosque...?❩[516] This is the correct way to arrive at an understanding of the two verses, as the scholars have mentioned.

He ﷺ is the Messenger of mercy, and the Prophet of mercy, as is narrated in *Ṣaḥīḥ Muslim* on the authority of Abū Mūsā al-Ashʿarī ﷺ, who said: 'The Messenger of Allah ﷺ would name himself with many names, saying: "I am Muḥammad, and Aḥmad, and the Seal (of the Prophets), and the Gatherer, and the Prophet of Repentance, and the Prophet of Mercy."'

Muslim narrated on the authority of Abū Hurayra ﷺ that the Messenger of Allah ﷺ was asked to pray against the idolaters. He replied: 'I was not sent to curse; I was sent as a mercy.'

More than this, he ﷺ is the gift of mercy that Allah ﷻ gave to the world: Ṭabarānī and Bayhaqī (in *al-Dalā'il*) narrated, on the authority of Abū Hurayra ﷺ, that the Prophet ﷺ said: 'I am nothing but a gift of mercy.' Ṭabarānī's narration has it: 'I was sent as a gift of mercy.'[517]

HIS MERCY ﷺ WITH HIS FAMILY AND HOUSEHOLD

Muslim narrated in his *Ṣaḥīḥ*, on the authority of ʿAmr b. Saʿīd, that Anas ﷺ said: 'I never saw anyone more merciful with their household than the Messenger of Allah ﷺ. Ibrāhīm ﷺ[518] used to be nursed in a house in the elevated area of Medina. He ﷺ used to

---

[515] Qur'ān 8:33
[516] Qur'ān 8:34
[517] See Zurqānī's *Sharḥ al-Mawāhib*.
[518] The Prophet's ﷺ son ﷺ.

236

go, and we would go with him, and enter the house, from which smoke was rising (for his wet-nurse's husband was a blacksmith), and pick up his son and kiss him, and then go back out. When Ibrāhīm died, the Messenger of Allah ﷺ said: "Ibrāhīm is my son, and he died whilst still at the breast.[519] He had two wet-nurses, who will complete his nursing in Paradise."'[520]

An example of his ﷺ mercy with his family is that he would help them with the household chores, as was mentioned in the Ḥadīth of Aswad, who said: 'I asked ʿĀ'isha what the Prophet ﷺ used to do around the house. She replied: "He was at the service of his family; and when the time for the prayer came, he would go to pray."'

He ﷺ was not one of the oppressive men; rather, he ﷺ would often serve himself: It is narrated in the *Musnad* of Aḥmad, and elsewhere, that ʿĀ'isha ﷺ said: 'The Prophet ﷺ would sew his clothes, and cobble his shoes, and do all the work that men do in their houses.'

HIS MERCY ﷺ WITH CHILDREN

Bukhārī, Muslim and others narrate, on the authority of Anas ﷺ, that the Prophet ﷺ said: 'I sometimes begin to pray,[521] intending to lengthen it, and then hear the cries of a child, and so lighten the prayer, because I know the severity of his mother's angst.'

Another manifestation of his mercy with children is that he would pat their heads, and kiss them: It is narrated in the *Ṣaḥīḥ* collections of Bukhārī and Muslim that ʿĀ'isha ﷺ said: 'The Messenger of Allah ﷺ kissed Ḥasan and Ḥusayn, the sons of ʿAlī, whilst in the company of Aqraʿ b. Ḥābis al-Tamīmī. Aqraʿ said: "I have children, not one of whom I have ever kissed!" The Messenger of Allah ﷺ looked at him, and then said: "Those who do not show mercy will not be shown mercy."'

---

[519] I.e. at the breastfeeding age.
[520] I.e. they will complete his two years of suckling, for he died at the age of sixteen months, or seventeen months. (*Sharḥ al-Nawawī*)
[521] I.e. the communal prayer in the mosque.

It is also narrated in the *Ṣaḥīḥ* collections of Bukhārī and Muslim that ʿĀʾisha said: 'A Bedouin man came to the Messenger of Allah and said: "You kiss children, but we do not kiss them!" The Messenger of Allah replied: "Can I avail you aught if Allah has removed mercy from your heart?"' This means that those who have mercy in their hearts for children are driven by that to kiss them; and those whose hearts are bereft of mercy refuse to kiss them.

Bukhārī, Muslim and Tirmidhī narrate that Barāʾ said: 'I saw the Messenger of Allah with Ḥasan on his shoulder. He was saying: "O Allah, I love him, so love him!"' Tirmidhī narrated, on the authority of Anas, that the Prophet was asked who from amongst his household was the most beloved to him. He replied: 'Ḥasan and Ḥusayn.' And he used to say to Fāṭima: 'Call my sons to me!' and embrace them.

Another manifestation of his mercy with children, and his love for spreading joy amongst them, is that when the first crop of fruits were brought to him he would give them to any children who were present: Ṭabarānī narrated, on the authority of Ibn ʿAbbās, that when the Prophet was brought the first harvest of a fruit, he would place them on his eyes, and then on his lips, and say: 'O Allah, as You have shown us the first of it, show us the last of it!' Then, he would give it to any children that were present.[522]

Another manifestation of his mercy was when his eyes shed tears for the loss of his son Ibrāhīm: Anas reported that the Messenger of Allah entered upon his son Ibrāhīm when he was close to passing away. The Messenger of Allah's eyes began to shed tears. ʿAbd al-Raḥmān b. ʿAwf said to him: 'Is this you, O Messenger of Allah?' The Prophet replied: 'O Ibn ʿAwf, it is mercy!' Then, another tear fell, and he said: 'The eyes shed tears, and the heart grieves; yet we say not except that which pleases our Lord. O Ibrāhīm, for your loss we are deeply saddened!'[523]

---

[522] Ibn al-Sunnī also narrated it on the authority of Abū Hurayra. Ḥāfiẓ al-Haythamī said: 'It was narrated by Ṭabarānī in *al-Kabīr* and *al-Ṣaghīr*, and the men of the chain of transmission in *al-Ṣaghīr* are rigorously authenticated.'

[523] Narrated by Bukhārī; parts of the Ḥadīth are narrated by Muslim.

Usāma b. Zayd 🕊 reported that one of the nephews of the Messenger of Allah 🕊 was close to death. As the baby was handed to him 🕊, his eyes welled with tears. Sa'd said to him: 'What is this, O Messenger of Allah?' He 🕊 replied: 'It is mercy, which Allah placed in the hearts of His servants; and Allah only shows mercy to those of His servants who are merciful.'[524]

Another manifestation of his mercy 🕊 is his weeping for the severity of the illness some of his companions suffered: Bukhārī and Muslim narrate, on the authority of Ibn 'Umar 🕊, that the Messenger of Allah 🕊 visited Sa'd b. 'Ubāda, accompanied by 'Abd al-Raḥmān b. 'Awf, Sa'd b. Abī Waqqāṣ, and 'Abdullāh b. Mas'ūd 🕊. The Messenger of Allah 🕊 began to weep, and when the others saw his weeping, they too wept. The Prophet 🕊 said: 'Do you not hear? Allah does not punish for the tears of the eyes, or the sadness of the heart; rather, He punishes for this, or shows mercy,' and he pointed to his tongue.

Another manifestation of his 🕊 mercy is his weeping for the death of his companions: Tirmidhī narrated, on the authority of 'Ā'isha 🕊 that when 'Uthmān b. Maẓ'ūn died, the Messenger of Allah 🕊 kissed him, and wept. Ibn Sa'd narrated that 'Ā'isha 🕊 said: 'He kissed 'Uthmān b. Maẓ'ūn when he died, and I saw the Prophet's tears roll down 'Uthmān's cheek.'

Ibn al-Jawzī's narration in *al-Wafā'* has it that 'Ā'isha 🕊 said: 'When 'Uthmān b. Maẓ'ūn died, the Prophet 🕊 unwrapped the shroud from his face, and kissed him between the eyes, and wept a long while. When he had been lifted onto the bier, he 🕊 said: 'You are blessed, 'Uthmān! This world did not clothe you, nor did you seek its garb.'[525]

As for the mercy he 🕊 showed to the poor and the destitute, we have already mentioned the narration of Bukhārī, in which Anas 🕊 said: 'If a servant-girl ever took the Messenger of Allah's 🕊 hand, she would lead him wherever she wished.' Aḥmad's narration has it: '...she would lead him to her need,' that is, so that he would fulfil her requirement, whether buying her food, provisions, or the like.

---

[524] Agreed upon by Bukhārī and Muslim.
[525] *Jam' al-Wasā'il.*

Nasā'ī narrated that Ibn Abī Awfā ﷺ said: 'The Messenger of Allah ﷺ used to remember Allah often and chat seldom, and lengthen the prayer and shorten the sermon. He did not disdain to walk with widow and poor people, and fulfil for them their needs.' Sahl b. Ḥunayf ﷺ said: 'The Messenger of Allah ﷺ would go to the weak from amongst the Muslims, and visit their sick, and witness their funerals.'[526]

HIS MERCY ﷺ WITH ORPHANS

Allah ﷻ said: ❴As for the orphan, oppress him not.❵[527] The Prophet ﷺ would treat orphans well, and be kind to them, and enjoin their fostering and good treatment; and he clearly elucidated the merits of actions.

Bukhārī and others narrated on the authority of Sahl b. Saʿd ﷺ that the Messenger of Allah ﷺ said: 'I and the one who fosters the orphan will be like this in Paradise,' and he twisted his fingers together. Ibn Mājah narrated, on the authority of Abū Hurayra ﷺ, that the Prophet ﷺ said: 'The best of the houses of the Muslims is the one in which there resides an orphan who is well treated; and the worst of the houses of the Muslims is the one in which there resides on orphan who is abused.'

The Prophet ﷺ also described the virtue of the woman who, upon the death of her husband, devotes herself to raising her children, and does not marry: Abū Dāwūd narrated in his *Sunan* collection, on the authority of ʿAwf b. Mālik al-Ashjaʿī ﷺ, that the Messenger of Allah ﷺ said: 'I and the grey-cheeked woman[528] will be like this'—and he indicated his index and middle fingers—'on the day of judgement: the woman of high standing and beauty who loses her husband, and devotes herself to raising her children until they either reach adulthood, or die.'

---

[526] Narrated by Ṭabarānī, Abū Yaʿlā and Ḥakim.

[527] Qur'ān 93:9

[528] Mundhirī: 'This means the woman whose colour has darkened because of long widowhood, because she has devoted herself to her children, and not remarried, so has had no need to make herself up for her husband.' (*Al-Targhīb*)

Abū Hurayra 🕮 reported that a man complained to the Messenger of Allah 🕮 about the hardness of his heart. The Prophet 🕮 said to him: 'Pat the heads of the orphans, and feed the poor.'[529] Bukhārī and Muslim narrate, on the authority of Anas 🕮, that the Prophet 🕮 said: 'The one who strives for the sake of the widowed and the poor is akin to the one who fights Jihād in Allah's cause.'

Anas 🕮 added that he thought that the Prophet 🕮 also said: '...and like the one who stands in prayer without flagging, or the one who fasts without breaking.'

Ibn Mājah narrated it with the wording: 'The one who strives for the sake of the widowed and the poor is akin to the one who fights Jihād in Allah's cause, and the one who prays all night and fasts all day.'

HIS MERCY 🕮 WITH ANIMALS

The Prophet 🕮 would enjoin mercy to animals, and forbid their owners from starving them, wearing them out, making them carry loads constantly, overburdening them, or treating them in any way that caused them suffering.

Abū Dāwūd and Ibn Khuzayma narrated that Sahl b. al-Ḥanẓala 🕮 said: 'The Messenger of Allah 🕮 passed by a donkey that was severely emaciated. He 🕮 said: 'Be mindful of Allah where these beasts are concerned: take care of them when you ride them; and take care of them when you eat them.'

Imam Aḥmad and Abū Dāwūd narrate that 'Abdullāh b. Ja'far 🕮 said: 'The Messenger of Allah 🕮 let me ride behind him one day. He entered an orchard, belonging to a man of the Anṣār, in which there was a camel. When it saw the Prophet 🕮, it cried out, and its eyes shed tears. The Messenger of Allah 🕮 went to it, and patted its head, and it became quiet. He 🕮 said: "Who owns this camel? Whose camel is this?" A boy from the Anṣār approached, and so he 🕮 said to him: "Do you not fear Allah for the sake of this beast, which Allah has given you? He complained to me that

---

[529] Narrated by Aḥmad; Mundhirī declared the men of its chain of transmission to be rigorously authentic.

you starve him, and wear him out!'" So, we see that the Prophet 🕰 forbade the starving of animals, and wearing them out; whether by working them too hard, or by forcing them to carry heavier loads than they can manage.

Likewise, he 🕰 forbade overburdening of animals by stopping and sitting on them without any need: It is narrated in the *Musnad* of Imam Aḥmad, on the authority of Anas 🕰, that the Prophet 🕰 came upon a group of people, standing upon their mounts.

He said to them: 'Mount properly,[530] and dismount properly, and do not take them as chairs upon which to chat in the streets and marketplaces. Many a mount was better than he who mounted it, and more abundant in remembering Allah.'[531] So, we see that the Messenger of Allah 🕰 prohibited people from sitting on a mount whilst it is standing, in order to converse.

'Allāmah Munāwī said:

> The kind of standing that is prohibited here is that which is long, and needless. It is permissible at times of battle, and at the standing at 'Arafat,[532] and the like. The Ḥadīth also implies the necessity of the rider's making remembrance of Allah. Some of the people of truth have said that this lightens the burden for the mount.

'Abd al-Raḥmān b. 'Amr al-Sulamī 🕰 reported that the Prophet 🕰 said: 'Allah entrusts these beasts to you;'—he repeated it twice or three times—'so, if you travel upon them, give them time to rest.'

---

[530] 'Allāmah Munāwī said: '*Properly* here means without causing any hardship or fatigue. Haythamī said that one of Aḥmad's chains of transmission is composed of rigorously authentic narrators, except Sahl b. Mu'ādh, whom Ibn Ḥibbān trusted, although he has some weakness ascribed to him. Dhahabī said that Sahl was somewhat lenient in his narration. However, the Ḥadīth was narrated by means of several chains, and this strengthens it.'

[531] It is also narrated by Abū Ya'lā, Ṭabarānī, and Ḥākim in *al-Mustadrak*, which indicates its authenticity. (*Al-Jāmi' al-Ṣaghīr*)

[532] During the pilgrimage. [t]

It is narrated in the *Sunan* collection of Nasāʾī that ʿAbdullāh b. ʿAmr said: 'The Messenger of Allah ﷺ forbade the killing of frogs, saying: "Their croaking is glorification (of Allah)."'[533]

Ibn ʿUmar ﷺ reported that the Messenger of Allah ﷺ said: 'A woman entered Hell because of a cat that she tied up. She neither fed it, nor let it eat beasts from the floor.'[534]

He ﷺ also forbade setting animals upon one another, and baiting them: It is narrated in the *Sunan* collections of Abū Dāwūd and Tirmidhī that Ibn ʿAbbās ﷺ said: 'The Messenger of Allah ﷺ forbade the provocation of animals.'

HIS MERCY ﷺ WITH BIRDS

The Messenger of Allah ﷺ forbade people from frightening a bird by threatening its young, due to the depth of his ﷺ mercy: It is narrated in the *Sunan* collection of Abū Dāwūd that Abī Masʿūd ﷺ said: 'We were travelling with the Messenger of Allah ﷺ, and he went off to answer a call of nature. We saw a small bird with two chicks, and so we picked the chicks up. The bird began to flap her wings in agitation. The Prophet ﷺ came back, and said: "Who has caused this bird to fret about her brood? Give them back to her!" Then, he saw a hive of bees that we had burned, and said: "Who burned this?" We said: "We did." He said: "It is not for anyone to punish with fire but the Lord of the Fire."'

He ﷺ also forbade the killing of birds for sport, without any beneficial reason such as eating them: Nasāʾī and Ibn Ḥibbān narrated, on the authority of Sharīd ﷺ, that the Messenger of Allah ﷺ said: 'If anyone kills a sparrow, it will declaim before Allah on the Day of Resurrection, saying: "O my Lord! So-and-so killed me for mere sport, and did not kill me for any benefit!"'

Ibn ʿUmar ﷺ reported that the Prophet ﷺ said: 'No one will kill a sparrow or anything larger without just cause, but Allah will ask him about it on the Day of Resurrection.' Someone said:

---

[533] Ibn Kathīr also mentioned this Ḥadīth in his commentary on Allah's ﷻ word: ❲There is not a thing but glorifies His praise...❳ (Qurʾān 17:44)
[534] Narrated by Bukhārī, and others. 'Beasts from the floor' here means insects, birds and the like. (*Al-Targhīb wal-Tarhīb*)

'O Messenger of Allah, what is just cause?' He ﷺ replied: 'Just cause is that you slaughter it and eat it, and that you refrain from cutting off its head and throwing it around.'[535]

He ﷺ also enjoined gentleness and kindness when slaughtering animals: Ṭabarānī and others narrate, on the authority of Ibn ʿAbbās ☙, that a man lay a sheep down on its side[536] whilst still sharpening his knife. The Prophet ﷺ said to him: 'Do you wish to kill it twice? Would that you had sharpened your knife before laying it down!'[537]

He ﷺ also forbade the taking of any animal or living being as a target for archery: Bukhārī and Muslim narrated that Ibn ʿUmar ☙ once passed by a group of youths from Quraysh who were using a bird, or a chicken, as a target to shoot with arrows, giving every arrow that missed the mark to the bird's owner. When they saw Ibn ʿUmar, they scattered. Upon seeing this, Ibn ʿUmar said: 'Who did this? May Allah curse whoever did this, for the Messenger of Allah ﷺ cursed the one who takes any living being as a target!'

REFLECTIONS ON ALLAH'S WORD ❨AND WE HAVE NOT SENT YOU EXCEPT AS A MERCY TO THE WORLDS❩

Those who reflect on Allah's word ❨And we have not sent you except as a mercy to the worlds❩, and ponder the meanings of this noble verse, will be illuminated with the realisation that everything that the Muḥammadan Message brought and encompassed, of commandments and prohibitions, and acts of worship and social transactions, and conduct and morality, and

---

[535] Narrated by Nasāʾī and Ḥākim, who declared it rigorously authentic. (*Al-Targhīb wal-Tarhīb*)

[536] To slaughter it.

[537] Ḥāfiẓ al-Mundhirī said: 'It was narrated by Ṭabarānī in *al-Kabīr* and *al-Awṣaṭ*, and by Ḥākim (and the wording here is his), who declared it to be rigorously authentic according to the criteria of Bukhārī.'

rights and responsibilities, is all built upon the foundation of mercy to humanity. This extends even to the legal penalties and punishments that the Muḥammadan Message enjoined.

All of this is nothing but mercy to the worlds, and mercy to all nations and peoples, because in it lies protection against those who would immerse themselves in corruption and evil, and spread it amongst others. If any of a person's limbs becomes infected, it is a merciful act to remove the limb before the infection can spread to the rest of the body. Likewise, society as a whole can be compared to a single body in the eyes of the Sacred Law; yet this is not the place for a detailed exposition of this.

The essence of all this is that the Muḥammadan Message came with mercy, and for mercy's sake; and this is why the language of the verse is that of encompassment, so that the sagacious person could see that the entire content of this message, and all that it encompasses, is nothing but mercy to humanity, in this life and the next; and within it is their happiness, and their rectitude, and their success, in this life and the next. The Muḥammadan Message did not come to bring felicity, rectitude and success in the hereafter alone; it provided the means to them all, both in the life of this world, and in the hereafter.

For this reason, the Prophet ﷺ alerted the sagacious, the perceptive, and the wise to the position he ﷺ held with respect to the search for happiness and righteousness in the world, providing an analogy to elucidate this position by means of a tangible example: It is narrated in the *Musnad* of Imam Aḥmad ﷺ that Ibn ʿAbbās ﷺ said: 'The Messenger of Allah ﷺ was visited by two angels in his sleep. One of them sat at his feet, the other at his head. The one sitting at his feet said to the one at his head: "Draw a metaphor for this man and his community."

He replied: "A metaphor for this man and his community is that of a group of travellers who arrive at the brink of a desert wasteland, none of them possessing provisions enough to cross it, nor to return home. As they are in this state, a man comes to them wearing a fine cloak,[538] and says: 'Tell me, if I were to lead you to fruitful gardens and orchards, and refreshing pools, would

---

[538] The significance of the cloak is that it denotes a man of fine and noble standing, upon whom are present the signs of honesty and sincerity.

you follow me?' They say yes, so he takes them to fruitful gardens and refreshing pools, and they eat and drink until they are satisfied. He then says to them: 'Did I not find you in that state, and offer to lead you to fruitful gardens and refreshing pools, if you would follow me?' They say yes, and so he replies: 'Indeed, before you there is a pasture more plentiful than this, so follow me!' One group rises, saying: 'He is truthful, by Allah! Let us follow him;' another group says: 'We are satisfied with this and will remain here.'"[539]

The Messenger of Allah 🕌 came with a general message, which encompassed and fulfilled all human requirements, and guided to their felicity in this life and the next.

The true believers accepted all the principles of the Muḥammadan Message, in relation to both their worldly lives, and the hereafter, and so attained felicity from Allah in this life and the next. Others accepted the principles of the Muḥammadan Message only with regard to that which brought them benefit in their worldly lives. In doing so, they attained their share of happiness, comfort, and order in this world. They did not, however, accept that by which their afterlives were set right, and by which eternal felicity is obtained; and so they have no share of the hereafter. In addition to this, Allah's word ﴾And we have not sent you except as a mercy to the worlds﴿ encompasses the world of humanity, and the world of the jinn, and the world of the angels, and all other worlds that exist.

As for his 🕌 mercy for mankind: it can be found in the sum of what was said before about his mercy for all kinds of people.

As for the world of the jinn: their situation is akin to that of humanity, for he 🕌 was sent to the jinn, too, with a message of religious responsibility, and he delivered it to them, and issued them with commandments and prohibitions, and explained to them the message on many occasions.

---

[539] Narrated by Aḥmad, Ṭabarānī, and Bazzār with a sound chain of transmission; Ḥāfiẓ Ibn Kathīr also narrated it in his commentary on the last verses of Sūrat al-Tawba. (*Majmaʿ al-Zawāʾid*, 8:26)

Likewise, they flocked to him 鬱 and listened to him; the details of this can be found in our book *al-Īmān bil-Malā'ika wal-Baḥth Ḥawla 'Ālam al-Jinn*;[540] refer to it for evidence of all this.

As for his 鬱 mercy encompassing the world of the angels: It is agreed upon by the vast majority of scholars and people of knowledge, who explain it thus:

1. Either, he 鬱 was sent to them with a message containing religious responsibilities, and commandments and prohibitions, which many scholars of Ḥadīth and jurisprudence assert.[541]

2. Or, he 鬱 was sent to them with a message of ennoblement, so the generality of his mercy encompassed them, and by means of him they attained much knowledge, and many great secrets, from the scripture that Allah 鬱 sent down to him 鬱, and the revelations that He revealed to him. Allah 鬱 said: ❨Nay, it is nought but a reminder, so let whosoever wills pay heed to it; on honoured pages, exalted and purified, in the hands of scribes noble and diligent.❩[542] 'Scribes' here means the angels, for they recite that which Allah 鬱 permits them to of the noble Quran, recorded upon their own pages, and by means of this they increase their knowledge and understanding of Allah's majesty, glory and wisdom. Bukhārī and Muslim narrate, on the authority of 'Ā'isha 鬱 that the Messenger of Allah 鬱 said: 'Whoever recites the Quran adeptly is with the noble diligent scribes; and whoever recites the Quran with difficulty has two rewards.'

All this is only a summary we have made of the discussion of this noble verse, because we will discuss it further, Allah willing, in the second part of this book. There, we will examine the position that our Master Muḥammad 鬱 occupies in relation to the world, part of which is that he 鬱 came as a mercy to the worlds; the details of this will be found there, if Allah wills.

PRAISE BE TO ALLAH, LORD OF THE WORLDS

---

[540] 'Belief in the Angels, and a Study of the World of the Jinn'
[541] See *Sharḥ al-Zurqānī 'alā al-Mawāhib,* and Ālūsī's commentary on this verse, and elsewhere.
[542] Qur'ān 80:11-16

BIBLIOGRAPHY

* Ālūsī, *Tafsīr Rūḥ al-Maʿānī*
* Aḥmad b. Ḥanbal, *Musnad*
* Aḥmad b. Ḥanbal, *al-Zuhd*
* ʿAbdullāh b. Aḥmad, *Zawāʾid al-Musnad*
* Ibn Athīr, *Jāmiʿ al-Uṣūl*
* Abū Bakr b. al-ʿArabī, *Qānūn al-Taʾwīl*
* Ibn ʿAbd al-Barr, *al-Istīʿāb*
* Bayhaqī, *al-Dalāʾil*
* Bayhaqī, *al-Madkhal*
* Bayhaqī, *al-Shuʿab*
* Bayhaqī, *al-Zuhd*
* Bayjūrī, *Ḥāshiyat ʿalā al-Shamāʾil*
* Bazzār, *Musnad*
* Bukhārī, *al-Adab al-Mufrad*
* Bukhārī, *Ṣaḥīḥ*
* Dāraquṭnī, *Sunan*
* Daylamī, *Musnad al-Firdaws*
* Abū Dāwūd, *Sunan*
* Abū Dāwūd al-Ṭayālisī, *Musnad*
* Ḍiyāʾ al-Maqdīsī, *al-Mukhtāra*
* Dārimī, *Sunan*
* Haythamī, *Majmaʿ al-Zawāʾid*
* Ibn Ḥajar ʿAsqalānī, *Fatḥ al-Bārī*
* Ibn Ḥajar ʿAsqalānī, *al-Iṣāba*
* Ibn Ḥajar ʿAsqalānī, *al-Maṭālib al-ʿĀliya*
* Ibn Ḥajar al-Makkī, *Sharḥ al-Arbaʿīn al-Nawawiyya*
* Ḥākim, *al-Mustadrak*
* Ibn Hishām, *Sīra*
* Ibn Ḥibbān, *Ṣaḥīḥ*
* Qāḍī ʿIyāḍ, *al-Shifā*
* Ibn Isḥāq, *Sīra*
* Ibn al-Jawzī, *al-Wafāʾ bi-Akhbār al-Muṣṭafā*
* Ibn Kathīr, *Tafsīr*
* Ibn Kathīr, *al-Bidāya wal-Nihāya (Tārīkh Ibn Kathīr)*
* Kattānī, *al-Tarātīb al-Idāriyya*
* Khafājī, *Sharḥ al-Shifā*
* Ibn Khuzayma, *Ṣaḥīḥ*

* Ibn Mājah, *Sunan*
* Mālik b. Anas, *al-Muwaṭṭa'*
* Maqrīzī, *Khiṭaṭ*
* Munāwī, *Fayḍ al-Qadīr*
* Munāwī, *Sharḥ Shamā'il al-Tirmidhī*
* Mundhirī, *al-Targhīb wal-Tarhīb*
* Muslim, *Ṣaḥīḥ*
* Yūsuf al-Nabhānī, *al-Fatḥ al-Kabīr*
* Nawawī, *Sharḥ Ṣaḥīḥ Muslim*
* Nawawī, *Tahdhīb al-Asmā' wal-Lughāt*
* Nābulsī, *Sharḥ al-Ṭarīqat al-Muḥammadiyya*
* Nasā'ī, *Sunan*
* Abū Nu'aym, *al-Dalā'il*
* Abū Nu'aym, *Tārīkh Aṣbahān*
* Abū Nu'aym, *al-Ḥilya*
* 'Alī al-Qārī, *Jam' al-Wasā'il*
* 'Alī al-Qārī, *al-Mirqāt Sharḥ al-Mishkāt*
* 'Alī al-Qārī, *Sharḥ al-Shifā*
* Qasṭalānī, *al-Mawāhib*
* Ibn Rajab, *Jāmi' al-'Ulūm wal-Ḥikām*
* Rāghib al-Aṣbahānī, *Mufradāt al-Qur'ān*
* Ibn Ḥajar al-'Asqalānī, *al-Maṭālib al-'Āliya*
* Ibn Sa'd, *al-Ṭabaqāt*
* Sakhāwī, *al-Maqāṣid al-Ḥasana*
* Sanūsī, *Sharḥ al-Muqaddima*
* Muḥammad b. Yūsuf al-Shāmī, *al-Sīrat al-Shāmiyya*
* Ibn Abī Shayba, *Muṣannaf*
* Suhaylī, *al-Rawḍ al-Unuf*
* Ibn al-Sunnī, *'Amal Yawm wal-Layla*
* Suyūṭī, *al-Durr al-Manthūr*
* Suyūṭī, *al-Itqān*
* Suyūṭī, *al-Jāmi' al-Kabīr*
* Tabrīzī, *Mishkāt al-Maṣābīḥ*
* Ḥārith al-Tamīmī, *Musnad*
* Tirmidhī, *Shamā'il*
* Tirmidhī, *Sunan*
* Ṭabarānī, *Mu'jam al-Awṣaṭ*
* Ṭabarānī, *Mu'jam al-Kabīr*
* Ṭabarānī, *Mu'jam al-Ṣaghīr*

* Wāqidī, *Maghāzī*
* Zarkashī, *al-Burhān*
* Zurqānī, *Sharḥ ‘alā al-Mawāhib*
* Zurqānī, *Sharḥ al-Muwaṭṭa’*

Author's Bibliography

* Ḥawla Tafsīr Sūrat al-Fātiḥa
* Ḥawla Tafsīr Sūrat al-Ḥujurāt
* Ḥawla Tafsīr Sūrat Qāf
* Ḥawla Tafsīr Sūrat al-Mulk
* Ḥawla Tafsīr Sūrat al-Insān
* Ḥawla Tafsīr Sūrat al-‘Alaq
* Ḥawla Tafsīr Sūrat al-Kawthar
* Ḥawla Tafsīr Sūrat al-Ikhlāṣ
* Hadī al-Qur’ān al-Karīm ilā Ḥujjat al-Burhān
* Hadī al-Qur’ān ilā Ma‘rifat al-‘Ulūm wal-Tafakkur
* Tilāwat al-Qur’ān al-Majīd
* *Shahāda Lā Ilāha Illā Allāh, Muḥammad Rasūl Allāh* ﷺ
* **Sayyidunā Muḥammad Rasūl Allāh** ﷺ
* Al-Hadī al-Nabawī wal-Irshādāt al-Muḥammadiyya ﷺ
* Al-Taqarrub ilā Allāh Ta‘ālā
* Al-Ṣalāt fī al-Islām
* *Al-Ṣalāt ‘alā al-Nabī* ﷺ
* Ṣu‘ūd al-Aqwāl wa-Raf‘ al-‘Amāl
* Al-Du‘ā’
* Tarjamat al-Shaykh Muḥammad Najīb Sirājuddīn al-Ḥusaynī
* Al-Īmān bi- ‘Awālim al-Ukhrā wa-Mawāqifuhā
* Al-Īmān bil-Malā’ika wal-Baḥth Ḥawla ‘Ālam al-Jinn
* Al-Ad‘iyya wal-Adhkār al-Wārida
* Sharḥ al-Manzūmat al-Bayqūniyya fī Muṣṭalaḥ al-Ḥadīth
* Ada‘iyyat al-Ṣabāḥ wal-Masā’
* Manāsik al-Ḥajj wal-‘Umra
* Al-Ṣiyām
* Mawāqif Sayyidinā Muḥammad Rasūl Allāh ﷺ ma‘a al-‘Ālam
* Durūs Ḥawla ba‘ḍ al-Tafsīr Āyāt al-Qur’ān al-Karīm
* Muḥāḍarāt Ḥawla Mawāqif Sayyidinā Muḥammad ﷺ

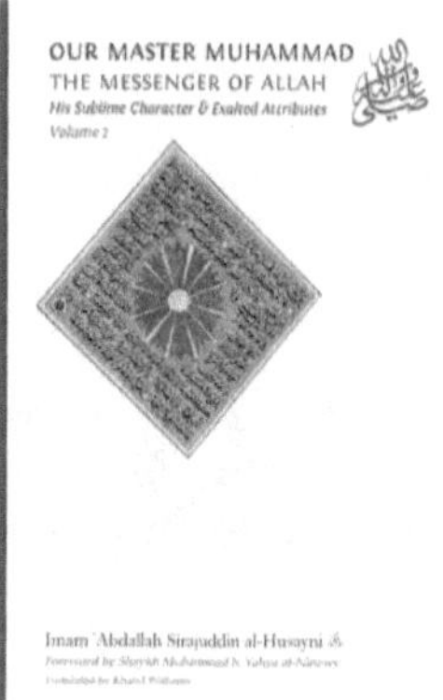

In this day and age, it is essential for the Muslim community and humanity at large to acquire a detailed description of the Best of Creation, the Messenger of Allah ﷺ. *Our Master Muhammad, the Messenger of Allah* ﷺ, is a book of devotion written from the heart and addressing every heart that yearns to draw closer to best of Allah's creation.

In this second volume of the book, the author details the exemplary character traits of our Prophet ﷺ, his devout worship, his noble lineage and progeny, and the blessings of his physical-self and personal effects, and his infallibility in both religious and worldly matters.

This expression of Prophetic love and longing was written by the 'Pole of Prophetic love in our times', the venerable saint, Ḥadīth scholar and exegete: Imām 'Abdallāh Sirājuddīn al-Ḥusaynī ﷺ. His book is an exceptional demonstration of sound scholarship and spiritual realization.

O you who love the Messenger of Allah ﷺ! Time has isolated us, tribulations have spread amongst us, the charlatans have spoken, and many people have preoccupied themselves with that which relieves neither hunger nor thirst. We have lost the warmth of the love of the Messenger of Allah ﷺ, the warmth that those who love him feel, and which those who yearn for him desperately seek, and in the beauty of which the most knowledgeable ones in Allah lose themselves. The reality of this love is absent, whilst claims to it are many, and the way of the Companions and the model of their love have been reduced to mere stories and legends. So let us renew our covenant with the Messenger of Allah ﷺ, and bear the banner of love to the most sincere and lasting love, and the most enduring and faithful reverence, and the brightest and most resplendent light, and the Beloved and Chosen One of Allah ﷺ.

—*Shaykh Muhammad b. Yahya al-Ninowy*

⟨*Indeed, Allah and His Angels send prayers upon the Prophet. O you who believe! Send prayers and abundant salutations upon him.*⟩ *[Sura al-Ahzab 33:56]*

Sending Prayers upon the Prophet ﷺ is an extraordinary work of scholarship infused with Prophetic love that expounds upon the command of Allah ﷻ and His Prophet ﷺ to send abundant prayers and salutations upon the Master of the Messengers ﷺ and details their deeper meanings, great virtues, numerous benefits and different rulings.

Steeped in spiritual insight and profound love and devotion, Imam ʿAbdallah Sirajuddin unravels the secrets of this noble act and elegantly explains its high status by drawing extensively from the Qurʾan and Hadith traditions and the understandings of the scholars of the past.

Sending Prayers upon the Prophet ﷺ will satisfy students of jurisprudence and the spiritual path alike, inspire them to act out of love for our Master Muhammad ﷺ, and intensify their yearning for him ﷺ.

> *Live happily with never-ending union*
> *With the one you love, with the veils of distance raised*
> *Witness the utter beauty of the one for whose sake*
> *The hearts of the lovers split asunder from its light*
> *Be of good cheer for attaining what you hoped for*
> *Upon the brow of the Elect Prophet has the sun of the forenoon shined!*

Imam ʿAbdallah Sirajuddin al-Husayni ﷺ was an exegete of the Qurʾan, scholar of Hadith, master of the spiritual path, expert of the Sacred Law, lover of the Prophet ﷺ and the Light of Aleppo.

> "You [Shaykh ʿAbdallah] are surrounded
> by the vision of our Master the Messenger of Allah ﷺ."
> —*Shaykh Ahmad Harun al-Dimashqi* ﷺ

Written by the renowned Scholar and Sufi of Aleppo, Imam ʿAbdallah Sirajuddin al-Husayni ﷺ, *The Testimony of Faith* elegantly portrays the beauty of the *Shahada*, the Islamic testimony of faith: There is no god but God and Muhammad ﷺ is the Messenger of God. Going beyond cursory explanations, the author provides a precise explanation of its meanings and conditions, and presents an exhaustive discussion on its merits, virtues, and benefits in this life and the Hereafter.

Effortlessly taking readers through the depths and details within this basic tenet of faith, Imam ʿAbdallah Sirajuddin unravels the secrets of *La ilaha illa Allah*, showing how it can purify minds, hearts, and bodies, uplifting them to lofty spiritual realities that are often veiled from man.

Called by his contemporaries '*the Pole of Prophetic love*,' Imam ʿAbdallah demonstrates the inseparable link between affirming Allah's Oneness and affirming the primordial rank of the Messenger of Allah ﷺ as the first of the Messengers created, the last of them sent to mankind, and the first of them to be resurrected.

With the precision of a Hadith scholar and the love of a Gnostic, Imam ʿAbdallah Sirajuddin ﷺ presents readers with this outstanding work: an authoritative look at the first pillar of Islam that will satisfy students of Islamic theology and spirituality alike.

> *How strange it is, how can God be disobeyed*
> *And how can the obstinate disbeliever deny Him*
> *When in every movement and stillness*
> *There is always for Him a witness*
> *And in everything there is a sign*
> *Showing that He is One*

"I begin with praise, sending prayers upon Muhammad ﷺ, the best of Prophets sent"

From the most noble of sciences is the science of Hadith. It is the key to unlock the Sunna of the Prophet ﷺ through his words, actions, qualities and tacit approvals. Allah ﷻ says: "Follow him so that you may be guided." The Messenger of Allah ﷺ said: "May Allah illuminate the one who hears my speech, understands it and conveys it."

For this reason, the scholars of Hadith have spared no effort to establish the principles by which to verify narrations and deduce—with the utmost precision—what can and cannot be attributed to the guide of mankind ﷺ. Facilitating this quest for the beginning student, the erudite Imam 'Umar al-Bayquni al-Dimashqi ﷺ (d. 1080 H.) succinctly defined thirty-four categories of Hadith in his famous thirty-four verses of poetry.

"Completed, with goodness they are sealed!"

Numerous commentaries upon this treatise followed, of which one of the most sought after in recent times is the masterpiece we have before us, written by the master [*hafiz*] of Hadith and exegete of the Qur'an, Imam 'Abdallah Sirajuddin al-Husayni ﷺ. In his unique and eloquent style, the saintly Imam takes the reader on an illuminating path of learning, guiding him towards the guidance of the most beloved ﷺ.

Sufism is good character
He who is ahead of you in good character
Is ahead of you in Sufism

The late Shaykh 'Abd al-Qadir 'Isa was one of the revivers of the Sufi tradition in the Levant. In a time of gross materialism and imported profane ideologies into the Arab world, Shaykh 'Abd al-Qadir 'Isa provided the keys for a reclamation of Islam's spiritual riches and revived the spiritual path, imparting guidance and instruction to scores of people from all strata of society.

Realities of Sufism, the Shaykh's only book, takes readers on a journey to the heart of Islam. Expositing on the foundations of Islam's spiritual path, Sufism, Shaykh 'Abd al-Qadir simultaneously describes the workings of the path of excellence—*ihsan*—and answers the doubts of the orientalists, modernists, and would be Islamic revivalists. Some of the topics in this book include: the history and etymology of Sufism, the conditions of a true spiritual guide, the proper manners of a spiritual seeker, the outer manners of the path, the inner manners of the path, the deeds of the heart, spiritual unveiling, miracles, oneness of being, and historic testimonies to Sufism's key role and efficacy in purifying the souls and elevating the Sacred over the profane in the lives of man.

"Our Shaykh was a Sufi of the old persuasion: the Sufism or purification indicated in the Book of Allah Most High, and which the Messenger of Allah was keen to teach. Our Shaykh used to say: 'The spiritual path has five pillars: remembrance, instruction, knowledge, struggle, and love.'"

—Shaykh Muhammad b. Yahya al-Ninowy

OUR MASTER MUHAMMAD
THE MESSENGER OF ALLAH ﷺ

HIS SUBLIME CHARACTER & EXALTED ATTRIBUTES

VOLUME I

IMAM ʿABDALLAH SIRAJUDDIN AL-HUSAYNI

Foreword by
Shaykh Muhammad b. Yahya al-Ninowy

Translated by Khalid Williams

SUNNI PUBLICATIONS